My Life in Three Centuries

My Life in Three Centuries

Autobiography of a Nobody

Irvin Bussing

VANTAGE PRESS
New York

Copyright © 1995 by Irvin Bussing

Published by Vantage Press, Inc.
516 West 34th Street, New York, New York 10001

Manufactured in the United States of America
ISBN: 0-533-10975-2

Library of Congress Catalog Card No.: 93-94271

0 9 8 7 6 5 4 3 2 1

Contents

Prologue

I started this commentary on my ninety-second birthday (October 13, 1990). If I manage to hang on for ten years from that date, this tale of a life in three centuries will not be a complete misnomer. Also at that time it will be interesting to round up others in the same age group and form a Three Centuries Club, since all of us will have lived *in* three centuries.

There's more humor than history in this review; it had to be that way because I think life is too important to be taken seriously. Chapters 2 to 8 should amuse you; chapter 11 inspire you, as it did me, to bring about the virtual rebirth and renovation of yours truly. So great was the change that you may justifiably consider the tale almost incredible. But it's true.

Then you will find a series of misadventures that will seem even more unreal, and if that is the case, be advised that they are as inexplicable to me as they are to you. But they happened. After this sorry tale, I took the advice of my granddaughter, who told me to "juice it up"; so I put in chapter 30. If that doesn't entertain you, chapter 34 might. Likewise chapters 36 and 38.

Then the tale becomes a bit more analytical than anecdotal as a few rather controversial forecasts are made relative to the economic and employment outlook for the United States in the decades ahead, how they may affect you, and what, if anything, you can do about it.

As a result I'll probably be called an anarchist, an atheist, a Republican, or un-American by some readers. (How a person can be an "un-American" I don't know; I can be undressed—which has never impressed anybody—but I've never heard of an un-Frenchman, or an un-Canadian.) However, I might not be around much longer if my internist has his way. The other day, when he was taking my blood pressure, I mentioned casually that I have buried four doctors in my lifetime; whereupon I got the impression, subliminally, that he was damned well not going to be the fifth even if he had to violate his Hippocratic oath in "caring" for me.

You can perform a public service if you peruse this abbreviated tome, in addition to amusing yourself, by deciding whether I ought to be put into one of those places cluttered with half-dead, helpless old people instead of being allowed to roam at large (writing books with interesting biographical beginnings and prospectively perilous endings). I hope your decision will not be that I and the book should be (ecologically) recycled immediately, because I would like to be here when the Three Centuries Club is formed.

Incidentally I might add that if you do not prematurely recycle the book, you may derive an additional, unadvertised benefit if you place it on your bedside table, where it may serve as a nonaddictive, inexpensive, everlasting substitute for sleeping pills, although I have tried to make it inappropriate for that purpose.

My Life in Three Centuries

Chapter 1
Background

Two people exerted a profound influence on me as a youngster—my mother and a grade school teacher. This may not seem particularly noteworthy: but in the tale I am about to tell, I think you will agree, they played an unusually important part.

First, a bit of background. Mother, though a person of considerable ability, never attempted to break out of the narrow environment that women in the early twentieth century were expected to accept. (This could be a partial explanation of her lifelong addiction to migraine headaches.) As a kid in elementary school she received an Honor Card, year after year; and elementary school was as far as she went. In her married life she managed the household so efficiently that our standard of living must have been above the level of my father's income; however, she never evinced the slightest sign of dissatisfaction with her choice of a husband; and he, a devoted and dependable mate, always seemed to be satisfied with what he had and saw no reason to aspire to more. I did get the impression as I grew up, however, that she hoped I would turn out to be "somebody," as she probably hoped she and her husband would one day—which never materialized.

Her aspirations, and efforts at realizing them, can be seen in the way she managed to move up to better neighborhoods as time went on. When she and father were married, on November 10, 1897, they moved into a rented house on Governor Street in the city of Evansville, Indiana, a neighborhood that was "redeveloped" during the 1930s.

Some of the furnishings for this little house in which I was born, were as follows. The first purchases were made on November 16, six days after the nuptials, inasmuch as the newlyweds went to Niagara Falls (like everyone else?) for the so-called honeymoon:

                1 bedroom Suite and commode............................... $33.00
                Sideboard... 18.00
                Tables and Chairs... 21.40

The grand total came to $72.40 (but the sales clerk made a ten-cent mistake, charging $72.50). Fifty dollars was paid at the time of purchase and the balance on December 21. Two other purchases, one for $41 and the other for $17.70, brought the cash outlay for setting up housekeeping to $131.20. Other items must have come as wedding presents. In terms of 1990 dollars, these purchases probably amounted to several thousand dollars and, please note, were paid for in cash—like everything else they ever bought.

A year or so later they moved to a somewhat better neighborhood and a larger house (Cherry Street), probably to have a bedroom for the kid (me). A few years after that, in 1905, mother decided that it was time to make the big move. The two rentals (on Governor and Cherry Streets) were short on indoor plumbing, and besides, by this time my sister had been born and three bedrooms would soon be desirable.

So my mother began looking at new, upcoming subdivisions in the city and soon decided that the place to a buy a lot was in an area a block from Washington Avenue (which was next in snob appeal to Riverside Avenue where the really "rich" people lived). After buying a lot in this Bayard Park area, she contracted with J. R. Anderson (father of Roy, one of my playmates) to have a house built to her specifications. I don't think there was ever anything more than a verbal agreement.

The house had seven rooms (three of them bedrooms), hot and cold water in the bathroom (but hot water in the kitchen was provided by the tea kettle), central heating, gas lights (a big improvement over kerosene lamps), two porches, and in the rear of the backyard, a laundry, storage space for the coal and kindling for the kitchen, and a privy (which may have been insurance against a back-up in city sewers when the river was at flood stage).

The cost of the house and lot came to $2,508; it was paid for in full, in cash, on July 5, 1905. (Mother considered mortgages a sign of weakness; she said no one owned anything if there was a lien against it. I don't think she and father ever borrowed.) If she were alive today,

I think she would say, "I told you so," as we increase the federal deficit of $4 trillion by about a billion dollars a day. "Debt and depression are two sides of the same thing," she would add.

Just how much $2,500 was in terms of 1990 dollars is difficult to say; we have no cost-of-living index with a base of 1905 = 100. But we do know that a seven-room house today is likely to cost not less than $100,000 and that few buyers plunk down the full amount of the purchase price in cash. But the Bussings did.

I have no idea what the family income was at this time. Father was in the retail men's clothing business at Third and Main Streets. (In the latter part of the nineteenth century, his father had had a dry goods store, Schapker & Bussing, at Second and Main Streets.)

The family valued security above all else. They had a savings account to take care of emergencies. They considered it thoughtless to buy now and pay later; their method was the other way around. Their financial independence, acquired through work and economy, provided a degree of social security a quarter of a century before the national government set up such a system, since individuals hadn't on their own.

It was some time before I was able to understand why we had bicycles when some of our neighbors had horses and automobiles; why father smoked a corncob pipe when he might have had a meerschaum. Or why he smoked stogies after dinner during the week and limited himself to a Havana after dinner on Sunday. Also, why we were the only people in the neighborhood who had a small flock of chickens. The chickens were fed goodies that other people consigned to a garbage pail: in return, the hens gladly gave us eggs. And the rooster obligingly saw to it that the eggs we allowed a hen to set on were fertile so that in due course we would have more chickens, and later on more eggs and more chicken-and-dumpling dinners.

The quality of the Bayard Park neighborhood where our house was located is to some extent confirmed by the behavior of the children. In the summertime, for example, it was a ritual for youngsters to vie with each other in the riverboat game. Steamboats carrying passengers and freight plied up and down the Ohio River on regular schedules. Somebody got the idea, and the children became interested, in making three- and four-deck boats out of suit and shoe boxes. Windows would be cut and covered with colored tissue paper, and candles would be placed inside. After sundown during summer evenings, the boat owners would light the candles, fall in line, and pull their boats up and down the sidewalks for the entertainment of neighbors sitting on their front porches. It was an original, fascinating, and creative activity that kept the children busy.

The boys put on circuses in the daytime. They would perform and cavort in real clown costumes made by their parents; others would be acrobats. A parade would take place in the morning, and the performance, in Erroll Byington's large stable where there was a horizontal bar and trapeze, would take place in the afternoon.

When we weren't making riverboats or rehearsing for the circus, we were tinkering with our push-mobiles, which we made out of wheels from baby carriages and cracker boxes. Our steering mechanism was made of rope, a broomstick, an improvised fifth wheel (to mobilize the front axle), and a steering wheel consisting of a barrel hoop fastened to the broomstick with a cross bar. The motive power was the pusher, and one mobile would race another, the speed of each depending in part on the quality of the wheels and axles salvaged from the junkyard, the amount of cup grease we'd smuggled out of Roy's father's garage, and, most of all, upon the capacity and enthusiasm of the runner-pusher and what he'd had for breakfast. (Wheaties?)

If there is any doubt as to whether a project of this sort will keep boys out of trouble, my suggestion is that you try putting such a contraption together, using only junk or discarded materials. It is totally absorbing, calling for creativity and ingenuity, leaving little time for mischief.

When we got tired of racing (or if the steering mechanism malfunctioned, a common occurrence), we might start a game of street hockey (ice hockey on asphalt). The puck would be a crushed tin can, and the stick would be a dug-up sapling with enough root structure at the end to constitute a club. Instead of ice skates, we had roller skates. Traffic in those days was light, and besides, Blackford Avenue dead-ended a block away from the hockey block.

If the hockey game was called because someone broke his stick or developed a hot box in one of his skates, we might play duck-on-the-rock. That also was a homemade game: a smaller rock would be placed on a larger rock in the middle of the intersection of Blackford Avenue and Evans Street. If I am the one "at bat," I lob a rock at the duck on the rock; and if I knock it off, I try to run around the four corners of the intersection and get "home" before the next one in the throwing order manages to put the duck back on the rock and get there before I do. In other words, we created our own games.

No, we were not always good boys. We experimented with smoking—such stuff as dried corn silk, penny royal, and pulverized grape and various tree leaves. We compared pipe smoking with cigarette smoking. Our pipes were made of hollowed corncobs and stems of any kind of plant or weed, if they could be made to draw.

We never liked these "weeds," so we decided to try something sophisticated—Cubeb, which is a derivative of an Indian piper-aceous (pepper) shrub. But we didn't take to this either, although we thought we ought to start smoking because that was an indication of manhood. So one day at a picnic of the Knights of St. John, to which father belonged, I saw an open box of cigars, which I clandestinely decided to sample. Shortly thereafter, I was too ill to take an interest even in apple pie and ice cream; the picnic for me turned out to be a punishment. I never touched anything thereafter that had tobacco in it.

We were not little angels in other respects either. If we were not the ones who stole the ice cream from the backporch of the mother who had arranged a birthday party of little girls for her daughter, who did do it?

And on Halloween, who dumped the family's pail of garbage on their front porch? Who put those pieces of porch furniture into one of the trees in front of someone else's house? And how did the porch furniture of one family happen to turn up on the front porch of those people in the next block?

So now, to get back to our house, I found eighty-five years later that it not only stands straight and tall but may even be in better condition than the only remaining member (me) of the first family to occupy it. And instead of bicycles, the present owner has a new model Cadillac.

I didn't have the temerity to ask him if he owned it or if, according to mother's way of thinking, it would be his only after he paid off the loan. Why would I even think of raising such a question?

Did I think that her economic philosophy had so permeated the woodwork that, like radioactive material, it affected the minds and behavior of those who occupied the place after us? No, I have long since come to believe that experience (rather than nagging by the woodwork of a house haunted with an outworn philosophy of sacrifice and saving) is the more effective if not the only teacher.

And my peers—the duck-on-the-rockers, the push-mobiliers, the asphalt hockeyers, and the circus clowns and acrobats—they no longer answer the phone.

Chapter 2
Religious "Education"

Both sides of my family, mother's side and father's, were at least nominal Roman Catholics. Grandfather Bussing emigrated from a little town on the border between Germany and Holland; and although he married a little Dutch girl (aged fourteen), his naturalization papers give his origin as Germany.

Grandfather Mace emigrated from Alsace-Lorraine when it was French territory. He married Sophia Ulsas, whose family had settled in New Orleans (Louisiana Territory, a French possession at that time). He had landed in French Canada. We assume that they must have had some family connections in Alsace; otherwise, how explain that both landed in French territory and later connected with each other on the vast American continent in Evansville, except that it was accessible from French Canada via the Great Lakes, a canal in Ohio, and the Ohio River. And from New Orleans via the Mississippi and the Ohio.

Both families became members of the same Catholic church. Marriages, baptisms, more marriages and baptisms, and, eventually, funeral services, took place in this parish church. (If that isn't provincialism, what is?)

All of this would be of no particular importance were it not for the fact that my mother was about to throw a monkey wrench into this ecclesiastical conclave. Although, as I have noted, neither side of the family seemed to be totally hidebound by the preachments of the high priests, none of them had run the risk of disobeying the basic requirements. One of these rules was (and is) that children born of Catholic parents, or even if only one parent was Catholic, must attend at least an elementary Catholic school. (There was no Catholic high school.)

Thus, in due course, the hour of decision arrived in our family.

Until I was about eight years of age, I had attended the public school in our new up-scale neighborhood, where I was with my playmates and the kind of people Mother preferred. Somehow or other, however, the question came up as to why I was not attending the parochial school affiliated with our parish church. I don't know whether the Reverend Father, pastor of the congregation, brought up the matter or not, but I strongly suspect he did.

If he didn't, he should have, for the thinking of the church at that time was that if a youngster was educated (indoctrinated) at an early age he would be a faithful member of the church for life. It was the duty of the parish priest to see to it that the children of members of the congregation were properly enrolled in the parish school so that they would receive the word of God and the pope, five days a week in the school (plus whatever they could understand of the sermon on Sunday if they went to high mass, which was primarily for adults). We youngsters attended the eight o'clock service, which left us free to paint the backfence or do anything else the Methodists considered inappropriate on Sunday. Besides, we heard "the Word" every day during the week in school, unless we were too preoccupied with shooting spitballs at the ceiling or doodling on our slates.

At all events, my parents got the message, which was that I had better be sent to the parochial school without further delay—or else. The pressure must have come not only from the church but indirectly and subliminally from members of our extended family; for if I had not been sent to the school, I would be the only member of each side of the family up to that point to have failed to heed the command of the hierarchy. And my cousins had suffered no serious consequences from toeing the mark, so why would I?

The priest prevailed, of course; he had God, hell, and damnation on his side. Therefore, at about the age of eight, after I had received a bicycle as a Christmas gift, I was yanked out of Chandler School three blocks from home and sent to the church school about a mile or so away.

My first impression was that one teacher seemed to be in charge of several grades of pupils all in the same room. This person, a nun, dressed (or confined) in her starched head gear, had to handle all the subjects from the catechism, which was priority one, on up to worldly subjects, whether she knew anything about them or not. (At this stage the question had not occurred to me as to whether she was a nun because she wanted to be a teacher, or whether she was assigned the job of teacher by the Mother Superior because she didn't know how to cook or was not needed to do laundry and housework.) Much later I came to the conclusion that the choice of a religious vocation usually came first, and that as a religious she had taken a vow of obedience. Therefore, if the order decided she should be a cook, she would be a cook. If there was a need for teachers because members of the faith were taking the mandate seriously to be fruitful and multiply, she would be a teacher, whether she had the educational qualifications or not. She did have the most important credential of all—to make good Catholics out of those of us who were exposed to her indoctrination in the name of education.

The first order of business on Monday morning was to report individually and loudly how diligently we'd served God on Sunday. The most sanctified members of the class were those who could report that they'd attended all of the Sunday services. They would report proudly, loudly, and rhythmically, "early mass, rosary, high mass, and vespers." That would be good for an A on the pupil's record of "deportment." (Note that no mention was made of Sunday school. That is because there wasn't any, the reason being that we had "Sunday school" every day in class.)

Academic "progress" was based on age not accomplishment. I have no recollection of the application of scholastic requirements; pupils advanced to the next grade at the end of a school term. There were no such things, as far as I can remember, as final exams. Maybe there were, but if so, they were not determinative of whether Willie or Mary was "promoted." At least I can't recall that anyone was ever left behind because of deficiency in one or more subjects.

In the sisters' school most of us were preadolescent, and it was coed. When a certain stage was reached, the boys were transferred to a building on the other side of the church and greeted by a man, in this case not a member of a religious order but a well meaning, overworked German immigrant who, like the sisters, had not been chosen for his qualifications as a teacher.

Chapter 3
The Boys' School

There was one room for about fifty boys, in six columns of desks; the first two columns were for the boys who had most recently been "promoted" by the sisters from the coed school, say about twenty. The next two columns were occupied by last year's "freshmen," and the last two columns by the "seniors," the smart alecks. As a result of dropouts, this was the smallest group; but what they lacked in numbers they more than made up for in devilish decorum.

Between the teacher's desk and those of the pupils was a large coal-burning potbellied stove, which, when properly stoked with paper, wood kindling, and soft Indiana coal—in that order—took the chill off the room—unless the kindling failed to catch fire, or the stove didn't "draw" because no one had removed the ashes. In other words, janitorial duties were the second order of the day, the first being to attend the early morning holy mass.

The latter was usually a "low mass," unless it was a burial or matrimonial service. In that case our school master played the organ and we, the janitorial pupils of the boys' school, "sang," as best we could, the requiem (in Latin) if it was a burial service, or the musical responses of a Bach mass (in German) if it was a wedding ceremony. The latter was important in that it enabled members of the parish, in good conscience, to be fruitful and multiply, if they had not already started to do so.

Occasionally the boys found themselves singing a cappella, if the one who was supposed to be pumping the bellows for the organ succumbed to a daydream. When that happened, the disharmony of the choristers became more audible. Fortunately, however, in a nuptial service the couple for whom the music was being performed were usually too eager to get it over with so they could get down to more important business to complain, while in a burial service the honored guest presumably couldn't hear it; or, if he did and if he was in the slightest degree musical, he probably turned over in his coffin, but to no avail. Those who were still alive couldn't do much more than the dead man could.

We not only couldn't read the notes of the musical score, we didn't know the difference between a requiem and a revival. Nor could we translate the Latin of the burial service or the German of the nuptial. But if the ceremonies were to be performed they had to be sung one way or another; and since many priests were not much better at carrying a tune than we were, and since there was no record of anyone's marriage ever being annulled or his burial botched as a result, we carried on.

By about nine o'clock these noneducational beginnings of the day would come to an end and we would march, two abreast, to our classroom. If the fire in the stove had been lit earlier by one of the more thoughtful boys, it would be dead by this time, not unlike the unfortunate principal in the burial service; but, unlike the deceased, it could be revived by a process not totally different from what was probably going on in the minds of the newlyweds while we were trying to chant like little cherubs for their benefit.

Likewise, the master would come down to earth, shake off the spell of the religious service, and cope with problems that were far more troublesome than those of mere musical discord. Although I never heard it said, I feel sure that the master would have been delighted to play a requiem for at least a fifth of the boys in the room.

The usual procedure was to start with the group in the first two columns, while those in the other columns "studied" until it was their turn to recite. This is where the system broke down. There was an unwritten code of behavior, in which the boys who caused the greatest amount of disturbance received the highest "academic rating" from their peers. Disturbance was measured by the amount of frustration the master exhibited.

The ringleaders showed considerable ingenuity in devising and timing their strategies to distract him. Sometimes it would be easy to flip off a shot of paper pulp or pull off a prank, as when he would do what the organ pumper sometimes did—that is, he would fall into a condition of cataleptic suspension, a daydream. At such times he would be walking up and down the aisle, oblivious of his whereabouts, his hands folded, his lips moving, his eyes on the ceiling (or heaven?) unaware of the spitballs that had stayed put on the ceiling and the halos left by those that had fallen. At such times, some pupils would likewise sit by idly, waiting for something to happen, while others who saw an opportunity to intensify their extracurricular activities, one of the favorites being spitballing.

A spitball is a wad of paper that has been reduced to pulp gastronomically, i.e., by chewing. The gastronome must not be squeamish, but rather willing to masticate any kind of paper that is available, including newspaper (which might not be too bad if there happened to be a spicy story on the page next to the part that was to be prepared for the mission to the ceiling). Besides, these academic marines were not to be daunted by a little disagreeableness in the line of (dirty) duty. Distasteful as newsprint was, it was frequently all that was left, after the fire in the stove had been laid, because we used slates instead of paper in case we happened to be called upon to write something.

Makers of spitballs had to work fast, because the master usually "came to" after a while, suddenly and without warning, and did his best to pick up where he'd left off. There was usually enough time, however, to produce a wad of pulp, load it onto the end of a ruler, and flip it upward, hopefully with enough force to cause it to stick to the ceiling and surround itself with a salivary halo—not unlike those around the pictorial heads of famous people, said by the pope to have been God-fearing when they were alive and worthy of his sanctification now that they are dead—assuming, of course, that God agreed but had not gotten around to it. (We were given to understand that popes are indispensable to religion; that they are uniquely qualified and always ready to do any of God's work, should the latter have been too busy or perhaps forgotten to do it himself.)

Success in spitballing and other kinds of misbehavior were applauded by most members of the classes and automatically entitled the culprits to "membership" in the mythical Mischievous Order of Merit. Even a brat whose wad had failed to stick could still be admitted to membership if, for example, the blob fell on or near enough the old man to shock him out of his somnambulism. It was the courage and daring that counted.

A few boys were sufficiently adept to get a shot off even when the master was alert. But if they failed all hell would break loose, for he would then become uncontrollably excited and frustrated. All tutorial activity would come to a halt, and everyone in the room would either stop carving his initials in his desk, promoting a prize fight, trading marbles, comparing pornographic postcards, or whatever, to see what the old man would do next.

If the rascal caught in the act was within arm's length of the master, the latter would haul off and box his ears. (If no one has ever boxed your ears, let bygones be bygones; not only is it a very painful punishment, but it can injure permanently the delicate parts of the inner ear. No one has attempted to find out how many hearing aids have been required, later in life, by kids who tormented teachers and had their ears boxed, but it is about time for the Congress of the United States to act. When it does, we can expect to see an item in the federal budget appropriating a hundred million dollars or so to find the answer. That will be followed by appropriate legislation creating a Department of Audiophonics, with offices throughout the country staffed by skilled audiophiles—provided they are members of the president's party and contributed to his political campaign.)

If the brat was not within arm's reach, and thus was spared a whack on the ear, a whip that the old man kept at his desk would enable him to make the punishment fit the crime in a different manner. Flushed with anger he would charge up to his desk, muttering characterizations of us as "Bohemians" (a racial slur?), scratch about until he found the broken buggy whip (which was about twenty inches long), and then command the offender to come forward, put out his hand, and take whacks across his fingers—as many as were considered appropriate. If the offense seemed to warrant it, both hands got the treatment.

The kid who flinched the least in taking this punishment received the highest commendation from his classmates. When one of the bullies got caught, he would try to walk away from the experience in a nonchalant manner as if nothing had happened, even with a forced smile, showing that he had the stuff required to be a bully.

Shortly after relating this relationship between punishment and pedagogy in a private school, I was surprised to learn that in a public school attended by Robert MacNeil (of MacNeil-Lehrer fame) in Nova Scotia the same kind of disciplinary practice was a part of the curriculum when he was a boy (as told in his recently published book, *Wordstruck*).

It is not unreasonable to suggest, however, that an ingenious instructor could have shown the spitballers how they were confirming the principle of the lever that Archimedes propounded more than twenty-five centuries before. That is, the functional relationship between the spitballer's ruler and Archimedes's lever is that both obey the same law of physics. If anyone had told this to the boys while they were chewing up a cud of flavorful newsprint, they would probably have said something to the effect that it sounded like one of those religious mysteries they didn't have to understand—only believe.

But the plain fact is that when a kid loaded up his ruler for a shot at the ceiling, the thumb of his left hand, which he held at one end of the ruler (lever), served as a fulcrum; then, as the right hand pulled the other end of the ruler down to increase its tension, the energy needed to overcome gravity would be generated when the ruler was released and the wad sent to the ceiling. But no one saw this connection; thus the possibility of utilizing a pointless prank to open the eyes of the pranksters to the fascinating subjects of physics and mechanics was overlooked.

It should be obvious, however, that it would take something of a genius to be able to (1) play the church organ for all religious services; (2) train and rehearse the adult choir; (3) create a weekday choir of boys whose only qualification was that they were enrolled in the parish school; (4) conduct three grades of pupils in one room in the "three R's," physics, catechism and bible history; and (5) maintain at least the semblance of an acceptable educational curriculum. Needless to say, Professor Stein's qualifications would have fallen far short of even a smaller list of requirements but not many people knew it, including the Bussing family, and they did not realize it until several years of their son's life had been wasted.

Chapter 4
Extracurricular Activities

During the school day the primary purpose of about half of the pupils seemed to be to torture the teacher. After school their main interest was in tormenting the nonconformists among the student body. A nonconformist in this sense was one who did not overtly participate in disrupting what decorum there was in the class room, preferring instead to devote at least some of his time to reading Bible history, a watered-down version of biblical narratives (folklore); a bit of arithmetic; and geography, including a discussion of the Golden Gate off the California coast (not imagining in my wildest dreams that I would look at it day after day in my old age from my living room window).

The disturbers of the peace felt that the nonconformists who were disinclined to participate in antipedagogical pranks in the classroom should be "dealt with" after school in the streets. A favorite way to do so was to arrange a fist fight between a rebel and one of these better-behaved sissies of the class.

I couldn't have become a member in good standing of the rebels if I had wanted to because, as my father was in the mens' clothing business and my mother an aspirant member of a respectable social class, I wore white shirts, white celluloid (hand washable) collars, a necktie, decent-looking coats, knee breeches, and shoes that were polished almost as often as my collars were washed; whereas the rebels generally wore colored shirts with neckbands but no collars, stockings that sometimes had holes in them even where they could be seen, bandanna handkerchiefs (unless they wiped their noses on their sleeves), and shoes that may have been polished before they left the shoe factory but seldom thereafter.

Besides which I was a lousy spitballer (one of the requirements of membership in the "club" of recalcitrants) for the additional reason that I disliked chewing up newspaper flavored with printers' ink, plus the fact that church mice, which are notoriously poor, evidently came to the schoolroom at night to feast on leftovers of brown-bag lunches and then apparently took siestas and sometimes left deposits on newspapers in the wood box.

The punks (troublemakers) who preferred turmoil to tutelage held "strategy" sessions from time to time for the purpose of selecting the next "pretty boy" to be "dealt with" after school. I was obvious fodder for their frolicking and took my share of the indignities meted out. On a cold winter's day, for example, one's cap with ear flaps might be missing when it was time to go home or a pair of overshoes (if snow had turned to slush). The space for such items was in a cloakroom through which a pupil, heeding a "call of nature," would pass on the way to an outside toilet (where if the temperature was not below 32 degrees Fahrenheit neither the water nor the waif would freeze), but that would not prevent the prankster from picking some article of "pretty boy's" clothing and stowing it away in some unlikely place or even parking it outside the building where it would get wet if it happened (fortunately or unfortunately, according to one's point of view) to be raining or snowing. A boy who pulled off a stunt like this would receive an accolade or suitable service stripes from his pesky pals.

Pranks of this sort were routine; occasionally an event of greater importance would be arranged by the more restless members—those who wanted to see action. The most popular form of harassment was a fist fight between one of the sissies and a member of the roughnecks. The ring leader of the latter or several members would decide who the two contestants would be; the challenger was usually a husky kid who liked to demonstrate his prowess, the defendant a "mamma's boy" who had no prowess to purvey.

The defendant would get his notification by way of an underground note that would pass from desk to desk when teacher was looking the other way, announcing that after school bantamweight A would meet defendant B in such and such alley in a five-round, bare-knuckled fight.

The defendant probably knew he would get at least one black eye, a bloody nose, and possibly even lose a front tooth, so his first reaction to this perilous promotion usually was to sneak out as if responding to a "call of nature" at the outside privy. But if it was a cold day, he would then have to go home capless and coatless because these had been secretly removed by the crime syndicate. If coats and caps were not necessary because the weather was warm, the escapee, if successful up to that point, was in danger of being rounded up by the promoters and treated more effectively, not to say savagely, by several of them than he would have been by the challenger.

When my number came up the news flash announced that after school that day, in the alley between Oak and Cherry Streets at Seventh Street (one block from the school), bantamweight Louie Fuchs would meet Bussing in a bare-knuckle fight. No one had to be urged to come; everybody loved a fist fight—well nearly everybody.

Louie was shorter than I, and, looking back, I wonder how the promoters could be so sure that he would knock me out. I had longer arms, and, if reach meant anything, I should have been able to paste him in the nose while keeping mine at a safe distance. Before school let out, however, I began thinking of a psychological angle, which interfered with whatever resolution I might have had to defend myself regardless of the consequences. The problem was that on that very corner of the alley at Seventh Street, my grandparents owned and rented a house to a man who built skiffs in the backyard, which overlooked the alley. So he would have a ringside seat, and would be able to give my grandparents a blow-by-blow account of the match; they would tell my parents, and that would make my life at home as difficult as it was about to be in the alley.

All of which did nothing to stop the rapid flow of events. School ended, the gang stuck together, surrounding and "ushering" me to the spot beside Grandpa's house. Then the promotor of the scrap—a husky kid, whose family owned a grocery store and butcher shop and who, I surmised, was big and strong because he got so much to eat—this ringleader stepped forward and placed a chip on Louie's shoulder and told me to knock it off—which I did in order to prevent his knocking me off.

Then Louie went after me. I managed to stay on my feet while also dealing him a glancing blow to the head. That didn't do much good. The more experienced onlookers started shouting instructions to Louie. "Give him an uppercut, Louie," one of them shouted. (An uppercut is a blow under the chin for the purpose of throwing the defendant off balance, at which time a well-placed sock to the eye or nose might floor him for the count. This is generally known as the one-two punch.)

Although I had not done much damage to Louie up to this point I was still on my feet and swinging, but not decisively. Inexperienced as I was, I did not capitalize on my height. Instead, I lowered my head at one point and thus enabled him to deal a couple of punches to my face, one of which landed squarely on my nose. Soon I began hemorrhaging. That was the pièce de résistance of the afternoon: now the boys were beginning to see a real fight, a bloody one. Maybe the knockout was about to come. Even the boatbuilder joined the applause (the SOB! Grandma ought to raise his rent, thought I to myself).

I was neither down nor out, but I was unmistakably a bloody mess. I tried, unsuccessfully, to keep blood off my shirt and necktie with my white handkerchief. (If I had bloodied Louie's nose, his handkerchief would probably have been a concealing red bandanna.) There was a lull in the one-sided contest of bestiality and an apparently unanimous agreement that Louie was entitled to the decision, as he showed no signs of defeat—no blood, no swollen eyes, no intention of backing away and calling it quits. And he could now go home, as usual.

But me? I had another problem, probably as troublesome as the one just ended. It was my custom to park my bicycle at my grandparents's house a block from the site of the fight. I could hide my handkerchief but not my bloody shirt. How could I explain that ugly sight when I fetched my bike? Would I have to admit that I'd behaved like a member of a street gang? What on earth had I been up to? I don't recall how I handled this situation. I do remember that they couldn't call up Mother before I got home because they had no telephone, not even a party line at that time.

I am a bit vague, also, as to how I handled the shirt problem when I arrived home; my handkerchief I could hide in the laundry room, where Mother would not see it. In any case, I must have been more adroit at fabricating than fighting—at least until Monday, wash day, when the laundress saw evidence of so much blood and duly reported it to Mother.

When Father got home that evening I was invited to give testimony and respond in a quiz session with him and Mother, mostly with him. However, although I was reprimanded and scolded, something else, I found out later, was germinating in their minds, something that lightened their punishment of me. In other words, they had begun to wonder, evidently, if this was the kind of educational environment to which they should be sending their son, for whom they had held such high hopes. Should the dictum of the church rob them of their freedom to choose another school, if they were dissatisfied with the one the church provided?

Soon the matter came to a head, a confrontation of dictum versus discretion, between a priest, who had God on his side, and a parishioner, who had no one of any influence at all on his side (except, perhaps, the devil). This altercation of course was psychological, not physical. The reasoning of the priest was persuasive, not punitive (at least) in the here-and-now; if there *was* to be any punishment, it would, of course, be meted out in the afterlife soon. That was the church's dictum; it was my parents' dilemma. How this case of Bussing versus Church, or Layman versus the Lord, was decided, we shall see.

Chapter 5
Gabriel and the Girl

The most important reason for going to a Roman Catholic parochial school is to receive religious instruction—not only religious instruction of a generalized nature, but also the kind of indoctrination that can be best provided by the members of the clergy (the spiritual successors of the Apostles, so they say).

In addition, we supposedly received instruction in the secular subjects taught in public schools. So, for only a moderate fee, we youngsters learned how to make a living *and* get to heaven. Not a bad deal, eh what?

Well, yes and no. For me, at least, it didn't turn out to be a particularly good bargain. If you had the patience and fortitude to read chapter three you got some idea as to the quality of instruction in the secular subjects; now how about the class given by the priest on the creed, sin, and salvation?

The deportment of the pupils was much better in the class conducted by the priest: no spitballing or teacher baiting, partly because there was only one class in one room and one subject.

We were introduced to the Holy Gospel and expected to accept it, without question, as an act of faith. Reluctance to do so would indicate that we were under the influence of the devil—that dirty bastard who is always at work as the ubiquitous adversary of God and his (her?) earthly representatives. And nobody wants to admit that Satan influences him.

The boys listened to the Gospel, some of them with thinly concealed indifference; if any of them considered it folklore, or something worse, he did not admit it; nor would whatever a pipsqueak in a Bible class thought have anything to do with the facts revealed in Scripture.

We began with the Nicene Creed, the first item of which relates to monotheism—a complete break with the polytheistic "religions" of the time. What concerned us at the moment, however, was the Holy Ghost and the fact that he (or she?) apparently came from nowhere, had neither an ID nor an IQ, was commissioned, evidently by God, to see to it that Jesus, though the "begotten son of God . . ." would be "incarnate . . . of the Virgin Mary and . . . made man," which evidently called for more than an obstetrical miracle and certainly much more finesse than anyone would expect a ghost to possess. So he (she) must have been given supernatural powers in spite of his mysterious or unrevealed origin. How come?

In fact, ghosts generally had an extremely bad reputation. They were variously thought to be souls of dead persons, or disembodied spirits that wandered among and haunted living persons. By no stretch of the imagination could an ordinary ghost perform the feats that the creed implies this one did. So he must have been something unusual; therefore we might as well believe it. That's what the word *creed* means: "believe."

So the die was cast: Jesus, though the Son of God, was to be born (again) of an earthly virgin; and the Holy Ghost was the one to accomplish somehow this biogenetic, obstetrical feat. Now when a group of youngsters comes up against an idea they can't readily assimilate they are inclined to fantasize a parody of it. Although I do not recall precisely what tomfoolery the boys invented in connection with the virgin-birth story, the commentary which follows is a reasonable facsimile of their interpretation of this coalescence of cosmology, theology, and genetic physiology.

The first problem, as they saw it, was to find a virgin. (Does this question indicate that they probably were precocious? Some probably were.) But it is a reasonable question to ask in a land occupied by an army of rapacious Roman soldiers and slave owners.

So they concluded that someone in the heavenly hierarchy must somehow have heard about a girl in Judea by the name of Miriam, or Mary, who, in spite of her rapacious environment, had probably managed to retain her virtue and was qualified to shoulder the awesome responsibility the hierarchy had in mind. Very little was known about her or her family, except that she had a brother, Lazarus, and a sister, Martha. A detective agency, or posssibly a Roman spy who was willing to do a little moonlighting, must have been employed to find the maiden and inform the Holy Ghost of her whereabouts, thus enabling him to arrange a meeting at which she would be informed, gently (and, hopefully, without shocking the pantyhose off her) that, of all the women in this world, she had been chosen by a supreme authority to become the virgin mother of a male who would, in turn, found a new religion that would become so popular it would replace all of the polytheistic, inhuman humbug mankind had been stuck with since time began.

Even the Holy Ghost got cold feet when he contemplated this awesome assignment. He not only feared the possibility of failing to find the girl, but also that his message might scare the living day-lights out of her, and worse still, God forbid, shock her into a state of sterility. If that happened, Satan would ridicule the whole idea, the Holy Ghost would be branded as a fraud, the hierarchy in heaven would become the laughing stock of the gods and their followers throughout the pagan world; and the "new religion" would die aborning. "Good riddance," the pagans would shout against this assault on their sacred gods, who had served them so well for so long.

But this was no time for vacillation. The decision had been made: a new religion was going to be started on planet earth and its priestly progenitor would make all other "gods" obsolete; this new God would be a human being, like you and me, but born of a virgin, unlike you and me, this having been made possible by the interven-tion of the Lord God of creation, the master of the universe. His would be a unique and priceless gift to all earthlings. Be thankful.

So, in spite of the difficulties, the Holy Ghost came to the only conclusion that was possible: get on with it. Which he did.

He evidently had been sufficiently indoctrinated, since his mys-terious arrival in heaven, to understand the power of prayer. So one morning while he was thus engaged, an idea popped into his head. (His prayer had been heard, he said, although he didn't know who heard it.) The idea he got was that a Syrian by the name of Gabriel had recently arrived in heaven. There was some doubt as to whether he had been clubbed to death by one of those rapacious Roman policemen or whether he had lost his life in the melee following a bitterly fought soccer match between the Sodom Suckers and the Gomorrah Gonads. Whatever the cause of his death, Gabe was there, in heaven; he was young, good looking (as you can see from his recently washed face in the Sistine Chapel; whether his thoughts were equally dirty we do not know), and he was familiar with the geography of the area where Mary was thought to be living.

Furthermore, as he was now an angel he was less likely to take advantage of the young girl and rob her of the very attribute that made her eligible to become the mother of the Messiah, namely her virginity. However, one of the wags among the heavenly residents who liked to throw monkey wrenches into the messianic machinery started the gossip that even a messenger from heaven like Gabe might take advantage of the poor girl if Satan got to him first. But the celestial campus cops got to this rumor-monger before the devil got to Gabriel, and slammed him into the purgatorial prison.

So the next step was for the Holy Ghost to approach Gabriel and tell him what the heavenly hierarchy had in mind. By this time, in view of the importance and complexity of the objective, it had been decided that the annunciation should involve two visitations: the first by Gabriel, who would gently break the news, to be followed later by the Holy Ghost, who would, so to speak, plant the spiritual seed. It was hoped that, by thus delivering the overwhelming message in two installments, serious shock would be avoided and tranquilizers unnecessary. Gabriel would simply tell her that she had been selected; the Holy Ghost would be more specific in explaining to her that by his power Jesus would "become incarnate from" her and thus be made man.

The heavenly promotion and public relations department thought they had all the bases covered and that there would be no breakdown between annunciation and parturition—no miscarriage, so to speak, either physically or psychologically—so the word went out: "All systems are go."

While the Holy Ghost was busy arranging the ecclesiastical details, Mission Control was taking care of liftoff and landing arrangements for Gabriel. The intention was for Gabriel to touch down in a pasture on the outskirts of Nazareth when the moon was full. At this point, another disrespectful wag in heaven (probably an angel who had been rejected for the mission) suggested that they should rush completion of the star of Bethlehem and use it as a landing light in Nazareth. But this idea was shot down as readily as the one the devil had planted in the mind of the other angel a few days before. The star of Bethlehem was to be used in conjunction with the advent of the Messiah and not otherwise. And besides, it was not ready yet; a design flaw had been found in one of its reflectors that necessitated dismantling some of its components. Articulating the completion of this wonder in the sky with the birth of the Messiah placed enough responsibility on the prime contractor, he said, and he was not about to change plans and run the risk of a cost overrun and an apostolic audit of his books.

Despite the uneasiness associated with this unusual undertaking, Gabriel lifted off on schedule and landed without incident and so quietly that a shepherd less than a hundred cubits away didn't know about it until he saw the story in the *Nazareth News* that afternoon.

After landing, Gabriel finished his can of K-rations, emptied his thermos bottle, and set out to find Mary's place of residence. The first person he saw was a Roman policeman who, with surprising decency, gave him a general idea of the way to go. Soon he located a house and, on a hunch, he knocked on the door. Someone from within asked, "Who is it?"

"A messenger from heaven," said Gabriel.

"From where?" she said, with an air of utter incredulity.

"From heaven."

"I'm sorry," the voice said, "I haven't time to talk to you. I'm getting ready to go to work. And besides, nobody in his right mind would leave heaven for even a day and come to a God-forsaken place like this where the Romans are making life even more miserable. Besides, I've got to milk the goats and get to work in less than an hour. Get lost."

This left Gabriel a bit shaken and at a loss about what to do next. Did he have the right house? Was that the woman God really intended to be the mother of the Messiah? Had the devil outsmarted us again? He walked slowly and pensively down the street.

A few blocks ahead he saw a huge M sign. *That certainly looks familiar,* he thought, so he went in. Indeed, it was a fastfood restaurant of the Maccabean chain. The menu consisted of Big Macs, knishes, and lox and bagels. He ordered the latter and then got into a conversation with the counter girl. The name tag on her uniform was that of Miriam; and she sounded somewhat like the person who'd given him the brush-off earlier. It's a long shot, he figured, but he must find out. Could *she* possibly be the Mary he was looking for?

"Are you by any chance betrothed to a man named Joseph, of the house of David?" he asked.

"Yes," she said, as Gabe almost choked on his sandwich. "But why do you ask?" she said. "And who are you, anyway?"

Regaining his composure, and feeling a measure of exhilaration at the possibility that he had stumbled on the girl he was looking for, he said, "My dear young lady, I wanted to tell you early this morning that I have a very important message for you, from heaven, which I must deliver before I return. This is no humbug. So I ask you, once more, if you will give me a chance to talk to you privately for at least a few minutes."

"Okay," she said. "I have to work here until four o'clock—I'm on an eight-hour shift. I'll be home shortly after four this afternoon. But I don't want to let you into the house. You will have to talk to me at a window of the lower room, where the animals are; but they will not bother you—not as much as you are bothering me. *You* sound like a deranged donkey, but I'll give you a chance."

"Thank you. I'll be there."

He was most certainly at the window at the appointed hour, as was Mary. He then told her that, of all the women in the world, she had been chosen by God to give birth to a Messiah who would found a new and more advanced kind of religion—one that would not relate to animals, inanimate objects, and junk like that, but a religion based on the worship of a living God—his son. "The son in this set-up will be the important link between heaven and earth in the new system. He has not yet been born on earth, but he will be and you will be his mother if you cooperate with the Lord. That is the important message that I came here to deliver to you."

"Sounds utterly ridiculous," said she. "I'm not married yet. Joe and I probably shall be, sooner or later, but he hasn't much of a job at present; and after deductions for social security, mine leaves hardly enough take-home pay to cover my expenses and feed the goats. The rabbi keeps telling us to be fruitful and multiply but he doesn't tell us how to pay for it. (Just between you and me, I don't understand why they want us to keep on increasing the population. There are enough people in this barren country now.)

"In fact, the best thing you could do when you get back would be to tell the people up there that, instead of promoting population growth, they should enable us conveniently and safely to *stop* the growth of population without having to sacrifice sex.

"The trouble is," she continued, "that you people have given us the physiological equipment and made it so much fun to use that the growth of population is almost inevitable. It should be obvious to you that somebody up there screwed up: first they give us sexual parts and then they tell us not to use them. How stupid can you get?

"Can't they see that if we multiply we impoverish ourselves? If there are a thousand acres and a thousand people there is an acre per person: but if we are fruitful and multiply our numbers to two thousand there will be only half an acre per person. So then they tell us to be patient, for the meek 'will inherit the earth,' but they don't admit that if there are too many of us eventually we'll inherit inches, not acres.

"The most 'fruitful' thing you guys up there could do would be to modernize the female sexual organ, limiting its productivity to two or (on average) 2.5 per lifetime. If you are not willing to go that far you ought to be able to think of some way of making it possible to use those sexual organs you have given us without converting this world into little more than an overpopulated, overpolluted ante-room to heaven.

"But since you are too stupid to do something about the real problems of the day, Joe and I are going to have to wait until we have a better income before we get married so we'll not have to apply for food stamps and stuff like that. So, even if what you're telling me is true (and it sounds like a harebrained, crackpot idea), I can't give you any assurance that I'll be able to pull it off any time soon. In fact, Joe might say nuts to the whole thing."

"The Lord God has a solution for all of your problems," said Gabriel. "He knows all about your circumstances, and He has made all necessary arrangements to take good care of you, so that you will not be a problem to Joseph. Jehovah is going to make an exception in your case: the child will be legitimate, even though Joe will not be its father; God will be the child's father.

"And as far as the neighbors are concerned, and the people at the Big M, we've thought of that too: arrangements will be made for you to spend the time of your pregnancy in seclusion at the house of Zacharias. As to the cost of bringing up the child, forget it. You will be Human Being Number Two and Jesus Number One. You will have enough food stamps for the entire household and as many credit cards as your heart desires; we'll take care of the monthly billings. Don't worry about the 13 percent interest on the unpaid balance; the usurers will wind up in custody of the devil.

"Now, one final note. You must realize that I am only a messenger boy; I can tell you what will happen, if you cooperate, but only the Holy Ghost can make it happen. So he (she?) will be along in a few days to get you started biologically. They are waiting up there now for me to return and tell them whether I have succeeded in delivering the message to you without causing permanent cardiac arrest. After I report positively, the Holy Ghost, a 'right-to-lifer' if ever there was one, will come down, put on the finishing touches (you should pardon the expression), and you will rejoice and give thanks to God for allowing you to become a member of the heavenly family, holy Mary, Mother of God. Thank you ever so much. Good-bye."

Chapter 6
Now—from the Horse's Mouth

Gabriel's return flight went according to plan. Despite jetlag, and the loss of a few feathers, he went directly to his superior, the Holy Ghost, and reported that he had delivered the message to a girl who, he had reason to believe, was the one they'd had in mind. But wishing to keep his residency in heaven he felt impelled to tell the whole truth, which included the fact that she'd been skeptical about the entire scheme.

The Holy Ghost said he knew that would be the case; which is why he planned to break the news to her in two installments, the second of which he would deliver personally. Whereupon he bade Gabe good-bye, hopped out to the launch pad, rubbed a little oil on his feathers, and took off. In record time he glided down to the Nazareth sheep pasture, where he headed for the town.

He was able to go directly to Mary's house, using the map of the town Gabe had picked up at a donkey watering station. As usual at this hour in the morning, she was in the lower room, at street level, attending the animals and curing feta cheese, which she made for her consumption and for sale. The upper half of a door was open and the Holy Ghost stuck his head in. (Down here he was just another bozo; upstairs everyone stopped to do homage to him.) So when Mary saw the stranger poking his head into the room she was somewhat apprehensive. She thought to herself that maybe she just ought to take Joe's advice and keep a German shepherd dog for her protection.

The Holy Ghost tried to start the conversation, but she would have nothing to do with him while she was doing her chores. She finished, and proceeded to "wash" her hands, without benefit of soap, in a jar of water that had evidently been recycled several times. Wiping them on a rag, which had been treated likewise, she said to the stranger, "You are the second person who has come here in the last few days. The guy last week told me that they want to make me the mother of a child who will grow up to be a God. I told him that he sounded like a deranged donkey, which he said sounded to him like a jackass and I agreed with him. I told him I couldn't understand the combination of gynecology, Jehovah, virginity, and Jesus. When I told our rabbi about it, he said, 'We do expect a Messiah, but there have been impostors before and this sounds like another one.' He also told me not to endanger my Jewish religion by listening to such heretical humbug."

This kind of talk had no effect on the Holy Ghost. Anybody who could come out of nowhere and ride roughshod over everybody and sell himself to God successfully enough to become his left-hand man (the position on the right-hand side being reserved for Jesus)—such a super salesman would not be baffled by a backward little farm girl. He knew what to do, and he did it.

First, he convinced her that he was the number-two man in creation, and that Gabriel, as he admitted, was only an errand boy. Second, he therefore had the power to bring about the gynecological, gene-splicing, chromosomal alteration in her that was necessary in order for her to become the virgin mother of the son of Jehovah.

With this, he took her hand and gently pressed it to his chest, holding it there for about half a minute as if in silent prayer. For an instant the two were in spiritual harmony and all thoughts of heresy vanished from her mind. The Holy Ghost then told her that all of the promises and pleasantries Gabriel had uttered unto her had been dictated by him, H.G., and they now had become a part of her spiritual being. He had put the finishing touches upon her and she henceforth would indeed be a member of the holy family, just as Gabe had said she would; and that in due course (without inter-course!) she would become the mother of the Son of God.

Without pausing long enough for even a taste of her feta cheese he hopped back to the pasture, waved to the shepherd, flapped his wings to get some altitude, and headed for his heavenly home. At the heavenly heliport a large crowd was there to greet him, although it is never a problem to round up a lot of people in heaven because they have practically nothing to do all day long, all their wants being satisfied without effort as a reward for leading a sinless life on earth and abstaining from certain pleasures, such as sex, except for the purpose of adding more people to the earth's population, for what reason nobody knows.

The Father Almighty, naturally, would not come out for an event of this sort but someone on the administrative staff decided that as a token for his grueling mission to Nazareth they should give the Holy Ghost a memento, which turned out to be another halo. (What else can you give the tripartite deity, who has everything?) It was presented to him by a little girl-angel who, it was said, had been abandoned by her mother at birth.

Meanwhile, down in what the heathen called their Holy Land, where Mary lived, the news media got wind of what they called her "seduction" by another one of those impostors, who had misled her into believing she'd been chosen to bring forth this all-important person, the Messiah. This threw the entire Hebraic community into an uproar, not only because they considered it a hoax, but also because whoever was responsible for the fraud had completely ignored the rabbinical hierarchy of the Israelites.

While the religious community was fuming over the assault on their theology, the medical profession grew equally perturbed about the method by which the charlatan said the Messiah would come into existence. The loudest complaint came from the obstetricians, who demanded the immediate enactment of a law that would impose the death sentence on any quack who would bribe innocent Jewish girls to serve as human guinea pigs (pigs? contrary to Mosaic law?) so that they might practice their heretical humbug.

It so happened that, when the news of this biological travesty broke, there was a convention of the Provincial Society of Obstetricians meeting at the Intercontinental Hotel in Jerusalem. The story that appeared in the newspapers so disconcerted the delegates that the regular program was tabled, and the rest of the convention was devoted to what the delegates considered a major threat to their profession.

What they feared was that this new cult would not only change the reproductive process, but might also sabotage the highly profitable be-fruitful-and-multiply mandate. Either would diminish their professional importance and bring about a decline in their medical practice and income.

So the president of the OB Association, at the urging of its members, left the meeting and called up the surgeon general of Judea and asked him to come to the meeting in Jerusalem to discuss this impending crisis; which he did, immediately. His twofold message, however, was most reassuring.

"In the first place," he said, "you can forget about a repetition of the humbug that the Holy Ghost perpetrated on that little girl in Nazareth, whom he duped, deluded, and deceived. That will never happen again." (The surgeon general was a student of comparative religions as well as a doctor of medicine.) "The reason why it will not happen again is that the handful of troublemakers who are trying to invent a new religion intend that it shall be monotheistic; they insist that there not be more than one god. Therefore, there will be no more incidents like the one that occurred last week in Nazareth.

"The second fact that should allay your fears," he said, "is that if the girl doesn't have a miscarriage or an abortion, or if the fetus is not stillborn, the heresy will probably be validated in the minds of many people and a new religion *will* emerge. Then, to increase its membership, the adherents will be exhorted to be fruitful and multiply, just as we are, except that they will work harder to multiply faster in order to catch up with us sooner. But the number of obstetricians can't be increased as fast and as easily as the number of pregnancies, so I don't think you have anything to worry about."

The OB men (no midwives or women obstetricians?) joyfully and enthusiastically agreed, so much so that the hotel concierge said he never saw a ballroom empty so fast. About half the delegates headed for the cocktail lounge, there to treat each other with drinks in celebration of the good news. (These would later show up on their expense accounts as tax-deductible items they hoped the IRS [Israeli Revenue Service] would approve.)

However, things were not going so well up in heaven: even there, when you think you have settled all your problems something troublesome can, and often does, rear its ugly head. In the present situation, just when they thought they had solved the problem of having a savior, Jesus, born of a virgin, their euphoria was diluted, if not downright destroyed, by the arrival of a man who, on earth, had been a college professor of Roman history.

(Incidentally, he had been murdered by a disgruntled student who felt that he was entitled to a better grade than the one the professor had given him. He is in prison for life, and will probably be in hell for an eternity after he dies, but that's not the point of the story.) The relevant point is that the ex-professor went to the heliport to find out what was going on, and was told that the assembled multitude had gathered there to welcome back the Holy Ghost, who had just completed the biogenetic virgin-birth arrangements with that little Jewish girl in Nazareth. When he heard that he practically flipped his lid and said, "Do you people up here really believe that unholy hokum?"

"Calling it 'unholy' and 'hokum'—that's blasphemy, man," said one of his listeners. "The Holy Ghost is the number-two man, next to God himself. If you don't believe in *him* and what he says, then somebody is going to say a mistake has been made in your case and you belong in the same prison as the kid who shot you in the head. You don't belong up here in heaven. You're a nonbeliever."

Being a Christian at heart, the ex-prof's mental reaction was "forgive them; they know not what they do," but his verbal response was definitive. He told those who would listen—some of whom were high school dropouts, while others were ex-college students, many of whom had gotten poor grades but had not shot the teacher—that "according to eye-witness accounts, Mary was three months pregnant when Joseph married her; and worse yet, Joseph was not the caused of it."

"Inconceivable," said one of his listeners.

"Quite conceivable," said the professor, "if you know the circumstances. What you have not been told is that Mary had been the slave of a Roman landowner. As his property, she was subject to his wishes; and one of the wishes or property rights of a slaveholder is to have sexual relations with female slaves whenever the spirit moves him. (That's an interesting and inexpensive way for a slaver to increase his property.) Consequently it is dishonest for you Christians to cover up the fact that she was not a virgin when the Holy Ghost planted the spiritual seed in her at the Annunciation."

"Well, how come she was given her freedom by the slaver? A herdsman seldom sells a cow in calf."

"It's hard to say," said the professor. "Some say that Joseph, her fiancé, paid for her release. All we know is what Matthew (1:18–25) tells us, i.e., that although Mary 'was espoused to Joseph, before they came together she was found with the child of the Holy Ghost. Then Joseph, her husband, a just man and not willing to make her a public example . . . put her away privily.' The angel of the Lord then appeared to him in a dream, saying 'Joseph, fear not to take unto thee Mary thy wife: for that which is conceived in her is of the Holy Ghost. And she shall bring forth a son, and thou shalt call his name Jesus: for he shall save his people from their sins.' "

This the heretics called the concubinarian cover-up. (Mary an ex-concubine—wow!)

Chapter 7
Confusion and the Creed

Although it appeared that one of the most important of the various heavenly housekeeping chores had been taken care of when Mary was located, informed, and spiritually impregnated by the Holy Ghost, leaving her little to do but wait six or nine months (depending on whether you believed the slave-girl story or the official account in the Creed), as far as our confirmation class was concerned a few remaining ecclesiastical questions demanded attention. One of the bright boys in the class, for example, took the risk of suggesting that the committee that hammered out the creed did a poor editorial or proofreading job because, although the first words declare that we believe in *one* God, a few lines later it states that we believe also in the Holy Ghost "who with the Father and the Son is worshiped and glorified . . . "

"If this doesn't sound like three gods I'll eat your biretta," the boy said, at the risk of his academic welfare. Ivo Herman backed him up with the observation that perhaps the organizers of the new religion weren't able to break completely and immediately from the polytheism of the Romans and Greeks (who outnumbered them a thousand to one). That idea didn't set well with the teacher. He said, with an air of authority, that "What appears to you to be a trinity is in fact, a unity"; then, to clinch the point, "The three-in-one are one if we (the church) say so; we put it into the creed; it's the doctrine of the church. If you do not accept it you defy the doctrine and expose yourself to everlasting damnation."

Later on, one of the nuns (who must have been railroaded into the monastic life before she knew what she was doing) confided in me that nobody really understood the "three-in-one" doctrine but few were willing to admit it, not only because doubt was a sin, but also because it would indicate that one was under the influence of the devil. So on to the next "credible" conundrum.

That item, the crucifixion, presented no problem of verification inasmuch as practically everywhere we looked we saw crucifixes. We were also able to see the logic of the condemnation: that is, any ordinary citizen who would have the temerity to declare to street people and anyone who would listen, day after day as Jesus did, that he was the Messiah, was likely to be a fraud, a saboteur, an imposter, or a lunatic—if not all four.

It was, therefore, only a matter of time before the Hebraic hierarchy would demand that he be arrested, tried, and put to death. Inasmuch as the judicial system, like practically all departments of the government, was in the hands of the Roman conquerors, the prosecution had some difficulty in convincing the court of the righteousness of their indictment and their demand for the death penalty: the Roman officials were heathen, and, as far as they were concerned, the Jews and the Christians were both equally objectionable and subversive in their assault on the true gods, who had served the Greeks and Romans very satisfactorily for thousands of years. In the end, however, the court, in order to clear the calendar and get on to more important business, pronounced the sentence of death.

They had chairs, in those days, but no electricity; so death in an electric chair hadn't even been thought of, except by an early Greek philosopher (who was removed from society for reasons of insanity). Another Greek committed suicide by drinking broth made from a poisonous umbelliferous herb (hemlock). Some of this substance could have been imported from Greece (without upsetting the balance of trade), which, if administered to Jesus, would have alleviated his suffering and expedited his expiration. But no, the multitude wanted a slow, painful death; crucifixion was the method reserved for the worst criminals. (Getting a Roman [the Judge] to approve cruelty was the least difficult part of getting rid of this irreligious, impious imposter, whose purpose was to discredit and destroy the religion of the Jews and set up his own system, in which *he* would be the almighty godhead. What a schmuck!)

There continued to be considerable skepticism among us school boys, especially the Boehme kid (who incidentally walked at least five miles from the family farm to the school every day). One of his questions was, "Why didn't Jesus prove his divinity by performing a miracle or two after he was condemned? For example, he could have changed the heavy wooden cross into balsa wood, which weighs less than a tenth as much. Or, instead of trudging up the mountain on foot, why didn't he levitate himself and then laugh at the mob that was plodding along on foot?"

There were no soft-drink stands or Big M's on the way to Calvary, but a few cold drinks on that hot afternoon would have gone over well. There is no reason why he could not have duplicated the feat he'd performed at the wedding feast a few weeks before, when a crowd of unemployed street people crashed the party and drank so much wine that there was not enough for the invited guests. Whereupon Jesus, who was a pal of the groom, said, "Not to worry. Bring me a few skins of water." He then pronounced a hokus pokus, and not only did the water become wine, but the guests, unaware of how it had been made, praised it highly and asked the host how come he'd served "jug" wines first and the vintage wines last.

Why didn't the Savior pull off such a stunt that afternoon? He could have synthesized ice-cold lemonade, or Coke, or beer, enough for everybody, which would not only have been refreshing but could have caused many of them to wonder if their decision to crucify might not be a miscarriage of justice. Maybe they were about to execute a man who was, after all, the person he said he was.

But it was too late to change course; the die had been cast. So the trudge up the mountain continued without benefit of refreshment or relief from the heat. When they got there, at about three o'clock, the executioners were busy nailing two other convicts to crosses, after which they got ready for the last job of the day—Jesus.

Meanwhile, the Boehme kid hadn't finished his "work" of raising questions. If Jesus meekly passed up the opportunity to pull off a few miracles on the way up to Calvary, why didn't he produce a big one, which would have thwarted the execution and made his critics and haters look like monkeys? When they got out the spikes that were to be driven into his hands and feet, why didn't he convert them to rubber or something useless for the purpose? the kid wanted to know.

When he was on the cross and he asked for a drink and they gave him something that tasted like vinegar, instead of spitting it out and saying "to hell with it," why didn't he convert it to a glass of cold Budweiser and drink it without making any for the "carpenters" who'd nailed him to the cross? Neither Boehme nor the rest of us got answers to reasonable questions like these.

A large crowd of thankful pagans and crying Christians left the courthouse that morning to witness the execution, and many more joined them along the way when they heard the jubilant Jews and raucous Romans loudly announcing there was going to be a killing that afternoon. As in the bloody gladiatorial entertainments in Rome, admission would be free. "Come along; join the throng; watch the culprit die," the gang shouted to the onlookers, causing hundreds more to join the parade. As a result, far more people saw "the Suffering on the Mount" than were present a few months earlier for "The Sermon on the Mount."

After it appeared death had taken over, one Joseph of Arimathea took down the body and laid it to rest in a grave that very evening (for the next day was the Sabbath), while the loyal Christians walked away in silence, bereft of their leader, having had a brief but exhilarating and uplifting experience of religion with a human God, who'd understood and lived with them. Now they were left, once again, with the same old impersonal inhuman, uncommunicative, imaginary gods of their ancestors.

Even the kids in our confirmation class began to commiserate with these dejected disciples. But at this point our instructor sought to explain the significance of the crucifixion, which is the doctrine of redemption for the sins of the people of the world. Had we been told this in a language or dialect we'd never heard we would have understood it as well as we understood it in English. Did it mean that in the afternoon of so-called "Good Friday," the sinful misdeeds of every living person, pagan and all, were then and there nullified, washed away, forgiven? If so, what about restitution? If Joe Doaks raped a damsel and then robbed her of her last week's wages, was he redeemed without being required, as a result of the crucifixion, to pay a penalty or make some sort of restitution to the poor girl? If Jesus came down from heaven to save sinners, who compensated their victims?

If this was a course of instruction to prepare us for confirmation, be advised that it seemed more like an organized effort to compound confusion. But that didn't matter in the eyes of the church: we didn't have to understand; we had only to believe, have faith, accept the biblical background of this, the true religion.

Still, the gnawing question remained. The imposter—Jesus—had been removed from society via capital punishment. He saved others, but not himself. He cured lepers, rehabilitated the crippled, raised the dead; he was the real McCoy. Why, then, did he accept capital punishment so meekly? Did he have something up his sleeve? If so, when are we going to see some evidence of it?

Soon. Very soon. Within seventy-two hours, in fact. Although Lazarus couldn't raise himself from the grave, Jesus could—and did. And then, to further confuse everybody, he resurrected himself after three days! Or did he?

Leo Hermann was one of the more conscientious members of our class. At dinner one night he told his father and mother that at school that day the subject had been the resurrection of Jesus from the grave. Leo's father, a physician, and presumably a good enough Catholic to consider it desirable to send his son to our school, let the boy tell his story. After dinner the kid went upstairs to his room to do his homework having first helped his mother in the kitchen.

Dr. Hermann then told his wife about a conversation he'd had a few days before at luncheon with several other physicians, when one of them commented that the resurrection story might not be accurate. A person crucified, he said, doesn't die in a few hours: it's a slow death, which may not occur for one or two days or more, depending on the physical condition of the individual. It is therefore unlikely that Jesus was dead when he was removed from the cross a few hours after he was crucified, and even more unlikely that he was buried at that time, or at any time. If so, there was no miraculous resurrection.

"The church fathers have heard heretical ideas of this sort for two thousand years," said Mrs. Hermann, "but they take no stock in them. The resurrection, like the rest of the gospel, has come down to us from those who lived with Jesus and therefore knew what they were doing and saying. People like your luncheon friends rely more on imagination and guesswork," said she. Evidently the nuns in the school had done a better job on Mrs. Hermann than the male instructors had done on her husband, as far as convincing them of the validity of the gospel was concerned.

For us youngsters resurrection was a fact, as well as additional justification for accepting Jesus as the founder of the faith. He had then, we were given to understand, spent the next few months here on earth, training the apostles for the missionary work of spreading the gospel as he revealed it and establishing the Christian church as the only worldwide, true religion. (Apparently no one considered it worthwhile at this time to carry the newly revealed word of God to the Orient, despite the fact that the size of the market for converts in Asia was considerably greater than that of Judea, Samaria, and Galilee combined.)

No explanation for this indifference toward Oriental "heathen" was offered; they were allowed simply to stew in their own pagan juices. If distance was a barrier, it was a poor excuse in light of Gabriel's interplanetary flight and the fact that Jesus was able to travel (in spirit) from heaven to earth (with the help of the Holy Ghost before he was born), and from earth to heaven, without assistance, after his resurrection. If all else failed, the apostles could always have asked the Holy Ghost to get out of his heavenly hammock in the Garden of Eden and do something useful, such as enabling them to carry the solution for salvation from the near east to the far east—from the thousands to the millions.

It couldn't have been a case of racial prejudice, could it? Not if we accept Jesus's words literally: he told the apostles before his ascension that they should teach *all* nations. Just how they were supposed to do that was left to their imaginations. Evidently they ran out of imagination.

Another item in the creed assured us that Jesus would return to earth to judge the living and the dead, but there was no timetable for this, or any indication whether Christ's return would occur before the "end of the world" or at the time of the cataclysmic end. Nothing was said about what would be done to, or with, those who are judged unfavorably (as unrepentant sinners); it was assumed that those who are judged to be righteous will be escorted up to heaven because there won't be any earth left—only heaven and hell.

The creed also revealed that when Jesus arrived in heaven, following his ascension from Mount Olivet, he was assigned a seat on the right-hand side of his Father; therefore the Holy Ghost probably sits on the left (unless he has been given a place on the floor). Even so, to most of us this seemed to be substantial, if not excessive recognition for the Ghost—another indication of the amount of influence and persuasive powers this mysterious person had.

I remember that at this point one of the boys in the class, Benjamin Schroeder (whom we nicknamed Ben Jamin) brought up a question, which, in retrospect, I feel certain did not originate in his mind: he'd probably heard his mother expatiate on the subject. She was an ardent advocate of the women suffrage movement, and also an active campaigner in the WCTU, so she probably had plenty to say about the shabby way the hierarchy treated Mary while exalting the mysterious Holy Ghost.

So when young Ben asked in school one day why Mary was literally left behind and abandoned here on earth while the men took over the whole business up above, the teacher's first response was, "That's a good question." (Why do people always say that when they don't know the answer?)

After some delay, the response came that after Mary got to heaven she was given the job of "intercessor." Her function in that regard was to take the complaints of earthlings when their prayers of petition (those of the "gimme" type, practically the only kind most people say if or when they pray) ascended on high. The assumption, in such cases, seemed to be that somehow these requests got sidetracked or lost in the Christian computer, but that Mary, presumably, could use her connections to get access to a member of the trinity and tell him to pay more attention to his job and help petitioners get whatever they were praying for.

Although this function of Mary's was above the level of a housewife, an earth person campaigning for women's rights like Ben's mother would nevertheless consider it a subservient position. And indeed it was, and is. But heaven is apparently a man's world, and its earthly organization is only following suit.

Not surprisingly, while they were busy setting up the organization of the new religion, another discriminatory item was overlooked. That is, since Mary was born as an earthling she was infected with the virus of original sin. Had anyone seen to it that she was cleansed of it? Apparently not. At least there was no record to that effect. Horrible thought! Something would have to be done about that, right away. But how?

So here she was again, a sort of neglected step-child of the family. Ultimately, a detergent solution was concocted by the College of Cardinals with the assistance of a group of conscientious alchemists, which, at least in their opinion, would wash away this dirty diabolical dilemma that damaged Mary's reputation and the purity of the holy family. How was it done? Stay tuned.

Chapter 8
Credibility and the Creed; Sex versus Salvation

It's difficult to understand how those capable, competent, heavenly Christians managed to handle the numerous complicated details of organizing their new religion without realizing they were tripping themselves up by bringing in an earth person like the little girl from Judea. If they were determined to infect everybody born on earth with that lousy sin Adam and Eve committed in the Garden of Eden, how could Mary have been born without it?

The fact is that the holy higher-ups didn't think of it for eighteen hundred years; and when they did, it was because a woman raised the question. This may require elucidation. The woman referred to had been a prosecuting attorney in San Francisco until a felon, whom she had indicted, escaped from jail and gunned her down. In heaven she continued to think legally, argue logically, and carry on discussions with other lawyers (who were growing in number very rapidly in heaven, not because they were growing more religious but because they were becoming more numerous on earth. In fact, the number of lawyers in our town now exceeds the number of physicians, which may indicate that people are having rather more legal and fewer lethal problems, although oftentimes these days it's hard to tell which is which.)

Lawyers are nothing if not logical; so when our "lady" lawyer heard Sunday sermons about how Jesus' mother was the child of an ordinary earthling, she knew that that individual had to be infected with the original-sin virus and inevitably passed it on to her daughter Mary. Therefore, said our now angelic attorney, there must be an ecclesiastical court decision somewhere in the annals of the last eighteen hundred years of Christianity absolving Mary, the mother of God, of this blight of sin. But she found nothing.

Nor could the heavenly hoaxers fabricate another Holy Ghost-virgin-birth story and apply it to Mary, because they wanted the virgin birth of Jesus to be the one and only case of its kind. Its uniqueness would be cheapened if it were repeated. "Good thinking," said the law librarian. "Sound reasoning," said other lawyer friends; older angels and most of the staff members of the hierarchy, who were satisfied with the status quo said, "Don't bring the subject up; let sleeping dogs lie; we've gotten along perfectly well for eighteen hundred years."

Most of the women angels called the new female attorney a "troublemaker." They would have been delighted if some way could have been found to send her back to San Francisco. (Quite frankly, if that had been done she would be nearly as well off here as she was in heaven, San Fran being the only locale on earth that can compete with heaven as a place to live.)

Since they couldn't expurgate her by other means, they spread the rumor that she seemed to be under the influence of the devil; otherwise she wouldn't be casting aspersions on the mother of God. (Could there be such a thing as jealousy in the kingdom of heaven?)

More research by her, however, failed to turn up any evidence that Mary's mother might have had some kind of anti-viral vaginal vaccination; nor was there any record of her husband having been castrated by the Roman army of occupation or having been vasectomized by the Malthusians, the Philistines, or the Samaritans. He most certainly received no such treatment at the hands of the Jews, in view of their mandate to "be fruitful and multiply."

Notwithstanding all of these complications, the hierarchy felt a sense of guilt and above all, an urgency to resolve the matter before churchgoers could hear about it. Unfortunately, however, the question was referred to a committee. Ordinarily that would be a way to bury, not solve the problem. But this time the beatific bosses used their holy haloed heads and required the members of the committee to serve without compensation, and also be denied access to the deified dining table and the Papal Pub, so long as they delayed or deliberated unnecessarily. As a result, procrastination would be undesirable and unprofitable. (That's the language lawyers understand, at *mucho dinero* per hour.)

Lawyers not only tend to be logicians; the more successful

among them are also semanticists. That should make it possible for them to hypothesize and name some kind of sanitized, sinless circumstance surrounding the birth of Mary. Their first decision was not to advertise for a linguist or etymologist; at least not yet. First, they agreed, they should cogitate a day or two. Then, they should try that new idea the archangels had been urging on them, namely, to practice prayer, to see if, in due course (again without intercourse), their prayers would bring them a solution.

Sure enough, it did. A young lawyer, who had only arrived in heaven about a month before, having been shot to death by a husband, who accused him, unjustly, of alienating his wife's affections, offered what he said was a simple, practical solution. "Why," said he "can't the pope put out one of his bulletins and say that, after a careful search of vital statistics in the home town of Mary's parents, it was found that her birth was the result of an *immaculate* conception?"

The first reaction of the other members of the committee was one of silence, probably because they were not sure what the word meant and didn't want to admit it. Then one member spoke up. "What in hell, or rather what, in the name of heaven, is an *immaculate* conception?" said he.

"Hold on," said another. "I'll get a dictionary, if they have one up here." They did; and it defined the word as being "free from stain, from moral blemish and impurities."

"Hot diggity dog," said another member of the group. "*That's* the solution. Now all they have to do is to get the old man down in Rome to put out a little papal Bull—to the effect that Mary was conceived *immaculately*. It won't be necessary to explain anything. Just make it an article of faith, like the trinity; then everybody will have to accept it, even though it didn't come to light for 1,854 years."

Good. That seemed to dispose of Mary's birth. "Now can we go back to the deified dining room and the Papal Pub?" asked one of the committee. Where Mary's parents were 1,800 years after the event, or whether they were interested in these shenanigans, we do not know. One thing for sure—they were not in heaven, because, unlike their daughter, they did not join the Christian heresy.

We do know that they were quite upset when Mary, as a teenager, consorted with known Christians, but we also know that their displeasure was mollified when they saw how well the bums treated her after she became pregnant, seeing to it that she had plenty of the necessities of life and medical and hospital insurance, at least in the prenatal period. Beyond that, we know nothing about them.

After the committee of lawyers finished its work on Mary's background, and having little else to do but lie in heavenly hammocks all day long (or at least until vespers or evensong), they began to think about other ecclesiastical questions, such as, How come Mary, who had done so much to get the new religion started by giving birth to its founder, didn't seem to have anything to say about running it; whereas an apparent interloper—the one they called the Holy Ghost, who came from nowhere, had no credentials, no IQ or even an ID—had somehow elbowed his way up to the throne of the Almighty, with whom he now shares control of the universe. "And what is worse," said one of the attorneys, who had specialized in occultism while on earth, "calling him 'holy' doesn't cover up his shortcomings. If he's a ghost, he could be the soul of a dead person, or a disembodied spirit—the last kind of person needed to run a religion." (Strange how this Holy Ghost question keeps coming up.)

"Putting the Holy Ghost ahead of Mary in the heavenly organization chart," said an ex-vice president of an earthly conglomerate, "is not unreasonable: it is simply a continuation of the policy Jesus adopted of having only men in his apostolic apparatus."

Could it be that there is a bit of a human-rights violation going on here? Does the administration in heaven really want it to be totally masculine? If so, is it beyond our control, due to the separation of church and state?

This brought us to the end of the confirmation class. We were supposed to have learned the fundamental tenets of our religion; and, having learned them, we would presumably adhere to them; and as adherents, we would qualify for an afterlife of eternal bliss, peace, tranquility, health, absence of tooth decay, and all the other goodies that are scarce or hard to come by on this temporary jumping-off place called earth partly because there are too many of us. (Sounds like a damned good deal—one that anybody with even a modicum of common sense would buy.)

But did we? Did we graduate from this experience with a

behavior pattern different from, and morally better than, that of boys and girls who attended schools where God either took a back seat, wasn't in the room, or wasn't even mentioned?

In a word, No. Our behavior pattern was no better when we came to the end of the required period of "schooling" than it had been in the beginning; and for some of us it was worse. We may not have learned much from the nuns and the master, but we picked up a lot from each other. (Man is known by the company he keeps.)

Although there was no sex education per se (sex being taboo in a situation where it was supposed to be totally suppressed and where celibacy and virginity were considered to be the greatest of virtues), the subject, unfortunately from the viewpoint of the instructors, had to be dealt with in connection with the "original sin" myth, which some of the more knowledgeable boys ridiculed but which seemed to be a necessary part of creation.

Sexuality took a number of forms among the boys. Pornographic postcards, in color yet, were popular. Some were in layers that could be manipulated. If anyone was in doubt as to how Cain and Abel might have been generated, one could easily resolve the doubt (although it would be a sin) with the aid of one of these "adjustable" two-layered *demon*strations, produced, one might say, in the demon's print shop. All of this, of course, took place before *Playboy* magazine made it . . . sinless?

From time to time on his way home, one boy, I recall, would loudly yell "Holditinner." Did he really understand what he was saying? He did, probably, after watching the animated two-layered postcard, the prized possession of Eddie Andrus.

Better than shouting or looking at pictures that could be animated was a gesture a boy might make, although I never quite understood its purpose: a boy would cup his hand over his genitals and say "help yourself." My confusion arose from the fact that I couldn't figure out which of the two derived the greater benefit or if both found it worthwhile (making due allowance for sinfulness, of course). Living in San Francisco, I ought to know now what I didn't know then, except that I do not associate with members of that large group of people who could, without any hesitation, answer my question from direct personal experience.

It was equally difficult to understand how these boys handled such matters in the confessional, since anything having to do with sex was sinful. If one didn't confess it, one could not or would not partake of the Lord's supper at the next mass, and would have to explain the failure to do so to his superior. Or, if he *did* partake with the stain of sin on his soul, horrendous consequences could follow according to the doctrine doled out to us.

On the other hand, if one made a clean breast of it in the confessional the priest would then have the justification he needed to walk into the classroom and raise holy hell, succeeding, without mentioning a single name, in frightening the daylights out of the guilty one, with threats of eternal damnation.

I was not caught up in this sex play to an appreciable degree— not, however, because I was pure or obedient, but because I matured slowly. I think I was a year or two behind my age group in terms of my sexual development, but I also took the religious doctrine very seriously. In fact, I swallowed it hook, line and sinker. I would break away from my neighborhood playmates on Saturday afternoons about twice a month, as if I was doing an errand for Mrs. Rowe, go to church, and there humbly confess my sins to Almighty God through the intermediation of the priest.

After listening to what he had to say about my behavior and what I should do as penance (which usually consisted of so many "Hail Marys" and other prayers), he would give me absolution and I would be ready to partake of the Lord's supper the next morning— provided I didn't commit a sin during the night!

My narrow-minded sex education, however, was not limited to the repressive inhibitions of Catholicism. I was also a member of the Protestant YMCA (sub rosa, i.e., contrary to the wishes of our church), and this only made matters worse. If the church's teaching was intolerant, the Y's was bigoted. The Reverend H. R. Mott, of the Methodist persuasion, was head of the national organization at that time, and its primary spokesman and preacher. He exercised both functions with the conviction and persuasion of an evangelical zealot or a blathering Bible thumper, depending on your point of view.

When I heard him, or read his articles, I was left with the conclusion that in Protestantism, as in Catholicism, the only accept- able thing to do with sex was to suppress it, outlaw it, excise it, or call it by its proper name—a demoniacal disturbance—and thereafter bury it.

His degradation of sex was based on a dichotomy of morality and hygiene. On the moral aspect he was on the same wavelength as our parish priest and the Catholic hierarchy. They wanted us to behave as if there was no such thing as the sexual impulse. So did he. His second point was that the male endocrine system secretes a substance (semen) so precious and important that nary a drop should ever, ever, under any circumstances be lost. Our strength, our manhood, our physical, and yes, above all, our mental capacities are manifested in direct proportion to our conservation of this vital seminal fluid.

His double-barrelled denunciation of a dominating, imperious urge, one that was neither sought by us poor souls nor susceptible of severance, left me perturbed and perplexed, to put it mildly. It never occurred to me to ask a YMCA secretary whether Mr. Mott's recommendation applied to females. If so, how? Do women have somewhere in their bodies (less obviously than we men do) the equivalent of those hypergenerative gonads? If they don't, do they have spontaneous sexual urges, and, if so, are they free to give way to them? And if they do, do they suffer the same sort of debilitating consequences Dr. Mott said we men do? If so, how come? If not, why not? But I never asked the question. I couldn't; I was too bashful. This quandry was simply a part of the ambivalence and anxiety that accompanied my adolescence.

While trying to free myself from the self-flagellating restraints urged by the likes of priests and Motts, I eventually reached college age. Much more will be said about my collegiate life later; at this point, its relevance to the subject of sex is simply that, while I thought my adolescent period was complicated by extremist opinions before college, I found the attitude of the president of the university to be just as stuffy, restrictive, and overly ascetic as everything else I'd heard before that time. In fact, I concluded that I had jumped out of the frying pan of Puritanism into the fire of chastity.

Dr. B. (the president) was also a Methodist minister, and, although he did not preach the Gospel in a church, he couldn't refrain from doing so to us students. What he did to make life more complicated and miserable was to schedule Sunday afternoon convocations he called "smokers." (Why they were called that was never made clear, although, in those days, smoking and manhood were considered two sides of the same coin. He may also have wanted to give the impression that he regarded us as adults.)

Women students were excluded, because no one (especially a sincere Methodist) would ever *think* of discussing what Dr. B. had in mind in the presence of women, young or old, in those days. (Poor man; if there *is* an afterlife and cosmic communication with places like earth he must be suffering constant pain and sorrow, in view of the fact that Indiana University, following the lead of Professor Kinsey, has become the headquarters of sex education and sex research, out of which a liberal [Dr. B. would say a licentious], freewheeling national attitude toward sex has evolved. Even college dormitories and residence halls are co-ed in many places.

If Dr. B. were to become aware of *that* in his heavenly abode, and if he did not die of apoplexy upon hearing about it, then even I should have to admit that medical practice up there in heaven is much better than it is down here.)

If someone had asked me seventy years ago to make a guess as to where a philosophy of sexual freedom and libertarianism would develop in the United States I wouldn't have given the slightest thought to Indiana University, a middle-western outpost of Puritanism.

The net effect of Dr. B.'s system of sex hygiene was (or would be, if it was followed), about the same as that of the Reverend Mr. Mott's. The difference between the two was that, whereas Mr. Mott based his bias largely on physiological grounds, Dr. B. simply said "Don't," primarily because he and Methodism said so. And the reason he and his fellow theologians said so, as nearly as I could figure it out, was that sex, like any other kind of enjoyment, should be eschewed because it was pleasurable. In this respect Methodism and monasticism were similar: adherents of both seemed to believe that one's religiosity existed in direct proportion to one's willingness to forgo pleasure and endure pain and self-denial. Catholics called it asceticism; nuns, priests and monks were among the most ascetic members of the Church, because, in taking the vow of chastity, they eschewed sex.

So what was Dr. B.'s advice or recommendation to a group of

male students made up of all varieties of believers, from the lowliest of heathen to the grandest, most exalted of hell-and-damnation devotees, from lukewarm Protestants to conscientious Catholics and Jews? In a word, when he said "don't," he followed this injunction with his one and only solution or prescription, which was to *take a cold shower!*"

I knew this man because, as counter clerk in the Bursar's Office, I handed him his $500 paycheck every month and took back his signed voucher; I also lived in the basement of the apartment house he owned on Kirkwood Avenue, for which I paid two dollars per week. So I was not about to ruin my relationship with him by asking what one should do if a seizure occurred in a place or under circumstances when a shower was not possible—as might be the case in California, where there is a shortage of water due to a six-year drought and *too many people*. Can you imagine the amount of water that would be required to cool off the amorous inclinations of couples in this state in one day, not to say one *hour*?

Nor did I ask whether the Reverend Mr. John Wesley considered it necessary to offer women the kind of solution Mr. Mott and Dr. B. recommended for men, or whether Miss Maxwell, Dean of Women, had "smoker" convocations for women. (If she did, I daresay the discussion was about punctilio at a tea party or dress and decorum, with nary a word about anything even remotely related to sex.)

Notwithstanding their exclusion from sex seminars, the girls knew more than they were given credit for. They had an explanation for the ill health of Dr. B.'s wife: they said she was doubtless in that condition because her husband took too many cold showers.

Much more can be said about the connection between religion and sex; but that will have to wait until another day.

Chapter 9
Growing Up, More or Less

When the church school year ended in June, my thoughts turned away from the sex life of the holy family and capers in the classroom to the more important matter of trying to act like a grownup.

When I reached the age of about ten, the economical and far-sighted way of life of my parents began to make an impression on me.

My earliest moneymaking venture began when I became an errand boy for neighbors, especially Mrs. Rowe. This I would supplement by cutting grass. I would take the family lawnmower and shears and walk up and down the sidewalks in the neighborhood until I saw a lawn I thought was about due for a manicure. I would ring the doorbell and offer my services, usually for about fifteen cents for a normal-size lawn, not including clipping the edges; that would cost about fifteen cents more. On a good day I might net as much as one dollar.

Another business endeavor involved the sale of Christmas wreaths. A month or so before Christmas I would canvas the neighborhood offering holly wreaths, which I would deliver several weeks later. My mark-up was about twenty-five cents above my cost of fifty cents, making the price seventy-five cents per wreath. A 50 percent markup may sound like Scrooge economics. On the way to delivery, however, this product suffered from handling: berries would drop off, leaves would become dry, and occasionally, in the absence of a written contract plus a deposit, a customer could, and sometimes did, decline to take delivery. When that happened I had to absorb the loss. Thus I learned the importance of the risk-reward ratio; the only trouble is, I didn't pay enough attention to it later on in life.

My first real summer job was at Parsons & Scoville, a wholesale food company that handled nonperishable products (canned and bottled goods and other grocery items). My job was to get to the office before the bosses, open the mail, open the windows, turn on the fans, put ice in the water cooler, swat one or two of the flies that had mistakenly assumed a food company would provide at least a few goodies that could be devoured during the night; and run errands.

The only other event I recall in connection with this job is that, in opening the mail, I sometimes inadvertently stuck the letter-opener into the letter as well as the envelope, thereby disrespectfully dividing the communication into at least two parts. This tended to complicate deciding whether the letter was an order, a complaint, or a query. Either Mr. Parsons or Mr. Scoville delivered a firm lecture to me on the subject of prematurely converting business letters to waste paper; which left me almost as uncertain about my future in the business world as one of my dead flies must have felt about his future in the insect world when he saw me coming at him with a fly swatter. (Before the summer was over, I might add, the local newspaper, the *Courier*, offered five dollars in gold to the person who killed the most flies in the month of August. I won the prize, but my swatting experience at P & S is not what enabled me to win the contest. I'll explain that later. Some of my detractors allege that I still have the gold piece; the truth is, I had to turn it in for paper money when we went off the gold standard in 1933, so that the great Roosevelt administration could show us how it could spend money it didn't have by printing dollar signs on paper, the result of which is that five dollars is now worth about fifty cents and continuing to fall in value; while gold is rising.

The following summer I was not employed at P & S. Whether this was because they didn't need or want a person who lacerated letters before they were read, I can't say. But I *can* report that I was offered a most unusual job, for which I was even less qualified than I had been for the office-boy job at P & S the summer before. That is, the father of one of my playmates was in the milk-pasteurizing business. Farmers brought fresh milk to his plant daily and were paid a rate depending on the butter-fat content, which was deter-mined by processing milk samples in a centrifuge—a rotating con-tainer that, at high speed, separates substances of different densities.

The operator of the centrifuge would place a milk sample into a beaker, top it off with hydrochloric acid, and turn on the power. In less than a minute the cream would separate from the milk, which graded the milkman's product; he was then paid accordingly.

I knew nothing about the milk business, less about chemistry, and probably didn't even know how to spell hydrochloric or how it differed from other acids, or if indeed, it did. This soon became obvious: when I got the job my mother decided that my clothes were okay but that I needed new shoes. So I spent several weeks' future wages on a pair. A few weeks later I noticed that, despite the good care I was giving them, my new shoes seemed to be taking on some of the characteristics of sandals: the uppers were beginning to self-perforate. We were in the midst of World War I at that time, and substandard merchandise, such as leather goods, was not unusual. Consequently I simply took the matter "in stride," so to speak.

Until—until the same thing began to happen to my trousers. My father, being in the men's clothing business, took one look at my clothing and said, "Uh-uh, that's not substandard merchandise. That's something else. If you don't find out why working in the milk business is ruining your wearing apparel, if that's the cause, your summer's work this year will result in a negative cash-flow. Instead of adding to your savings account at Citizens Savings Bank, you'll have to draw money out."

Telling me to draw money *out* of my bank account—when I was trying to make it grow by putting in every dollar I had acquired by cutting grass, the five dollars I received for killing flies, and larger amounts from a real job working at the milk company—this was the practical equivalent of telling me to self-destruct, along with my wearing apparel. (Maybe that's how I got that reputation mentioned above.)

These strange happenings in the butterfat-testing department soon became known to the employees in the plant manager's department; but, instead of being sympathetic, they rather considered it instead to be the funniest bit of humor and their best relief from the monotony of the milk business since Jake, one of the clean-up boys in the plant, had combined fresh milk and butter milk, without benefit to either.

In a way, this should not be too hard to understand, because even a kid in high school, although his major interest might be, say, English literature or human physiology, ought to have enough common sense to know that stuff with a name as horrible as "hydrochloric" could be caustic and corrosive, and should never be combined with delicate substances unless the intention is to obliterate them. Although my degree of intelligence was not sufficient, at that time, to distinguish between a corrosive compound and a more salubrious substance, I learned the difference in a hurry—though not soon enough to prevent the loss of a perfectly good pair of shoes and an equally satisfactory pair of trousers, probably the equivalent of three or four weeks' earnings.

The rest of the summer went smoothly: I did no apparent violence to the dairymen in rating their product, and the milk company didn't go bust in paying them for it. September came in due course and I returned to school. There was no chemistry class (or any other kind of science course in my school), but if there had been I might have taken it to find out why the application of some substances polishes shoes and cleans fabrics and others make holes in them.

McFerson-Foster

Tempus fugit. Yes, before I knew it another school year ended, and I was again in the job market. The First World War continued, and, although the *Lusitania* had not yet been sunk, the United States was fully employed supplying goods to England and France and making up for shortages worsened by the submarine menace. This made it possible for youngsters like me to find jobs, even though they didn't always know what they were doing. This was definitely the case with the milk-company job; and also at the McFerson-Foster box factory, where I landed a job as soon as the next summer vacation began. A finished box was one that had been nailed together; unfinished boxes consisted of the pieces, cut to fit and tied into bundles called shooks. The customer would nail them together. The shop foreman was the husband of the Mrs. Rowe for whom I was errand boy, cherry picker, grass cutter and weed puller. When Mr. Rowe casually mentioned that he needed a shipping clerk, Mrs. Rowe said, "Why not try Irvin?—School's out now."

Mr. Rowe had some doubts. "He's only a high school kid; I'm not sure he could handle it," said he. But evidently he didn't discard the idea and he probably also spoke to the management about it the next morning because, that evening, he called me over to his house, across the street from our place, and told me that he would give me a job as shipping clerk if I would be ready every morning at seven o'clock to ride with him to the factory in his little low-slung, topless, two-seater, ground-hugging Saxon "motor car," which, as I look back on it, was actually not much more than a four-wheeled motor scooter. Of course, from my point of view, the ride to and from the factory in this little motorized equivalent of a pushmobile would almost be compensation enough. In fact, I didn't ask how much they would pay (probably because my mother advised me not to appear mercenary when offered a job; her view was that any job was preferable to unemployment).

So the next morning I appeared at Mr. Rowe's door step at 7:00 A.M. with a bag of lunch, ready to go. We dodged in and out of traffic, sometimes almost seeming to dart under rather than around the big rig trucks, until we reached the mill. I heard the siren song of giant circular saws, which were ripping logs into boards of varying thickness depending upon what kind of boxes were being made at that time. Obviously, in order for a Cook's Brewery box to hold twenty-four bottles of beer, it had to be made of thicker lumber than a box made for soda crackers or tea biscuits; even *I* knew that much.

Conveyor belts brought logs from rail cars, which were on sidings next to the factory; they moved from one work station to another. To avoid pile-ups and pandemonium the sawyers, planers, and joiners had to work at the pace set by the impersonal task-master—the conveyor belts and other mechanical movers.

Everybody was sawing or planing wood to minute specifications, creating a harmonious, high-pitched hum; a haunting, whining, and, in a way, rather mournful sound. The faster the blades of the planers and the teeth of the circular saws revolved, the higher the pitch, and prospectively, the income of the company. From the viewpoint of the people in the front office, this was the "sawmill symphony"—a melody in money making. If I could write music (I do try to compose and whistle it) I would like to do a *real* "Sawmill Symphony."

These whirring blades and saws would, however, unfortunately just as lief cut off the limb of a man as that of a tree, and for that reason the entire mechanical operation would be stopped, from time to time, to relieve tension and fatigue among the operators and reduce the danger of injury in this beehive of boxmaking.

I was not only given a job, I was given a title, shipping clerk. My first official act was to bill Cook's Brewery for a load of beer cases that were to be stacked onto a Cook's truck. I counted them as they were brought out of the factory to the loading platform. This caused considerable merriment for the factory employee—"Irish" was his name—and the truck driver, Sam, because they always stacked the boxes the same way on the same truck and the load was always fifty-seven. So my first assignment was probably unnecessary, unless the boss wanted to check up on the system. This might indeed have been the case, because I found out later that Cook's man usually brought a cold bottle for "Irish," and who knows whether the latter then added on another case for good measure.

I soon discovered that there was more to the job than counting. There were, in fact, three methods of delivering or shipping that I had better learn, and fast.

If the customer was a local company, it would probably pick up the bundles of shooks or the boxes. On the other hand, if the customer was within trucking distance and preferred McF & F to deliver, we would use our truck, or rent one if necessary, to suit the size of the order. This is where I had to begin to use my head. How big a truck was needed? That depended upon the cubic content of the shipment. If the order was too large for a truck and the distance too great, shipment would then be made by rail—but by LCL (less than a carload) or by a full-car lot? Same problem: what is the size (cubic content) of the shipment?

It didn't matter in school if we failed to understand the complexities of, say, the immaculate conception, or whether the spitballs stuck to the ceiling or dropped onto someone's desk or head. Box shooks and bible study had little in common, and I decided that I had better learn—pronto. We didn't have to calculate the cubic content of the loaves and fishes left over after the picnic in the public park; all we had to know, in that connection, was that more was left over than they had when they started, even after all the hungry had been fed, whether they were believers or not.

But in the box business, I discovered, we had to know the cubic content of a shipment. If I was unable to provide such information, I was in danger of being returned involuntarily to the comparatively juvenile occupation of cutting grass.

The fact of the matter is that I was beyond my depth. Fortunately the management didn't expect me to come up with an answer on the spur of the moment. Days before an order would be ready for shipment, calculations could be made as to the size of truck that would be needed; whether it would be less than a carload, if shipped by rail; and, of course, whether the order would be shipped knocked down (as shooks) or made up. Consequently, I could hide my ignorance and somehow find the answers before we ordered the vehicle of transportation. Mr. Rowe would also check any and all of my arithmetic on an important matter of this sort.

I didn't admit at the mill that I was unable or incompetent to make the calculation; instead, I would take the problems home and submit them to my parents. This is where trouble, real trouble, began, for my parents began to wonder what kind of education I was getting at the parochial school: if I was not learning arithmetic, was I at least making up for that deficiency in other subjects?

Much that has been said thus far has a bearing upon this situation; and more that will come later follows from it. The problem that was beginning to develop in the Bussing household was that my mother's hope and aspiration—that her children, especially her son, would grow up to "be somebody"—might not be realized. Now the first sign of failure seemed to have surfaced: my education was apparently substandard. Something would have to be done about that at once.

But that posed another, more serious problem. Catholic parents can't yank their offspring out of a parochial school at will: their children are supposed to stay there until the church feels that they have received proper and adequate religious training. (It is an interesting question—whether learning more about a subject, such as religion, causes one to become more devoted to it, or whether the opposite actually turns out to be the case. In the religious community, the prevailing opinion seems to be that religious indoctrination, and acceptance thereof, are two sides of the same thing. That was the view of the church when my parents had to cope with the problem. Let us see how they handled it.)

Chapter 10
The Cost of Confirmation

Suspicion gave way to surprise when Mother began investigating the school. Prior to this time she didn't seem to question its quality, much to my amazement in retrospect. That may be because she, and all of the other members of the Bussing and Mace families, had gone to the same school and all of them had managed to survive, though with admittedly varying degrees of success. Only two or three became "somebody," as she hoped I would.

She was, however, taught by the sisters, and I believe the quality of their work was better than that of the master in the boys' school. In any case I was adrift in a sea of indifference, being taught by someone who was either unaware of or unconcerned about the fact that I had no motivation to study. Unless there was a change of course, I was headed for a life of mediocrity and no one seemed to realize it—including me.

If I read anything it was Horatio Alger, *Peck's Bad Boy*, and the local newspaper. I was interested in tinkering, building a playhouse in the backyard, whittling propellers for weathervanes and for a new kind of thing called an aeroplane. I also experimented with dry-cell electric batteries, grinding the valves in Uncle Will's Model-T Ford, building pushmobiles—everything but book-learning. Electricity fascinated me. We had candles on the Christmas tree, but lit them only once during the season because of the fire danger. So I decided to put an electric light on the top of the tree, but there was no electricity in the house: we had gas lights. I had to find a way to bring in electricity. This I did by purchasing a dry-cell battery for twenty-five cents, which I placed on the floor under the tree, running two fine wires up to the tiny light. Having no light shade, I colored the shell of an egg and placed it over the little bulb; bravo! a colored light was aglow atop the Christmas tree.

In view of my interest in electricity, Mother was receptive to any suggestion I might have made as to a Christmas gift along that line; so when she took me down to Main Street to shop in one of the department stores and I saw what looked like a dynamo that was run by a belt from a toy steam engine, I became excited, but suspicious of its capacity to generate electricity. If it would, I could dispense with the dry cell and keep the little light aglow as long as there was fuel in the steam engine. So I asked the sales clerk if that dynamo really would generate electricity. He said it would, and so we bought the combination of steam engine and dynamo. Result? I continued to use the dry cell because the dynamo was too crudely built to do what the dynamos at your local public utility do. It was not a total loss, however, because I could still play with the old-fashioned part, the steam engine.

This kind of tinkering did little to cure the effects of mental malnutrition and the toxicity of spitball pulp in the "educational" institution in which I spent the early and formative years of my life. How the reformation came about is one of the reasons for writing this tale.

The chickens came home to roost (i.e., my deficiencies came to light) when I was unable to calculate cubic content at the box factory. Mother then began testing me in subjects other than arithmetic, such as spelling, grammar, history, civics, and geography, and found that I was as backward in these subjects as I was in arithmetic. This turned the latter part of the month of August into something of a traumatic turmoil. The problem was twofold: first, what should be done about it; and second, if the remedy was to take me out of the parochial school, how could this be done without running the risk of excommunication?

After considerable soul-searching, Mother (Father concurring, as he usually did with anything she wanted to do) decided to take me out of the church school and worry about the excommunication later. Even for a lukewarm believer, however, a decision of that magnitude took considerable courage; while I, almost a retardate, followed directions, which involved going along with whatever Mother told me was necessary in order to extricate me from this virtual non-school and get me into a public school.

I was eleven years old when this ruckus erupted, and I would be twelve in October. Chronologically, therefore, I was old enough to be in the sixth grade of an elementary school, and that is where Miss Bisbee, the principal of Chandler School, put me. However, it was soon discovered that the sixth grade was too advanced for me; so I was demoted to the fifth: but even some of the fifth grade work required a background I didn't have, so that some of my classes were at the fourth-grade level, at least initially—until Miss McCutcheon got into the act.

The feeling of being treated like a retardate was compounded by the fact that I was a tall kid for my age. What I lacked in educational development I more than made up with my long legs. I couldn't get my knees under the little desks; my feet stuck out in the aisle. That created a traffic problem if a classmate was called by the teacher to go to the blackboard to, say, diagram a sentence. (Diagram a sentence! What in heaven's name does that mean? Never heard of such a thing.)

Better the other kid than me, however; he could climb over my long legs and at least do something with that sentence. The only thing that came to *my* mind was what judges pronounce in court— sentences.

Later I concluded that diagramming a sentence is a system teachers of English use to find out if a kid knows the difference between what they call parts of speech; some words, I found out, are called adverbs and adjectives, while others are called verbs, without the "ad." Why this was important I did not know, but I was given the impression that if I didn't take it seriously I would be considered as rampant a renegade in the public school system as I had been (among the doubters) in the confirmation class: and as a consequence, I might be in for a "Protestant-style" excommunication—i.e., not promoted.

When I started to write this "true confession" on my ninety-second birthday, I said that two women had exerted a profound influence on my life—one being my mother, the other a school teacher. In refusing to follow the exact routine prescribed by the church relative to religious training and education, Mother did her part. The other person, Miss McCutcheon, was one of the teachers in this public school where I was in so much trouble; she took over where Mother left off. She heard early on about this big, new kid, who had come in from a Catholic school but was either retarded or had been neglected and was not making the grade.

She was a devout Catholic. (She and her sister, I feel safe in saying, had never been married or anything.) Therefore she had more interest than usual in this new kid, including, perhaps, a tinge of embarrassment if her associates got the idea, as a result of my ineptitude, that Catholics taught by nuns, priests, and monks either get an inferior education or are stupid to begin with.

While I was trying to adjust to this new life, Mother was having even more serious problems with the parish priest, because, when the school year began, I had not been present in the confirmation class. If I did not attend, I would not be confirmed, and that would defeat the whole purpose of the parochial school.

So it was inevitable that there would be a confrontation between my parents, especially Mother, and the reverend father. When it did occur, the verdict was handed down: either you bring the kid back to our school or you face excommunication.

Although the Bussings (my father's side) were relatively staunch believers or faithful followers, the Mace family (my mother's side) was less so. My aunts and uncles on the Mace side did take their religion seriously, and one of my uncles (Mother's brother) married—yes, married—a Methodist.

So it was not totally unexpected, though difficult enough, for Mother to tell the priest (in a ladylike manner) what he could do with his excommunication. The result was that we could no longer show our faces in our parish church, although we were not about to chuck the whole thing bell, book, and candle, for excommunication cannot be treated too lightly. One might have many reservations about the dogma of the faith; but, if a person is excommunicated, he is denied the sacraments of the church and consequently runs the risk of everlasting damnation if, indeed, the doctrine holds water. (Holy water?) We may not necessarily agree with these man-made rules, but is it worth taking a chance?

We could not transfer to another parish, because we were black-listed. However, there was a convent not too far from our house and, if I am not mistaken, a convent is not under the same degree of supervision by the bishop as a parish church is. The result was that Mother found we could slip into the convent chapel for services, which we did without fanfare and as far as I know, no questions were ever asked. (Incidentally, there was a high brick wall around the convent with broken glass embedded in concrete on the top of it. I could never figure out whether this impediment was designed to keep the nuns in or the rapists out. Religious practice seemed to bring up one question after another.)

Chapter 11
A Savior in a *Public* School?

The difference between this September and the Septembers of the preceding three or four years was that, this year, I would go to school with the same kids with whom I played street hockey, leap frog, duck-on-the-rock, and ran pushmobile races; i.e., with my neighborhood playmates. But while we would be in the same school, we would not be in the same classes; they were all ahead of me. If dunce caps had been in use, I would have worn one.

It is difficult to recall how I coped with this situation. Maybe I am an example of the Freudian thesis that we forget what is disagreeable. But I was not abandoned, alone, or ridiculed: Miss McCutcheon took a personal interest in me, for the reasons mentioned, and this more than offset any derogation there might have been toward this big fellow who, in social relationships, showed some signs of maturity, but who had very little to show in terms of academic achievement. Who was he? Where had he been? Was he an ex-truant the truant officers had brought back to school?

What light could his parents throw was the conundrum. This was the question that Miss McC. began to investigate: she visited my mother after school hours, unbeknownst to me, and got the whole story. Immediately thereafter I found myself in a new world. While the other teachers regarded me as a slow learner, or something worse, Miss McC. (who many months later suggested that I call her Betty) told me to stay after school. She was willing to sacrifice her afternoons to teach me what I needed to know to catch up.

In addition to the instruction, I began to feel a sense of rapport with her (she must have been in her late twenties or early thirties) unlike anything I had experienced heretofore—a consciousness of kind, which Professor Giddings of Columbia used to say, is a stronger bond than that of birth. If it is reasonable to think that a kid of twelve can be in love, then I was in love with Miss McCutcheon. What a change from the impersonal relationships of the past! And what a lift to my spirit to have the interest and confidence of a person who was not only mature, but who was also beautiful and cultured. I was mentally and spiritually transmuted; I became, literally, a different person.

Whether it was our religion that was beginning to bond us together, or a mutual sympathy, or simply her attitude of magnanimous helpfulness, I shall never know; nor does it matter. The plain truth is that, at a time when despair and disillusionment could well have dominated me and my outlook on life, a human being, here in my home town, was ready, able, and willing to guide and assist me and restore my self-confidence. Even now, at the age of ninety-four, my eyes become misty as I tell this tale.

The school day ended at 3:30 in the afternoon; from then until 4:30 or 5:00 P.M. she would sit with me in the otherwise deserted classroom and work on my weaknesses, which were mainly in arithmetic and grammar. After these sessions we sometimes walked through Bayard Park, which was near the school, and at these times she would talk to me less as a preadolescent and more as an adult— and as a result, I began to think more as an adult.

One Sunday afternoon she and her sister had arranged to go down to Second Street to visit Miss Rich, another teacher in the city school system. I was flattered beyond belief to be invited to join them. (Second Street was then, and is today, in an upscale area of the city.) I had not only reached the point where I was in the company of an adult in the classroom after school, I was now mingling socially with adults who were among the city's elite. I might not have known how to calculate the cubic content of a bundle of box shooks a few months before, but wow! look at me now. Believe it or not, at Miss Rich's apartment I was probably not much more than a stone's throw from where Mr. Clifford, one of the owners of the McFerson-Foster box factory, undoubtedly lived! Or from the Fendrich household, on Riverside, where I'd delivered cream from Mrs. Morden's Holstein cows years before.

The next social event was even more significant. One of Betty's uncles lived in Henderson, Kentucky, across the river from Evansville; he invited her for a Sunday dinner and she took me along. So, after church, we took the ferry across and were met by her uncle (or was it his chauffeur?) in his car, a Winton Six. (In case you have forgotten, the Winton Six was a competitor for fame of the Pierce Arrow and the Packard.) It was built in Cleveland, where one of my uncles had something to do with its manufacture, before the company went the way of hundreds of other automobile companies during the first half of the twentieth century. Unlike my uncles, her uncle, from the looks of things, had never had anything to do with any undertaking that suffered financial reverses.

The family domicile, surrounded by trees at the top of a modest incline, was quite as sumptuous as the highly polished, brass-and-nickel-plated Winton Six. I had come a long way, baby—from a classroom dominated by a pot-bellied stove and a ceiling decorated by spitballs dignified by halos of sputum, and fellow "students" who were more interested in disobedience than decorum—to a family setting of affluence, dignity, and rank.

Just how I managed readily to adjust to this rather substantial change in my social life escapes me. However, I recall that it was my parents' opinion, oft expressed, that children "should be seen and not heard," that older people "go first," that a boy always tips his hat in greeting an older person, male or female, that one says "sir" or "madam" in conversation, and that never, under any circumstances does a child seat himself before others have been seated; he sits on the floor if necessary. These social amenities certainly were of value in enabling me to adjust to my new social status; they must also have made it easier for Betty to take me under her wing as a protege. She even gave me the impression that I was her escort, not her ward, and it elevated my self-esteem enormously, although I evidently kept it from adversely affecting my manners.

Although I think I managed to keep it to myself, I had reached the stage where the sermons and articles of the Reverend Mr. Mott of the YMCA took on added significance. What would he say if he knew that I was beginning to have dreams, not about pushmobiles and hockey sticks, but about a lovable female—my teacher? After all, she was the only exogenous member of the opposite sex I really knew. Is that why she gently suggested, on one of our walks through Bayard Park, that I lighten up on my workload and get acquainted with girls? Was she trying to tell me that, sooner or later, emotional considerations would deserve as much attention as scholastic endeavors? Was she telling me that she had had a disappointing love affair, and that I should begin to think about trying to have a wholesome and satisfying one?

I wanted to, but never did ask any questions about her love life, or if there had even been one. I was too bashful. I do recall a remark she made, during one of our walks through the park, in connection with some sort of romantic story that was appearing in the news at that time. She characterized the individuals involved in the romance as "lovesick fools." I extrapolated that remark to the conclusion that she might have had an unfortunate love experience, which could account for the fact that she was not married.

In any case, I reasoned that although she was an affectionate, loving person, for reasons unknown she happily and devotedly bestowed her affections on those of us youngsters she considered deserving, rather than upon a mate of her generation. This seemed still to be the case when last I saw her, some forty years ago.

If you feel that I may be exaggerating her apparent personal interest in me, I might mention another item or two. During the early years of this century, painting china was a hobby among many people, and she took up decorating blank pieces of china with gold paint or gold leaf and color. As a Christmas gift in the year 1912 she gave me a piece of porcelain, in the shape of a wing collar with a lid, decorated with forget-me-nots and highlighted with gold. On the underside of the piece she inscribed in gold, *"Merry Xmas to I. B., B. McC."* This little memento was for collar buttons, which were used in those days to attach a collar to one's shirt. I wore white celluloid hand-washable collars, which were attached to my shirts by collar buttons. (No doubt you are saying that collar buttons are as antique today as some of us who used them seventy-five years ago.)

Her Christmas gift the next year, 1913, was a blue cream pitcher highlighted in gold, with the same inscription on the under-side. In December 1914, when I was about to depart for high-school (having completed in two years what probably would have required at least three had it not been for her help), her gift was a cup and saucer elaborately painted with gold and colors. All three of these prized possessions are on display in our china cabinet. Next time you come to everybody's favorite city we shall be glad to show them; but it will be impossible to convey the sentimental attachment they evoke for me every time I look at them.

The fact that she took up this hobby is one reason for thinking she may have had a nervous breakdown earlier, possibly as a consequence of an unfortunate love affair, and it may have been a part of her therapy. As I look back, I wonder where I got that idea. Freud had begun to influence our thinking, but I certainly was not reading books on psychiatry. I had more than I could handle, what with diagramming sentences, trying to understand the relationship between fractions and decimals, and making up for the three lost years in the parish school. But I still think that my "diagnosis" of her situation was not too far from reality.

Chapter 12
Hurrying through High School

I was now ready for high school, although two years late. Having done the three-year stint in the elementary school in two years, could I do the four-year course in high school in three? I would try.

To accomplish this it would be necessary to carry at least one more subject than required each year, and to attend summer school besides. I did both, with the approval of Mr. J. O. Chewning, the assistant principal.

I have nothing but praise for that school: it was as good an educational institution as the parochial was deficient. In addition to English literature, grammar, mathematics, composition, history, and other customary subjects, there was an excellent course in human physiology, which included laboratory experiments. What we learned in that course has been of great value to me throughout life. In addition to anatomy and physiology, it dealt with personal hygiene, the effects of narcotics, nicotine, and alcohol on the nervous system, with the digestive process; and with the essentials of good nutrition.

There was a course in bookkeeping. Would that I had stayed with that one, but I didn't, because I aspired to being much more than one of those people who wore black elastic arm bands and green shades over their eyes as they pored over ledgers. *I* would be a big shot: I would employ such people, not be one of them. (Is this the same kid who, about four years previously, was adrift in a sea of educational indifference, floating in a lifeboat without a paddle?)

Little did I realize that the so-called bookkeeping course would prepare me for the kind of life I would lead some years later. What I think threw me off the track was that the course began with an individual proprietorship, which sounded to me more like keeping accounts for the corner grocery store. That definitely did not arouse any enthusiasm in me, after I'd visited Betty's uncle in Henderson, or spent the afternoon with Miss Rich on Second Street, where the people lived who employed bookkeepers.

Too bad. Nowadays I have to rely on accountants (who probably took bookkeeping courses in order to become CPAs) to help me analyze balance sheets and income statements, to determine whether the amount reported as earnings per share of stock can be taken at face value. That's important, for if a stock is selling at ten times reported earnings per share and the earnings so reported are inflated, you might soon find that you can't afford a bookkeeper, let alone the kind of automobile Betty's uncle had. But the guy you bought the stock from might. Bookkeeping precedes accounting, an understanding of which is important in this monetary society.

There was also a course in touch-system typewriting. After completing this course one would be able to type without looking at the keyboard. I signed up for that course, too, but dropped out, because, again, I expected to hire stenographers, not replace them. Wrong again. I am now sitting in front of a computer keyboard, hunting and picking keys, at great expense in time, and time can't be recovered. When it's spent, it's gone forever. In fact, my failure to complete that typewriting course so long ago might ultimately contribute to my demise before I finish this piece of work (which you might think unimportant, but which would be a considerable disap-pointment to me—if I was aware of it, under those circumstances!).

The "manual training" section, under the supervision of Mr. Tinker, had to do with woodworking. I never used a buzz saw at the box factory, but I used one under his supervision in the shop at school. We learned how to make mortise and tennon joints, dovetails, and connections using dowel pins. I could have gone back to the box factory after completing this course and become shop foreman, but not having studied bookkeeping, I probably couldn't be office man-ager.

We also did mechanical drawings under Mr. Allison's direction, using india ink and a very special kind of draftsmen's instruments. If we made an ink smudge, we would have to do the drawing completely over.

I remember Mr. Allison, not merely because he wasn't much taller than the drawing boards we worked on, but also because on my way to school one day I had a slight accident, which made it desirable that I return to my home before going to school. That made me late for Mr. Allison's class. I don't recall precisely why, but I wrote a note, which I handed to Mr. Allison, saying "Please admit Irvin" and signed (by me) "J.O.C.," those being the initials of the assistant principal, J. O. Chewning. Mr. Allison smelled a rat. He showed the note to Mr. Chewning, unbeknownst to me, and after class told me that Mr. Chewning would like to see me. With considerable apprehension I presented myself to him in his office. He had the note in hand as he looked me over. (Frankly, and not for publication, it is my hunch that he was a little perplexed in a situation where a kid wanted to be *in* school, to the extent that he would forge the principal's name. He was more accustomed to dealing with pupils who tried to avoid going to school.)

He handed me the note and said, "Did you write that?"

"Yes sir."

"Do you realize that you have committed a forgery?"

I don't know how I responded; but I do remember his telling me that forgery is a serious offense, and that I should never do it, or anything like it, again. Did I understand?

"Yes sir."

Off I went to my next class (for which I was late), where I entered the room as furtively as possible, offering the teacher no excuse, either oral or written.

Incidentally, my last encounter with Mr. Chewning occurred on a hot afternoon in August 1917, when I took a history examination. In order to complete the requirements for graduation that summer, three years after I'd entered, I needed two additional credits. This I requested I be permitted to make up by reading for a history course and taking an examination. If I passed the examination, I would have enough credits for graduation. Inasmuch as the summer session had ended and the history teachers and others had gone fishing, only members of the administrative staff were in the building; so I was seated at a table in Mr. Chewning's office. There I racked my memory for an hour or two and evidently came up with enough right answers to justify Mr. Chewning's signing my diploma. Thus I graduated high school three years instead of four after I entered.

The reason why I was so eager to complete high school was that

I couldn't wait to enter Indiana University. Although Evansville High School was interesting, productive, and instructive, wouldn't college be even more so? I thought so. Nothing could have kept me from taking this next step.

Chapter 13
From High to Higher Education

Walking out of the high school office that afternoon in August 1917 marked the end of one phase and the beginning of another; like a butterfly, I had changed from the larva stage, where my purpose in life was undefined, to the current stage of being intellectually ambitious. There was little similarity between the kid who'd left the parochial school a few years previously and the one who walked out of Mr. Chewning's office after writing on that history exam to complete the requirements for graduation. (Whether or not Mr. C. remembered me as the brat who "forged" his initials, I don't know.) Had anything conspired at that time to prevent my going to college, I hesitate to contemplate the consequences.

Primary credit for this rebirth, you must know by now, goes to Betty McCutcheon. I don't think I paid adequate homage to her later in life, for which I do not forgive myself; my only lame-duck excuse is that I became so involved in academic work at the university, and later in business, that I neglected to keep in touch with her, and it's too late now. (If her religious belief is right and mine wrong, maybe I'll meet her somewhere in the cosmos in the not-too-distant future, provided they have telephone directories. Although I "didn't have time" here on earth there should be ample time up there, because as I understand it, there will be little or nothing else to do but try to find old friends—those who went up, not down, after death, according to "Scripture.")

The State University at Bloomington is the school I chose. Carl, one of my playmates, went to Ohio State, and Roy chose Illinois—in both cases, I think, because those schools had better football teams. I deplored the emphasis on intercollegiate athletics, and still do. I think M.I.T. does very well without that childish rah-rah stuff. Maybe I also agree with Merle Kessler, who says that football players, like prostitutes, are in the business of ruining their bodies for the pleasure of strangers.

I had hopes of accomplishing at least three objectives: (1) I wanted to "work my way" through college, i.e., not depend on remittances from home to cover expenses; (2) I would not try to exceed the speed limit, as I did in high school; I would do the four-year course in four years; and (3) I would try to achieve a high level of academic accomplishment. (Mind you, this is coming from the kid who used to leave his homework assignments at his grandmother's house, because he had no interest in either the subject matter or his scholastic record.)

The first objective was also the first one to be tackled. So within seventy-two hours after leaving Mr. Chewning's office I was on a C. & E.I. train enroute to Bloomington for the purpose of lining up a job of some sort.

I had a box lunch, which I preferred to the kind of food that was offered in the train by hucksters who came through the coaches with sandwiches and other items. (I was under the influence of the physiology and hygiene course I'd taken in high school, with the result that I preferred my bran muffins, cottage cheese and fruit—and still do—to ham on white bread, potato chips, Coke, and cake. Consumers of that kind of stuff evidently had not had as good a high school class in nutrition as had I.) When I arrived in Bloomington that evening a storm was brewing, so I took the first room I saw that was for rent, made do with what was left in my lunch box, and went to bed.

Next morning I started job-hunting. My first stop was at a grocery store on the public square, where I told the manager that I was looking for a part-time job so I could attend the university. He suggested a Saturday job delivering orders to households and I accepted it, starting in September.

At least, I said to myself, I'll avoid starvation. I also reminded myself that I had better not try another Kewson caper. Mr. Kewson, you see, had a food store in our neighborhood. On Saturday, Father would come home for lunch, because Saturday was payday for practically everybody and Main Street would be awash with shoppers that evening; Father might not have time even for a snack.

One Saturday morning, Mother sent me to Kewsons to buy a

porterhouse steak for Father's lunch. As I was leaving the store, and thinking that Mr. Kewson was still in the butcher section and unlikely to see what I might be up to, I pilfered a pear from the produce counter. Wrong again. I not only underestimated, in high school, Mr. Allison's ability to suspect a simulated signature, I failed again to realize Mr. Kewson was capable of seeing if anyone was trying to purloin some of his precious produce while he was still in the meat department. Indeed, he caught me red-handed.

His "advice" to me was physical, as distinct from Mr. Chewning's, whose admonition had been ethical. Or, to put it more succinctly, Mr. K. gave me a swift kick in the pants, repossessing the furtive fruit before I'd had a chance to conceal it in what was referred to in our physiology class as one's digestive tract. He accompanied this act of violence with language that left no doubt that, as far as he was concerned, my father could go without porterhouse steaks the rest of his life if he had to send me to buy them. He also characterized me as the son of quite a different type of woman than Mother was—the relevance of which, to the immediate situation, I failed to see. (I didn't tell Mother what Mr. Kewson thought of her, nor did I confess what he thought of me or the reason why he did. She did wonder, however, why I never wanted to go back to that convenient store.)

Getting back to Bloomington—while holding down a delivery-boy job at a grocery store would keep the wolf from the door, little more could be said for it, especially as I now know that it would be foolhardy to try to augment my earnings with a little income-in-kind from the produce department, or from any other part of the store. (Had I forgotten the priest's warning, that we couldn't conceal our sins: God knows all?) At any rate, after a few moments of soul searching in front of the grocery store, I bethought me thus: *Although such a job would keep body and soul together, couldn't I do better? How could my mother think I was on the road to becoming "somebody," if I was content to work in a grocery store? Why not make another effort? Why not go up to the university?* As I was as eager to see it as I was to get a job, I started up Kirkwood Avenue, which leads directly into the campus.

On this hot and humid afternoon in the latter part of August 1917, the campus was deserted. Summer school had ended. No work was being done on the buildings or the campus grounds, because all available manpower was either in military training camps or employed directly or indirectly in the war effort. In only one building was there a sign of life—Maxwell Hall, where the president, the registrar, and the bursar had offices. With considerably more trepidation than I'd had in entering the grocery store, I ventured into this beautiful Indiana-limestone building. The bursar's office on the first floor was closed; so I went up the iron stairway to the second floor, where the holy of holies, the president's office, was located, as was the registrar's, which was open. Having come this far I could not let timidity overtake me, so I walked in cautiously. The room was dark and quiet; the only sound, that of an electric fan. The window shades had been lowered to defeat the sun. Only one person was there, a youngish man, though he was old enough to have lost most of his hair. In a pleasant, soft-spoken manner, he asked me what my purpose might be and why had I chosen to interrupt his tranquility on this sleepy, sultry August afternoon when the university was closed.

In that famous course in human physiology, to which I keep referring, we learned that one's pulse rate rises at times of excitement or danger, this being a reflex action to supply additional oxygen to muscular organs, so better to cope with an emergency or crisis. For me, this particular interview was the practical equivalent of an emergency. If I had been wearing a black box at the time, the EKG would have registered about the same pulse rate as if I had been trying to outrun a hungry tiger.

In response to his question I said that I wanted to matriculate when the school year began, but it would be necessary for me to earn enough money to cover my expenses.

The next question pertained to my qualifications. I said that I had been working during my last year in high school as counter clerk at the *Evansville Courier* newspaper office from 6:00 to 9:00 P.M.

"What did that involve?"

"Operating the telephone switchboard; taking want ads; wrapping and mailing copies of ads to out-of-town advertisers; pasting late-breaking news stories on the windows at the sidewalk level (mostly war news and numbers of men drafted by the army), and anything else that Mr. Fehn left for me to do, being the only one still in the office on the first floor."

"What other work have you done?"

I didn't mention my confusion in trying to cope with cream and hydrochloric at the milk company. But I did say that after summer school last year I'd worked as a shipping clerk at a box factory, omitting reference to my arithmetical ineptitude in that job.

These responses seemed to elicit some degree of interest, as a result of which he told me to write a letter of application for a job, supported by letters from present and former employers and addressed to him, Mr. Claude Bolser. (How come I remember his name after seventy-five years? It's not simply because many people my age remember what happened to them decades ago better than what just happened a few minutes or hours ago—a common symptom of Alzheimer's. I remember his name, I feel, because of the importance this contact had to me, and the fact that, up to this point, the interview had gone extremely well. At least I was not told that I was wasting his time and mine, or that it would make more sense if I continued my stroll through the campus.)

So, back I go to the shabby Monon railroad station, where I was told a rickety "passenger" train (with a freight car attached) should be along "pretty soon," and that it would connect with a C. & E.I. train at French Lick, provided the latter had waited for the Monon in case it was late, as it usually was, and as the C. & E.I. usually didn't.

However, I had no choice. I had to get back, get in touch with Mr. Fehn at the *Courier* and Mr. Clifford at the box factory, and ask each of them to write the required letter to Mr. Bolser. School would begin soon. Missing connections at French Lick was SOP (Standard Operating Procedure), not a serious matter for some people but rather an opportunity to spend the night at the swank French Lick Hotel and Spa, there to partake of the spa's famous Pluto water. (Betty and her sister used to go there for a luxurious holiday and she would tell me about its sumptuosity.) I wouldn't dare suggest that there might have been a little collusion between the railroads and the spa. Nor will I question the curative properties of the mineral water (at least we never heard about it in our physiology class).

Needless to say, the Monon was late; the C. & E.I. didn't wait, and I didn't spend the night at the spa. There were fleabags in the village for people like me: if we wanted a swig of Pluto Water, we could buy a bottle with a dime. During the next few years, a misconnection at French Lick, for those of us traveling from Bloomington to points south, was more or less expected, largely as a consequence of the deferred maintenance of these coal-carrying railroads during the war.

Chapter 14
Of Money, Monks, and Matriculation

The letters written in my behalf must have been convincing, for, in the first week in September, I received a letter from Mr. Ulysses H. Smith, Bursar (who the students nicknamed Up High Smith because he was over six feet tall). With fear and trembling, I opened it to find that he was asking me to return to the university at once because, if I was found to be acceptable to him, he would want me to start work a few days later when registration for the fall semester would begin.

Overcome with joy, I raced up stairs, started emptying my bureau drawers and filling my handbags; I also should have a suit of new clothes, which, where necessary, I was able to acquire and have altered overnight with Father's assistance, so that within less than forty-eight hours I was again at the C. & E.I. station buying a one-way ticket to Bloomington.

On the train I met some boys who were I.U. bound also. They asked me why I was going so early. My answer was likewise: why are you in such a hurry? It turned out they were brothers in a fraternity and intended to get their chapter house into ship-shape condition for the "rushing" season. They also asked me what fraternity I planned to join. I told them that I hadn't given the matter any thought.

Whereupon they decided that, not only should I give it some thought, but that I should come to their house for dinner the next day. Which I did.

I was not impressed. The dinner would not have been approved by anyone who had learned the elements of nutrition in a high school course on physiology and hygiene, if you know what I mean. (*Yes, we know what you mean. We thought we weren't going to hear any more about that damned course, I can hear you saying.*) Although they didn't know that they flunked the dinner course, they proceeded to show me the study rooms. Three boys occupied each room. On one of the study tables there was a phonograph; on another, a large ash tray and a pipe, both of which showed signs of considerable use. Would such surroundings be conducive to study? Not in my opinion.

The dorm wasn't too bad. Plenty of fresh air; also alarm clocks, which could be a nuisance unless becoming a member of the club caused all members spontaneously to conform to the same circadian rhythm. (Years later, when my son entered a New England college, he became a member of this same national fraternal organization. So now, who had a phonograph on his desk? I'll give you three guesses. And who was his favorite composer? Bach. And how many of his brothers considered Bach and other classical composers a source of atmospheric pollution? Probably most of them, especially if they might want to do a little studying.)

The upshot of this was that I did not pledge, to this or any other group. I didn't have social life on my mind, and social life was a distinguishing feature of fraternities and sororities at that school in those days.

My mind was on Mr. Smith, who saw me the morning after I arrived in town. He at once put me at ease, evidently having decided beforehand that I would be able to handle the job they had in mind for me. What it involved did not differ, basically, from the responsibilities I'd had as counter clerk at the *Courier* office, except that here I would handle considerable amounts of money at the beginning of a semester, when fees were paid by students. I would also make up bank deposits and take them to the bank downtown (which was only a few yards from the grocery store where I might have worked had I not been so fortunate as to have met Mr. Bolser).

I would be under the supervision of Mr. Smith's number-two man, Mr. Thomas A. Cookson. When I was not busy at the counter I would post the fee ledger and do odd jobs for him. One particular function of the counter clerk was to hand salary checks to members of the faculty who called for them in person; I thus got to know many of them before I'd even registered for classes full-time.

There was a fly, as it were, in the ointment: the job was full-time, not part-time. I therefore was not able to do any academic work during the first year. This was somewhat troublesome, since I was already at least a year behind schedule on account of my setback in elementary school (which now seemed to have occurred back in the dark ages).

My salary at $0.375 per hour came to about $15 per week; my room rent, $2 per week. I worked for my meals as an agent for Mrs. Wellons's dining room, keeping twenty-two places at the tables as nearly filled as possible. Consequently, from my point of view, I was economically secure, but I was not a student. How was I going to combine a job and school work? I would discuss it with Mr. Cookson.

He said it could be arranged: he brought in a new employee during the summer, told me to show her how to take over the work I had been doing, and assigned me to posting and other jobs that I could do between classes starting in September.

Meanwhile, I had to cope with a completely different problem as an outgrowth of the war, which, incidentally, was going rather badly for us, as the Germans were making one last major assault before the American expeditionary forces became more numerous.

In October 1917 I became nineteen; at eighteen males were being drafted by the army; patriotic fervor was at such a high pitch that an able-bodied man in civilian clothes was called a slacker, or draft-dodger, or something worse. Although of draft age I was wearing "civies," and I was embarrassed—despite (or because of) the fact that, while I was ready and willing to "do my bit," as they said at that time, I was not considered "able" by the army, and had been classified 4F because I had an inguinal hernia—which, you know if you attended a good high school offering a course in physiology, may strangle the intestinal tract and cause death if not dealt with promptly—a complication the military doesn't need and their reason for classifying me 4F.

In the summer of 1918 I discussed this problem with Mr. Smith, who made monthly trips to the Indiana University School of Medicine and Hospital in Indianapolis. When he returned from his August trip he said that, as soon as summer school ended, I could go to Indianapolis and Dr. Gatsch would do the necessary surgery for me. I jumped at the opportunity. Two weeks later I was back in Bloomington, a few days after the fall term started.

During the summer the military decided that male university students would be drafted into a unit called Student Army Training Corps (SATC), be billeted in barracks on campus, (i.e., dormitories and gymnasiums), attend classes, and take military training. Result? I became Private Bussing, finally.

The commanding officer, Capt. A. T. Dalton, had been at I.U. in charge of the ROTC for years, and therefore knew me in the bursar's office and was aware of the fact that I was familiar with office routine (of which there is an overabundance in the Quartermaster's Department). Consequently he assigned me to that duty, as well as for the additional reason that I was not ready for physical training so soon after surgery.

One of the duties of a quartermaster is to equip a soldier with "general issue," which is the army's way of saying "clothing and accessories" (the origin, I guess, of the epithet "GIs" for soldiers). One of my jobs, therefore, was to outfit these "doughboys" (as they were called in the First World War), including yours truly. When I got into the warehouse I found a few uniforms and overcoats of the quality worn by officers. How they got into our shipment I never found out. I did not issue these to privates, but if you won't tell anybody I'll let you in on a little secret: I issued to myself two uniforms, one made for GIs and one of serge, suitable only for an officer. This could have gotten me into a lot of trouble because, on one occasion when I went home wearing an officer's uniform (without insignia, of course), I could have met an officer on the street and he could have had a few things to say to me. Fortunately, I had no such encounter. So how come I had a furlough so soon after joining the army and was able to abandon boot camp and go home? Is that a way to fight a war? The fact is, in 1918 we were fighting two wars—one in the mud of northern France and on the high seas, the other on the home front—the influenza epidemic. The danger was that, if the situation became worse at the university, there would not be enough beds and nurses to take care of us; at home, presumably, there would be beds and family members available. So, to reduce its liability, the university was shut down. That's when I left the "camp" in my officer's uniform. (One member of my family died; otherwise we came through this crisis without difficulty.)

A few weeks later, the eleventh hour of the eleventh day of the eleventh month arrived, and the guns of August fell silent for the first time in four years. In due course, we were mustered out; "peace" of sorts and a new world order, it was hoped, would come about with the assistance of the League of Nations. My "new order" took the form of a full-time course of study and part-time employment in the Bursar's Office. My study period was in evenings and on weekends. That was the routine throughout my college career. It was a somewhat rigorous and disciplined program, not totally unlike, in some respects, that of the monks I'd heard about in confirmation class. The main difference, I imagine one would say, was that the asceticism and self-flagellation practiced here on earth by those celibate men supposedly built up a balance of "brownie points" in their heavenly quartermaster's account (provided Satan didn't somehow worm his way into the heart of the heavenly bookkeeper and cause him to screw up the accounts).

My reward, on the on the other hand (if I earned one), would be realized here on earth, and would end with me; while that of the monks would be forever—provided the forecast of the fathers held (holy) water and the monks kept the faith.

No, I didn't wear a hair shirt, but I lived in something like a monk's cell. I mentioned above that my room rent was two dollars per week; for that one can't expect much, and I didn't. The room I had was in the basement of the apartment house that the president of the university owned—at least I think he owned it, and I paid the rent to him.

There's nothing necessarily wrong about a room in a basement, and this one was intended for the caretaker, who was not occupying it. It was also "conveniently" close to the coal pile, and there's nothing wrong with that either. But there is a disadvantage to this juxtaposition when a load of coal contains a sizable proportion of coal dust, much of which does not find its way to the coal bin but drifts to other parts of the basement and settles on, for example, a study table, a bed, a bureau, chairs, the floor, a typewriter, books and writing paper, your other suit of clothes if you have one, and anything else you touch.

Working half-time, my weekly earnings amounted to $7.50; my meals (such as they were) cost me nothing, because I was managing Mrs. Wellons's dining table; after paying $2 for rent I was able to squirrel away $5.50 per week for emergencies and a move to New York (if I decided to take that risk).

The room had another slight disadvantage: it was below grade;

if the window was open and a wind came along, a certain amount of dust and dirt, less black and oleaginous than soft coal dust but still obnoxious, would blow in and replace the coal dust if the latter had been wiped, washed, or swept away.

Although the room as a whole was below grade the window was at the grade level; it didn't, therefore, require one to be proficient in Newtonian physics to see that when the wind reached the interior of the room its velocity was insufficient to overcome the force of gravity, and the dirt fell. Consequently, if you didn't want dirt and dust to cover your bed, or you if you were trying to sleep, one solution would be to move the bed as far away from the window as possible and raise the bed as much as possible from the floor.

There was no way to lengthen the iron legs of the bed. I knew how to do woodworking, having built pushmobiles and play houses; but I was not a pipe fitter or metalworker. So instead, I went down to the grocery store (where I didn't go to work), and tried to get four wooden boxes (the kind whose cubic content I couldn't calculate at the factory) of uniform size; then I attempted to put the four legs on top of them without allowing the whole shebang to collapse in the process. Actually, getting four large boxes under four legs of a bed practically simultaneously required almost as much methodological insight as Mr. Newton needed to discover why an apple falls to the ground—if it is not eaten beforehand. (It was evidently left for others in high school physiology classes to explain what happens *after* the apple is eaten.)

I spent three years at I.U. as a student, during which I took the courses that interested me most. But the same kind of urge that impelled me to leave the provincialism of my hometown and go to I.U. now induced me to take another giant step—to an eastern university, preferably Columbia, where I could combine the academic life with as much activity in the business world as I might want or need. More about that anon.

Chapter 15
Of Faith, Fornication, and the Holy Fathers

A strange thing happened when I arrived in Bloomington: I fell off my horse of religious convictions, as Paul of Tarsus did, except that he substituted incomprehensible Christianity for inconvincible Judaism; but I was content to live in a religious vacuum unless or until I found a suitable replacement, which I hoped would be possible in the unbiased atmosphere of an institution of higher learning. However, if none was found, I was so close to being an agnostic that I didn't lose any sleep over it; hard to believe, but true.

Hard to believe in light of the fact that this was the same kid who, only six or seven years previously, never seemed to think independently, had no interest in book learning, and was adrift in a sea of intellectual indifference.

Hard to believe in light of the fact that dumping the doctrine of the church involved the danger of breaking the bond of love, friendship, admiration, and indebtedness I felt toward my earthly savior, Betty McC., were she to become aware of it. The only solution that would spare her acute disappointment in her protégé was to keep the facts from her, which is what I managed to do.

If I had any misgivings about my dropping out of the church they were dissipated as I delved more deeply into the history of the papacy. History was one of my favorite subjects, and when we completed the fascinating review of Greek and Roman civilizations in the history course I was taking at the university, we took up the equally interesting, if not even more absorbing and revealing study of life and living in medieval Europe.

The history of medieval Europe is, in effect, substantially a review of the history of the Roman Catholic church. Or, at least, one can say with little fear of contradiction that you can't study one without the other, because of the enormous influence the church had in governing western Europe from the early days of the Christian era until about the end of the fourteenth century.

If Jesus had come back during this period he probably would not have been able to believe what he was seeing; and, in his dismay, he would have said to the pope or cardinals or bishops or any other administrative churchmen, "What in the name of God, my Father, do you people think you are doing?

"How do you justify behaving like robbers, whoremongers, slavers, liars, gluttons, usurers, rapists, simoniacs, and heaven knows what else? Have you forgotten the instructions I gave Peter, Paul, Matthew, Mark, Luke, John, and the other apostles before I took off from the Olivian launch pad a few weeks after I rose from the grave? How, in my name, can you lead lives of lechery, treachery, and debauchery, and still hoodwink innocent people into believing that you are emissaries of mine? Do you hear confessions of penitent sinners? If so, who hears yours? One reason for my returning so soon is that we have not been hearing confessions from you bastards recently. This, among many bad reports we have been receiving from parishioners, prompted my father to send me to find out what in the hell you reprobates are up to. Yes, 'hell' is what I said, because your behavior is converting this world into an anteroom to hell instead of a stepping stone to heaven."

Pope John XXIII, for example, *permitted* and then taxed "prostitution, gambling, and usury," and according to his secretary, "seduced 200 virgins, matrons, widows, and nuns . . . " The historical record of the time is replete with accounts of this sort from the See of Rome to the land of Britain. In politics, the religious hierarchy utilized any kind of tactics necessary to gain their political objectives, not excluding murder, stuffing ballot boxes, bribery, or other gangster-like methods that would enable them to satisfy their lust for sex, power, influence and cash. This is not to say that every pope, cardinal, bishop, or priest was a scoundrel for a thousand years or so; there were good ones. But as an epoch, it was flawed by the breakdown of morality among an enormous number of those who were supposed to sustain it. In time, constructive forces got the upper hand and the Reformation took place, most of it as a result of nonclerical demands that Christianity be "restored," if necessary by the establishment of theological systems quite different from those then being purveyed by the corrupt custodians of Catholicism.

In this maelstrom of immorality and licentiousness, what happened to the sacrament of apostolic succession? If an ordained minister violated his vows did he retain, and could he pass on, the powers of consecration, absolution, solemnization, and others through the all-important sacred ritual of apostolic succession? Or had the devil so completely seduced him that he no longer could do so? If so, the primary difference between a Catholic priest and a Protestant minister would be lost, inasmuch as a Catholic looks upon a Protestant minister as little more than a well meaning layman—which is all a priest would be, if he had not received the rite of apostolic succession.

Putting the matter more concretely, and speaking only as a liberal layman totally ignorant of canon law, my question is, if all of the priests present at the consecration of a candidate for the priesthood were following the example of Pope John XXIII, and had to be awakened by their respective bedtime girlfriends and reminded of their appointment to consecrate at the cathedral, would they be able to do so in spite of the double life they were living? Or, if ten priests were present and one obeyed the rules, while the other nine were libertines who had adopted the decorum of the devil, could that one pass on the rite? Layman Bussing thinks, Presumably. If not, God help the millions of Catholics who are banking on that assumption in their struggle for salvation.

If my conscience bothered me at all after I shed the cloak of Catholicism, what I learned in this course in medieval history relieved me. But did it go so far as to induce me to join one of the successor reform groups—the Methodists, Presbyterians, Lutherans, Baptists, or one of the others? No. I still retained the notion that we have no reliable comprehension of the cosmos, and that our attempt to construct a relationship between us and the Lord of the inscrutable universe is folklore and wishful thinking, if not downright egocentricity.

Chapter 16
Still "Higher" Education

If the history course reinforced my biblical bias, the sociology course justified my population prejudice. Admittedly, sociologists do not have a discipline of their own, as physicists, chemists, economists, physicians, and others do, and therefore they have to draw upon the latter in formulating their philosophy and programs for social betterment. This tends to get them into hot water, because of the difficulty of applying the technical findings of others to a practical human problem; yet someone should do it for the good of all of us. This is the kind of thinking and debating that went on in our sociology class.

One of the first topics of discussion was the relation of population, and its rate of growth, to the amount and availability of the world's resources. If we were concerned in the early 1900s about overpopulation, what should our attitude be today? Were we wrong in 1919 when I attended my first sociology class? Since then, the world's population has increased from about a billion to something like 5.4 billion; at the present rate of increase, world population is likely to hit 6.3 billion in less than a decade, and, God forbid, 14 billion before a climax is reached in early-to-mid-twenty-first century. (In many areas of the world demographers have to estimate population data, because the natives are so busy increasing their numbers that they literally don't have time to count them. But the figures, we believe, are reasonably reliable.) It is difficult to think of any problem in this world that wouldn't be more amenable to solution if there were fewer human beings. The optimum population of the world was reached long ago.

We either don't believe or refuse to admit that space is limited, and that as our numbers increase at something like ninety million a year, a balanced diet for everyone is an unattainable ideal, unless we use incredibly large amounts of artificial fertilizers and pesticides—a short-term solution with long-term catastrophic consequences: chemical fertilizers ruin soil and pesticides kill people. (However, maybe the pesticide approach is the hidden solution. "Sodden thought," as Herb Caen would say.) When all's said and done, are we the most intelligent creatures on earth?

Yes, say the cornucopians. They will tell you that man has the ingenuity to cope with crises such as the pressure of a growing population on the carrying capacity and habitable area of the earth. Their philosophy may be condensed by quoting the Henry George aphorism to which they subscribe: "Hawks and people eat chickens. Increase the hawks and you *decrease* the chickens; increase the number of people and you *increase* the chickens." On the other side of the controversy are those who advocate a zero rate of growth of population—the ZPGers, whom the cornucopians call Malthusians.

If you are a cornucopian you believe that we'll "soon" find solutions to crowds everywhere, to insufficient parking space, urban sprawl, diminishing forests, growing deserts, to the soil erosion caused by cultivation of marginal land ill-suited to the agriculture necessary to feed 90 million more people every year, to falling water tables and the gradual depletion of aquafers, to widespread hunger, disease, and starvation. We will find solutions because of our intelligence and ingenuity, these worthies proclaim.

The ZPGers say "nuts" (not the edible kind) to this. The solution to the population problem, they believe, is to be found in testicles and tubes—fallopian that is—which have not been altered, modified, or adjusted since Homo sapiens came down from the trees. Our other features have been retro-fitted, more or less, to a new way of life: our forelegs (arms) are not necessary for hanging on branches, so they have become shorter, our brain power has increased, but unfortunately, not immunized against doctrinaire religious dogma, which has, in some inexplicable way, made salvation and sexual satisfaction incompatible or mutually exclusive.

It apparently doesn't worry the cornucopians that, despite the fact that about 2.5 acres would be needed for the purpose, less than one acre of arable land is available in the world today to provide a minimum diet and clothe each of us for one year. Heaven knows how many acres would be needed to provide a *balanced* diet for all of us.

They evidently have confidence that biogeneticists will come along with methods of production that will double, triple, or quadruple the output of an acre of land, and will also alter the genetic structure of seeds, prevent droughts, and kill pests without the use of pesticides (which, incidentally, they might prefer to use on us Malthusians!). They will cause deserts, which are becoming even larger, to become smaller and bloom; prevent droughts and crop failures; and restore a balance between man and his environment to the everlasting satisfaction of all.

The immediate purpose here, however, is not to belabor what so many thoughtful people know, namely, that at the present rate of growth of world population nothing but disaster lies ahead. The intention is merely to call attention to the fact that in our little class in sociology, in the backwoods of central Indiana in the year 1919, Professor Weatherly directed our attention to what was then an ominous trend that had the potential of becoming a worldwide problem, as it is today. Like any good teacher, he didn't tell us what to think: he simply exposed us to the pros and cons of the subject and let us make up our minds. As a result, some of us became ZPGers. At least one of us became a "sub-zero population growth" believer, having had only one child. (And now he is dead. "Serves you right," say the cornucopians.)

We sociologists might not have been considered then, nor may we be thought of now, as the most sophisticated intellectuals on a college campus. But I doubt if anyone, in any other department, dealt then or deals now with a topic more vital than the ineluctable perversity of human beings to complicate life on this earth by allowing our numbers to continue to grow, in spite of the fact that we have long since exceeded an optimum ratio between man and his environment. (Are people really the dumbest animals, or only the most stubborn?)

The sociology course in college was as great an eye-opener as the physiology course had been in high school. If I had to name the two most valuable educational experiences in my life, those are the ones I would mention.

There were other courses in the college curriculum that I enjoyed, such as history, where I ran the gamut from ancient to modern, and I never tire of reading, even today. I also gave a lot of attention to psychology, even to the extent of taking a course given by Harry Dexter Kitson dealing with the mundane, not to say mercenary, subject of "The Mind of the Buyer," a study of the "art" of salesmanship! Don't ask me why I did that. It may have been because Dr. Kitson was such a fascinating person.

Geology captivated my attention as much as history—which might not be too unusual, inasmuch as geology is a history of the earth. Every day one sees geological formations, and I find it delightful to try to "read" the history of a region by looking at strata and fossils. (Some of my so-called "friends" say they see a fossil every time they look at me; if that is true, it only confirms the importance of fossils, I say to them.) I enjoyed the courses in Shakespeare and Chaucer, withstood the tedium of memorizing Spanish and German, and neglected science courses because I wasn't able to see how, with my interest in the humanities, I could ever make much use of physics, chemistry, and advanced mathematics. I regret my ignorance in these subjects, but, like having another child to replace the one we have lost, it's a bit late, you might say.

On the less intellectual side, there were two strata of students at the university—the Greeks and the barbarians. If you were anybody, you would be a member of a Greek letter society. In these organizations, the taboos were such that a member of a fraternity would not be seen with a girl unless she was a member of a sorority; Greeks associated only with Greeks (sign of an inferiority complex?).

The reasoning behind this clannish attitude was that if a "Greek" associated with a "barbarian," there must be something wrong with him socially: he must, in fact, be déclassé. Maybe he shouldn't have been admitted to the club in the first place. Many students who were not members of this social set felt ostracized, if they'd ever had any desire or interest in becoming a member. Some were not members because they had been "blackballed." Others took no interest, or preferred to give all of their time and attention to what they considered the much more fascinating part of college—the intellectual side. But you never knew whether a nonmember had been rejected, ejected, or simply preferred independent status. In my own case, I was, or I felt like, a fish out of water. Had I joined the Delts, I could have sidled up beside the little Wolfe girl in Professor Nicholson's class in psychology. She was not only very attractive, but, like most attractive girls, belonged to a sorority. Consequently I hesitated to sit beside her. One morning, however, Professor Nicholson came into the room and, before calling the class to order, wrote in large letters on the blackboard, "Isle of use wheat art," whereupon the little Wolfe girl and I exchanged glances. But even after that, I failed to follow through.

In fact, I was romantically illiterate. I never had a close friend of the opposite sex until I met the one I married. I really didn't know, or understand, the young female mind, because I never got close enough to it. My excuse, in those early days, was probably that I was too busy keeping my head above water—earning a living and going to school at the same time. If I had it to do over I would associate more freely with women, even if I had to join a fraternity in order to meet girls like Jan Wolfe.

Chapter 17
So This Is New York?

I had a little reminder on my desk that encouraged me to carry on in spite of the pressures of the job in the Bursar's Office, keeping Mrs. Wellons's dining tables filled, and maintaining a high scholastic record. Its message was that "dreams in hours of insight willed, are in the hours of gloom fulfilled."

As a third-year student in our small freshwater college in the Midwest (as some New York highbrows like to call it), I began to feel that if I was going to "be somebody," to use Mother's phrase, it was probably time for me to begin thinking about my next move. Wasn't it as important to move on from the academic cove in the hills of central Indiana as it had been for me, several years previously, to go from my home town after high school to Indiana University? If so, what, precisely, should this next move be?

After the First World War there was widespread migration to the big cities, especially among the young people, who were more free to move. The country was awash in cash as a result of the war, and New Era psychology permeated the industrial and financial markets. Europe, endeavoring to rebuild its economy after four years of war, became our best customer (with borrowed funds, for the most part), and financial centers like New York reflected this activity.

So, said I to myself, why not find a way to get to New York? The answer was not too long in coming. Why not try for a scholarship at Columbia University? That would take care of the tuition fee (which was ten times that at I.U.); and surely I could find work in so large a job market. Was this a dream willed in hours of insight? Might it be fulfilled with a minimum of hardship and gloom? I thought it was worth a try.

I found immediately that I had the support of Mr. Smith, the bursar. He said, "You write the letter and I'll sign it." (He was a top-notch person.) Various members of the faculty also contributed to my dossier. The result was that, in May of 1921, I received a letter from Dean Hawkes of Columbia College, stating that I had been awarded a scholarship for the academic year 1921-22.

I was overjoyed; but still I had to find a way to keep body and soul together. My net worth was only $350. And that amount wouldn't go very far in New York (although the subway fare was only a nickel).

At this point, Vera, one of the more attractive girls in the Bursar's Office, for whom I had a suppressed fondness, no longer concealed her interest in my plans—especially in the fact that I would surely have an uphill struggle attending school and working, too. Not to mention the fact that, since I had been given a scholarship based on my scholastic record at I.U., I would feel duty-bound to do as well, scholastically, at Columbia; otherwise they might say that an A at I.U. was only the equivalent of a B at Columbia. I couldn't let that happen (as a matter of fact, my grades were just as good at Columbia as they had been at I.U.).

During the two years we worked together in the office, I had spent all of one evening with Vera. Although I admired her she was not a student, and that counted against her in my opinion. I also wondered if this was not a case of propinquity, which, in our eugenics class in sociology, was frowned upon as a way of choosing a mate.

One day she brought a copy of *Red Book* magazine to the office and showed me a story about a girl who accompanied her boyfriend to New York, and how the two of them, together, had enough income to cover expenses.

The temptation was nearly overpowering. Here was a beautiful, outwardly conservative, willing person who could greatly simplify my problems, on the one hand, but who could also greatly complicate them, on the other. She didn't flat-out suggest we would live together; in those days, that would have been on the border of the unthinkable, at least for a college student. (In fact, more than 60 years later, the Dean of Women of Barnard College of Columbia attempted to expel a woman student when it was discovered that she was living off campus, and not with her parents!)

One side of me wanted to take up her offer, but another side of me said *no*. And although I lacked experience in matters romantic, I was able to see the potential pitfalls in a liaison of this sort. What if she was not successful in the job market? And what if, God forbid, I chucked the admonition of the Reverend Mr. Mott of the YMCA, or the cold-shower solution of the president of I.U. and the dire warnings of the holy father of the parochial school? And what if, with the assistance of the devil, Vera became pregnant? Ye gods! In such a case I would have to support her, instead of the other way around.

I was also still struggling with that "be somebody" syndrome. If a man is known by the company he keeps, how could a little country girl from Bedford, Indiana, be of any assistance in my efforts to reach my goals? Why not hold off a little longer; take cold showers, if necessary; wait until I no longer had to wear cast-off clothing and unironed shirts. Then, might I not meet and marry somebody who was somebody?

Yes, in the end reason triumphed over romance. I continued my hand-to-mouth existence and poor Vera was left behind. (Years later, I heard that she and Della Williams went to California, without husbands.)

So now it was necessary to get back to the business of taking care of myself without the help (or hindrance) of a beautiful girl. So, first of all I wrote to the placement office of the university and asked if they might have a job available for a student. They did: Miss Casey had a dining room on the first floor of an apartment house at 119th Street and Amsterdam, directly across from the campus. She needed a kitchen boy, and she said she would look me over as soon as I arrived. Her clientele were business people, and she was open whether the college was in session or not.

And, as it turned out, her sister Margaret had an apartment on 118 Street and would rent me a room. All I needed now was a little income to pay for the room.

When the term ended at I.U. early in June I said goodbye to my friends in Bloomington, went home to do the same there, bought a coach ticket to New York, and left, nervously, for the relatively risky venture in the big city.

The Pennsylvania Railroad's coaches in those days were better than cattle cars: they had seats. The coaches were placed forward and the Pullman cars behind. The effect of this was to make certain that as much fly ash as possible from the coal-burning locomotive would blow into the coaches and onto the passengers, if any, thus leaving less to cover the higher-fare passengers in the sleeping cars. (You didn't think there was air conditioning in the Pullmans, did you?) They did put screens on the windows, but that only kept out the larger particles of fly ash. There was no inclination on the part of the railroads in those days to make passenger trains more comfortable; the roads wanted to get rid of them, because passenger traffic was unprofitable. Besides, the automobile was becoming a substitute of sorts.

By the time we got to Pittsburgh, I found that two or three other people and I were the only ones left in our coach. Whether the former passengers had choked to death and been cast off with other freight at the various stops along the way, I never found out. (I think the company police keep such matters quiet.)

At about daybreak a boy with a pot of coffee, some sandwiches, and fruit came aboard; but I still had some bran muffins made by Mother and a few other items in my box, so I was not a customer.

Toward afternoon we were roaring through towns in New Jersey, and I began to see what life was like in the kind of crowded communities we had been discussing in Professor Weatherly's class on population some months before. *This doesn't look too good, I thought to myself. Maybe the tranquility of our cove in the hills has a lot to recommend it after all. But I can't turn back; that would be an admission of defeat.*

About 4:00 P.M. we rolled into Penn Station, New York, more than twenty-four hours after leaving home. I had a suitcase and a handbag. I didn't know how to get to Columbia University. I looked like a hick; a porter agreed. He asked me if he could be of assistance as he took my suitcase. I told him I wanted to go to Morningside Heights. He'd never heard of such a place. I then said, "Columbia University." He'd heard of that. So he took me across Seventh Avenue and pointed to a double-decker bus going up Fifth Avenue to 110th Street; then to Riverside Drive and 116th Street, where I disembarked—at the acropolis, the uptown seat of learning, the place of my dreams, the campus of Columbia.

I'm a bit hungry; and tired from a night of acrid smoke, noise, and attempts to sleep while sitting on a surface not materially different from that of Riverside Drive. If states which use the electric chair for the purpose of capital punishment would like to adopt a simpler method and save electricity at the same time, I have a suggestion: find some of these old "passenger" cars, and require the condemned convicts to spend twenty-four to thirty-six hours sitting in one of them. That will be capital punishment. Call it the "Capital Express." The drawback is that it may well be declared "cruel and unusual punishment," and therefore unconstitutional.

As we rolled along up Fifth Avenue I noticed the bookstore of Harcourt, Brace, and Howe. The "Howe" was Dr. Will D. Howe, one of the faculty at I.U. until a year or so before, and a good friend. (I didn't feel totally isolated.) Dr. Howe's name has long since been replaced by others, as he is no longer of this world; or, at least, not in his original form as ex-professor of English Literature at Indiana University.

When we reached 116th Street I disembarked with my handbag and suitcase, which contained all of my worldly possessions, except my bank account, walked a block east to the Broadway entrance to the university, past the magnificent Seth Low Library to Amsterdam Avenue, turned left, and wound up at 119th Street, where I sought out Miss Casey. It was now well after five o'clock, and she was preoccupied with preparations for dinner. But she took time to look me over, and decided to take a chance. So I went to the kitchen, where I met Georgie the cook. She called me Mr. Buzzin. Soon three very recent Irish immigrant girls appeared, the waitresses. I was given the job of putting salads together, cutting pies and cakes, washing a dish or two if necessary, and generally trying to make myself useful. I wasn't wholly out of character in the food line, having been a counterboy in the high school cafeteria in exchange for lunch. So everything, so far, was clicking according to plan. I had hit a jackpot, of sorts.

After dinner I met Margaret Casey, who took me to my room in her apartment, which was on the first floor of a six-story building on 118th Street on an inside court never graced by a ray of sunlight. Although Professor Einstein told us that a ray of light bends in response to gravity, it would be too much to expect sunlight to stoop so low as to wend its way into such a dismal spot if it could possibly be avoided. However, this bit of space did, in fact, have a window, through which one could see the brick walls of other buildings that graced this enclosure, which would qualify as a dungeon except that it was open at the top. All buildings in the court abutted each other so there would be no "wasted" space.

In warm weather, occupants would keep their windows open most of the time to avoid suffocation, which enabled the residents to entertain each other with a cacophony of variations: One tenant might be drying dishes, piling them on each other none too quietly; another might have Caruso on his phonograph; a not-too-well mated couple might be venting their respective spleens on each other, or on the boss. An aspiring soprano might be trying to sound like Gali-Curci, who was in her prime in those days. Then there was the pupil of the nearby Julliard School of Music, who tried to render "Eine Kleine Nachtmusik" in the daytime. If Wolfgang Amadeus could have heard it, I'm sure he would have said that, not only was this not one of his compositions, it was not even written for the piano. All of the notes struck by this aspiring pianist sounded like dominant fifths, as far as I was concerned, because his piano was on the first floor of the adjoining building.

So, when Margaret showed me my room, I, being on the ragged edge of penury—almost a dependent, you might say, of the Caseys and unfamiliar with the ways of New Yorkers (after all, two million people lived here and *they* managed to survive)—I thanked her and started to unpack my bag. A few moments later she came back and told me that Edwin Franko Goldman was giving one of his famous free concerts that evening across the street on the Columbia campus, and mentioned that I might like to go to it. Indeed I would, although sleep might have been the better choice considering the fact that the Pennsylvania Railroad had kept me awake the previous night, and charged me for it besides. The concert, however, confirmed the good reputation of this bandleader, following which, as Pepys said, "and so to bed."

"Going to bed," however, soon proved to be something quite different from actually sleeping. And I'm not referring to Margaret, or the persistent pianist, the solicitous soprano, the quarrelsome couple, or the celebrated Caruso. No. Could it be mosquitos? No, they don't have mosquitos in New York. Mosquitos can't live there; only people can because only people are sufficiently intelligent to find ways of dealing with and overcoming obnoxious obstacles to decent living (as the cornucopians say).

So I tossed and turned until the garbage collectors (who were not on strike that month) start rattling metal garbage cans in the street. That occurred in this neighborhood at about daybreak. (It's difficult to tell when day breaks if you're at the bottom of an inside well of an apartment complex, and the scavengers make it worse by rattling garbage cans at all hours of the night.) But New Yorkers adjust to that and sleep through it. That's one kind of garbage they are able to get rid of—locally, at least. Where it goes after that is another matter. At that time they were dumping it into the ocean a mile or two from Long Island, in hopes that creatures in the sea would, after a billion years of prior evolution, be able to adapt their digestive systems (in true cornucopian fashion) to this new and gratuitous gastronomic offering.

When I decided that I would be no worse off dressed and scratching than in bed and itching I did indeed get up, took a bath (in a tub, there being no shower), and prepared to venture to the street, buy a copy of the *New York Times* (with two cents), and try to find a place for breakfast.

Before leaving my room, however, I noticed spots of blood on the sheets of my bed. Maybe they do have mosquitos, big ones, bigger than ours in Indiana. Then I noticed some reddish spots on my arms; then elsewhere on my body. These mosquitos certainly have a fondness for Hoosier blood, I thought to myself. Maybe they have learned in the evolutionary process that it is beneficial to the species to introduce new blood strains into their genetic makeup—a sort of muscatoid miscegenation—a biological transfusion of Mid-western blood with that of the richly diversified (melting-pot type) of the native New Yorker.

On my way to a lunch counter for breakfast, I passed a little hardware store where one of the displays was an adjustable window screen; one of these might be just what I need, I thought. It won't keep out the cacophony, but it might keep the blood-exchanging relatives *outside* my room from joining the pests *inside* and feasting on me at a kind of family dinner or seder. So I bought one of the screens and installed it in my window.

One disadvantage was that it was only about ten inches high, which meant that only ten inches of the window would be open; and that was hardly enough to relieve the stuffiness of this inhospitable four-walled space. But then maybe that's what one should expect, if one wants to live in New York.

That night about ten o'clock I went to bed hoping to get some rest, the first since leaving home. I would keep a sheet over me; then even the most ravenous of these dipterous devils, if they managed to get into my room, would hardly consider it worth the risk of injuring or breaking their proboscises trying to penetrate a sheet just to get one meal; better to go up to one of the other apartments and bite the piano player or the girl who tries to sing opera, provided they, too, haven't covered themselves with sheets. But the new screen at the window also made it difficult for the residents in my room to get out, in case they wanted to vary their sex lives as well as their diet, in one of the other apartments. Yes, mosquitos, too, have problems.

For a while, before falling asleep, I began thinking about the creative possibilities of living in this little room, especially if I had the ability of a composer of modern music. Practically all of the sounds necessary for a modern orchestral composition were within earshot of where I lay: the couple washing dinner dishes would comprise the tympanic section; the quarrelsome couple, the recitative; the aspiring (or expiring) soprano, the theme song; the pianist would double for the orchestra. The result would be sufficiently atonal to qualify as a modern composition. However, as I had much learning to do before mastering musical theory, harmony, and composition, I didn't try to put it all together and simply fell asleep instead.

But the latter, as usual, was short-lived. The tireless little torturers got to me in spite of the screen and the sheet. This time I got up, turned on the light, and began to consider the various options open to me. Something more fundamental than sheets and screens had to be found.

What I saw, now that the light was on, was not a winged creature. It did not fly away as those other nocturnal nuisances do; and the blood stains on the sheet gave the impression that these fellows were more like surgeons: they evidently were able to make incisions in the skin—not just holes—suck out at least one square meal's worth of the host's hemoglobin, and then go home and to bed without bothering to suture up the opening. Sloppy eaters, I thought to myself: if they were human they would have to take their silk neckties to the cleaners after every meal.

But wait a minute; haven't I heard of these creatures before? Aren't these the little SOBs (sons of bugs) that were discussed in (yes, you guessed it) our high school physiology class? Of course they are. These must be—brace yourself, be prepared—these must be hemipterous, blood-sucking bastards of the family *Cimex lectularius*, which, however, does not make them any less undesirable as bedfellows. They were, in plain, unexpurgated English, b-e-d-b-u-g-s.

So now I'm in a pickle; although I'm in a place that is infested with vermin, what can I do about it? If I leave, where shall I go? If I take the matter up with Margaret, will I be in trouble with her sister who has the dining room? Will I be out of a job that provides food and a place to live at the same time?

The first thing I did was to go to the dormitory office of the university where the office manager gave me the word I had expected, which was that there were no vacancies. Then I tried to find a solution to the next problem—food. After all, I could sleep on a couch in the mezzanine of one of the residence halls temporarily; but sooner or later a little sustenance would be desirable, assuming that Miss Casey might not keep me in her kitchen. So I went to the university cafeteria and accosted the nutritionist in charge, a Miss Riley. She could give me a job drying eating utensils but not until summer school started, which would be in about ten days. I'll not starve in so short a period.

Meanwhile, I heard from the dormitory dame. She told me that there was a room on the second floor of Hartley Hall that was intended to be a broom closet for the caretaker but was now being prepared for student occupancy. It had no window, but there was a skylight. (She thought that was a drawback and admitted it rather apologetically.) Little did she know that a windowless room was just what I was looking for. To my way of thinking, a window can be an abomination: it can be an open sesame for mosquitos and for raucous racket, both antithetical to sleep, and I was a too recently arrived New Yorker to have learned how to cope with such problems. She implied, however, that if I wanted it I would have to decide then and there. The cost was something like $110 per semester. Although that was about a third of my reserve for emergencies, I decided this *was* an emergency, of sorts, and I was ready to sacrifice almost any amount for a solution that would extricate me from bugs in a room and bedlam in a courtyard.

I didn't have the courage to tell Margaret Casey what the real trouble was: I simply told her that my "earlier" application for a dormitory room had been accepted. Her sister allowed me to continue working in the kitchen, which was preferable at this time because it was open, whereas the university cafeteria was closed during intersession periods.

So you might say that solutions had been found to a couple of critical situations; and by the middle of June 1921 I was breathing more easily.

Chapter 18
Mistake Number One

Not long after I got settled in my new broom closet I received a note from the admissions office of the university, advising me that my scholastic record was excellent but that I did not have enough credits in mathematics. It was suggested that I could take a course in, as I recall it, intermediate algebra in summer school; or, if I preferred, I could present myself for a special examination before the fall semester started. In either case, if I failed to make up the deficiency I probably would not have been permitted to register for my last year of college, and thus the scholarship and a Columbia degree would be left hanging in the balance. Evidently there had been insufficient coordination between the dean and the admissions office.

This bothered me almost as much as had the members of genus *Cimex lectularius.* I couldn't take the summer school course, because the Columbia bursar had given me a job in his office that would provide funds to pay for my dormitory room. Also, paying the summer-school fee would have created a hole in my reserve fund.

So I elected to take a chance: I would study for the lousy exam at night and on weekends during the summer and take the test early in September. If I flunked it, I would probably buy a one-way ticket on the Pennsylvania Railroad and check to see if as much smoke and fly ash comes in the windows going from east to west as was the case from west to east.

Early in September, I presented myself to a professor in the math department. He handed me a series of problems. I proceeded to solve them to the best of my ability. Frankly, I doubt if I passed that exam. If I did I am surprised. My hunch is that the dean's office was satisfied with my scholastic record and somehow managed to deal with the matter brought up by the admissions office. In any event, I took two more courses in math during the school year and got an A in one and a B-plus in the other.

So now I am a full-fledged student at the university, in my senior year, and eager to see if my grades would be as good here as they had been at I.U. I found the pedagogical process a little more formal, more impersonal, and the classes larger. Examinations were set up and supervised as if everyone taking them was a recently released convict on parole from that stone-walled institution to the north of the city commonly referred to as Sing Sing. The exams were given in the gymnasium. One column of chairs, set about three feet apart fore and aft, would be separated on each side by columns of vacant chairs; thus the escaped convict-student would be effectively isolated and unable to communicate with any other student. Then, to make certain that some ingenious member of the class had not found a way to circumvent the system, gumshoe monitors paced the aisles scrutinizing each person in the room. If he was diligently inscribing his responses from memory without referring to any clandestine information, also known as a "crib sheet," he would not be subjected to serious disciplinary action. It was a very commendable system, because it rewarded those who worked. I might add, that, as far as my grades were concerned, they were about the same at Columbia as they had been at I.U.; which must have pleased the dean, as it tended to justify the scholarship he had so generously awarded me; it also indicated that the educational process and grading system of at least one freshwater college was on par with that of the illustrious, age-old member of the Ivy League.

The committee that selected graduating students for membership in the PBK scholastic society also saw fit to admit me. I can't prove this by showing you my PBK key, however, because the moronic houseboy we had stole it, along with a bundle of flat silver, jewelry, and a newly tailored suit, in the year 1928. Thus, whenever I see someone wearing that coveted emblem of scholarship I wonder if he might have purchased it at the pawnshop, where the houseboy probably converted it to cash. One's name is engraved on the back, but I don't usually accost strangers and ask to see the backside of either themselves or their emblems.

So now the first of my educational objectives had been met here in the big city. What should come next? One reason for wanting to come to New York was my fascination with Wall Street. So, the day after graduation, I took the subway (for a nickel) down to the canyons of commerce in lower Manhattan.

A while back, when I started to write this whatever-it-is, I said that it would probably turn out to be a compendium of the mistakes I have made in my ninety-three years; which would amount to a rather lengthy bit of prose. Up to this point in my revelation I have not had many mistakes to report; but from here on in, they begin to crop up.

My first faux pas came this day. I passed the famous J. P. Morgan corner, observed the pockmarked north wall of the building, where a bomb had exploded several years previously; took note of the stock exchange across the street, and the old sub-treasury building at Wall and Nassau; glanced casually at 14 Wall Street, just another office building, totally unaware that fourteen years later I would be sitting at a desk on the twentieth floor thereof.

I continued walking. It was noon. I came to an eating place called Exchange Buffet. I went in. I saw people picking up food items, some eating at tables, others eating while standing at high tables. I thought they must all be brokers eager to get back and trade stocks. Interesting. Then I noticed something even more fascinating. As a person left the restaurant he passed a cashier; the cashier asked him what he owed. He either told the cashier or the cashier told him, based on the strength of his "disclosure." In other words, it's the honor system. On Wall Street, at the Exchange Buffet they trusted stockbrokers and others more than the university trusted us students taking our exams. I might add that I believe this system has since been discontinued, which, you could say, indicates a decline of honesty in the financial district and a preference for much bigger swindles, like insider trading; either that or they can't find cashiers who can add in their heads.

In any case, I reported to the cashier that I'd had a tuna fish on rye and a glass of milk; she said "thirty-five cents," after which I'd gone on my way until I'd reached a building, not really different from many others, but that somehow seemed to beckon me. A door was open on the street level, and I walked in. It turned out to be the head office of the Corn Exchange Bank, a branch of which was located at 110th street, the banking office nearest to Columbia.

Now don't ask me why in God's name I walked into that place; or why, when I got inside, I told the guard that I might be looking for a job. But that's what I did. And that is why he directed me to the Personnel Office.

Had I given a second thought to what I was doing I might have turned tail and returned to the street, at which point the guard might have thought I was a bank robber who had changed his mind. So it might be just as well that I stayed inside and took my medicine. When the personnel clerk found that I was a kid who had just been graduated from Columbia he seemed to take an interest. The only trouble was that I didn't know why I was there, and he didn't know where to place a casual interloper from the street. All he did know for sure was that Mr. Clark, the manager of the Twenty-eighth and Broadway branch, was desperately in need of a bookkeeper (ledger clerk), and it would be to his credit if he could send a qualified person up there at once to fill the job.

So, in short order he sent me with a note, and in I was. It all happened so fast that I didn't have time or the courage to confess that I didn't know what I was doing or why I'd walked into such a trap. Mr. Clark welcomed me with open arms, so to speak; which I thought somewhat unusual for a banker, until he told me that his wife was a Bussing. (He never introduced me to her.) He did introduce me to the assistant manager, however, who took me to the bookkeeping department, which was immediately behind the teller cages. There were three bookkeepers: Emily, Frank, and Howard. None of them had ever been inside a college classroom and, for all I knew, they might have been high school dropouts.

I can only imagine their incredulity; why, they must have agreed before I got there, would a Columbia graduate take a job like this? There's got to be something wrong. Could he be a spy, who might be trying to find out why one of the tellers comes up short so often? Is one of us three falsifying the balance of one of the bank's customers, and is the bank therefore trying to get the goods on us?

Before I arrived there must have been a conference among these three and the assistant manager, in which they'd decided to put this new guy on the largest of the four ledgers, the Q-to-Z book. The bank, at this time, was still using the old-style Boston ledger, a bound volume with ruled pages about twenty-one inches vertically by about twenty-eight inches horizontally. Names of the depositors were on the left, postings for every day of the week had to be made across the page, and on the right date. The net difference between the deposits and withdrawals, plus or minus, had to be added or subtracted mentally from the previous day's balance and extended to the totals column for that day.

If you think *you* are confused by this, imagine how you would feel if the three other bookkeepers had finished their posting by four o'clock, had proved their work, and were ready to run for the subway by four-thirty; while you—overeducated student of geometry, trigonometry, history from ancient Greek to modern American, taxation, economics, sociology, psychology, botany, physiology (as far back as high school), and God knows what else—were still posting, not even having *started* to prove your work? And, worse still, imagine that the assistant manager can't go home until you've finished, while the rest of the staff can—except, that is, if the teller (who is apparently as dumb as you or as cleverly dishonest) has a shortage in his cash.

In defense of my seeming ineptitude, I'll try to illustrate the challenge I was up against: say the Anti-Animal-Rights Fur Company (this branch of the bank was in the fur district) had a closing balance yesterday of $3,000.74. In today's exchange checks we received three debit items, $175.50, $68.70, and $122.00; $250 was deposited at our branch, a credit item. My first job is to post the exchange checks because, if there is not enough in the account to cover these items, one or more of them must be returned to the clearing house before three o'clock. We received the "exchanges" between eleven and twelve o'clock, while we were out for lunch so our work is cut out for us when we get back. We have to work fast.

After the exchanges are out of the way and the bank closes at three o'clock, we are ready to close the books for the day. My job, as bookkeeper, is to extend the new balances mentally. An adding machine and a Boston ledger have nothing in common. No one ever heard of trying to use an adding machine in this situation; only sissies would think of such a thing. Besides, it would be a waste of time. In fact, when some misanthrope designed the Boston ledger, adding machines might not even have been in existence.

The Anti-Animal-Rights Fur Company's debit items for the day totaled $366.20; a deposit (credit) of $250 also was made.

The previous day's balance was $3,000.74. So, mentally, I have to subtract $250 from $366.20 and subtract the difference, $116.20, from the previous day's closing balance, which gives me a new balance of $2,884.54 for this account.

If you have nothing better to do (which I hope is not the case), you may test your ability as an old-fashioned bookkeeper. Here are the amounts for the fur company as they would appear in a Boston ledger if correctly posted for one day:

Old Balance	Debits	Credits	New Balance
3000.74	175.50	250.00	
	68.70		
	122.00		

(Please extend the new balance without using a pencil, except to total the debits. This exercise is suggested only as a bid for your sympathy.)

Now, to make certain that I have not made any mistakes, I total *all* debits and credits of today's business and mentally apply the difference to yesterday's total closing for *all* accounts; and that amount must agree with the total balance of all accounts as of the close of the business today. If it does, I can go home, and so can the assistant manager.

However, I seldom managed to get done by five o'clock. Footing a column of figures, rapidly, is an art. I learned after a while that one adds by recognition, or cognition, not by conscious accumulation: you recognize an eight and a seven but you think fifteen. After you overcome your lack of confidence, you will be able to stop analyzing numbers and accumulate them faster than you could run a tape on the old hand-operated adding machines. Having lived through four years of college, where critical analysis of everything we studied was the approach, this seemingly carefree, if not careless, method of treating the bank balances of other people—customers of the bank—

was a hard lesson to learn. And it left me embarrassed and humili-ated.

But even after I had balanced the day's work, my troubles weren't over. Two or more posting errors could still be lurking in my ledger and totals would prove, so we wouldn't find them out until the end of the month. That is, I might have posted a debit or credit in the right column but on the wrong line, i.e., to the wrong account. Ledger pages were at least twenty-eight inches across and one could post an item or two above or below, which would have the effect of screwing up the balance of two customers' accounts at once. Still, my book would balance, because all items had been posted and correctly extended.

This awful truth would come to light at the end of the month, when statements of accounts would be verified and mailed to cus-tomers together with their canceled checks. Before sending them out, however, the statement clerk would compare his balance with the balance on the ledger. That is when the moment of truth would arrive.

This flurry of activity came on the last day of the month. At about 6:00 P.M., we would be permitted to go out to dinner at the expense of the bank. There would be no additional compensation for the extra hours of work. That was a part of the job. It was up to us wage slaves, and in our own self-interest, to get the work done as soon as possible.

So when the statement clerk found a difference in one or more of the accounts in the Q-to-Z ledger (or any other), he would have to review the month's postings to the accounts out of balance, find the error, correct it, cuss out the bookkeeper, and finally get ready to close up shop at heaven knows what hour.

I realized from that fateful day in June that I had made a dreadful mistake, and that it would be only a matter of time before I would extricate myself from a situation that was about as far from the academic world as one could get. I knew I was a fish out of water, and that my place was back in the academic world (where they hadn't found out how dumb I was?). But I didn't want to leave the bank until I had redeemed myself and erased the impression I felt I had given in terms of the mental ability of a college graduate. So I stuck it out until about mid-January 1923, having started this hapless hiatus from the academic world in June 1922. Why January? Because that was the time to register for the spring session at Columbia graduate school for the purpose of obtaining a master's degree in the disciplines of history, economics, and public law.

Chapter 19
Number Two: A Bigger One?

My vocational and intellectual interest continued to be in sociology—particularly in that branch of the subject having to do with the relation between the size of the world's population and the conditions under which mankind must live.

I was particularly aroused, at about this time, when some social-welfare organization came forth with a report deploring the plight of children in the United States, and recommending that a subsidy be paid to parents who have more children than they could afford.

My feeling then, and it hasn't changed much since, was that admittedly we should do whatever is possible for the benefit and welfare of children; but that we would be putting the cart before the horse if we let the matter rest there, as the report seemed to do. Any policy that makes it easier for parents to have more children is, and will be, counterproductive. After the existing brood of offspring is cared for, maximum effort should be exerted to limit the number of offspring per family—as some Asian countries have found it necessary to do, even to the point of penalizing parents who defy the long-run interest of society. Any program, such as a subsidy, which lightens the burden of a large family will lead to trouble, because it tends to foster fecundity and compensate for carelessness.

It was because of my concern with social questions such as this that kept me in the field of sociology in the graduate school; my minor subject was economics.

One of the courses in sociology was a two-hour lecture given one day a week by Professor Giddings. Over a hundred students attended this class; we were seated alphabetically to enable a clerical assistant to take attendance with dispatch while the lecture was delivered. At the end of the first fifty minutes there would be an intermission of ten minutes. The lecturer would go to his office and the students would be free to roam in the hall, where smoking was permitted, or stay in the room and talk to fellow students.

Sitting directly in front of me at these lectures was an attractive-looking girl, well dressed and much better groomed than the typical female graduate student. In fact, this didn't seem to be the kind of place where a person of her type ordinarily would be. The reason why she was sitting in the row in front of me was because her last name began with Ba and mine with Bu. And the reason why she was not out in the hall smoking a cigarette (as women had begun to do by this time), I was told later, was that her mother gave her only one bit of advice when she left home for the big city; that admonition was, "Don't smoke in public." (That would seem to give a girl quite a bit of latitude, you might say to yourself. But in this case I believe her mother, in all innocence, didn't think her daughter would do anything more risqué than that.)

The ten-minute intermission ended and the lecture resumed. Fifty minutes later the session ended, and we all went our separate ways; except that the girl in front of me seemed to be interested in finding out what I might be doing or where I was going, and my curiosity about her was no less. So, as we walked out together, she said that she was returning to her rented room in an apartment on 113th Street between Broadway and Amsterdam; I said I would walk that far with her, if she didn't mind—and she didn't.

She said she was from Omaha, Nebraska; was twenty-two years old; was not a graduate of a high school or prep school, let alone a college, yet here she was in the graduate school of Columbia University! That, I thought to myself, sounds like a mystery wrapped up in a conundrum; the rest of us have to go through myriad educational contortions to get to this point, but here's a gal who has managed, somehow, to circumvent all the rules and regulations. What's the explanation?

I was too timid to ask questions, and also too inexperienced in my relations with women to know quite how to handle myself. Remember, I was afraid of girls (which is about as accurate a description as I can give of myself)—partly because I feared I might become entangled in a relationship that could not be broken without traumatic consequences; and also because I was not interested in taking the kind of job that would provide enough income to support a family. I wanted to be free to follow my own intellectual pursuits without regard for the income they might provide. My lifestyle was sufficiently spartan to enable me to live as I chose, on the income of an intellectual; it probably would not support more than one person, especially if the second one had a champagne appetite. In a word, taking on the responsibilities of a husband was completely outside my realm of thought.

We reached the apartment house on 113 Street, and as we stood there on the sidewalk several children, who were playing hop scotch, paused long enough to entertain us with an impromptu vocalization (no worse, I might add, than the rendition by the sorry soprano a floor or two above Miss Casey's apartment) of "They're going to get married."

That left both of us speechless, and me a bit worried. So, before matters got worse, I took off for my dormitory. We didn't see each other until the next week in class, where I found I was still curious as to what Omaha people have that Evansville people lack. How was she able to get into the university without the proper academic credentials, when the rest of us had to go through contortions to do so?

Little by little, I began to get the picture. Mind you, all this time I'm trying to remain aloof. I don't want to become involved. But, as an amateur Freudian, I would like to psychoanalyze this situation. The story, as it begins to unfold, is about a grandfather, an Englishman, who, like so many Britishers in the early part of the nineteenth century, had what the Germans called Weltanschauung, or world outlook, also known as colonialism by some, or the last gasp of mercantilism by others. It was the basis for the expansion of tiny Britain into a colonial empire that, in its shear magnitude, rivalled that of the Romans two thousand years before.

So Grandfather Barker (there's the Ba which determined the seating arrangement) landed in the United States about the middle of the nineteenth century because, like a good colonial-minded Englishman, he thought it only a matter of a few years before the Union Pacific Railroad, which was being built from Chicago to Council Bluffs Iowa, would be extended across the Missouri River (by a bridge) into Nebraska territory, where a trading center would probably develop as a gateway to the east from the vast hinterland in the west. So why not buy some farm land on the Nebraska side in the area where the railroad would pass? Indeed, why not? So he did.

The land he bought later became part of the downtown area of Omaha. (Don't ask me how an immigrant Englishman could have anticipated that, if in fact he did. Maybe it was sheer dumb luck, or maybe he had some "inside information." No one knows; or, at least, no one tells.)

The family, as a consequence, became the equivalent of one of the FFV, i.e., the FFN (First Families of Nebraska); or rather one of the second families: the first families were the Omahas (the Indian tribe). But no one mentions that.

Or maybe their eldest daughter, the one I was talking to, did. In fact I would be surprised if she didn't, because she was a rebel. She had no interest in the so-called "high society" life of parties, and other forms of conspicuous consumption; as a teenager, she wouldn't behave like a member of the leisure class; instead of wasting mornings playing bridge and having lunch at the country club, she preferred attending a minor college in town and took classes in sociology and continued to look askance, in Veblenian fashion, at the lifestyle of her family and the social whirl in which they wanted her to take an active part. The conflict took its toll. She had, for lack of a better definition, a "nervous breakdown"—the recommended cure, psychoanalysis. But before the psychoanalyst could even get started, she told him where he could get off, that he was a tool of her parents, and that she was not about to let him bend her to their will. Result—he threw up his hands in defeat. She was as big a problem for him as she was for her parents. No solution was in sight. He lost patience and a patient.

Matters grew "worse" when she began dating an Irish Catholic who lived literally on the "wrong" side of the tracks. It was unclear whether her father objected more to the fact that the man had no "social position," or to his religion. (Her father's attitude toward the Irish and Catholics was inherited from his British father.) There were many other men in town, who belonged to the same affluent social and respected group as the Barkers; so why in God's name did she have to take up with people who simply didn't belong to her "class"? She knew, and occasionally dated another man, named Buckingham, who *was* in her "class." Her father would approve of anyone with a name like that. But she didn't. Was it more of her rebelliousness?

I didn't get *all* of this background from her in the spring of 1923 as we walked along Broadway from 116th Street to 113th Street, where she was living at the time. But it throws some light on the subject of how she managed to elbow her way into the graduate school of Columbia without having met any of the usual entrance requirements. I should, however, absolve the university of any irregularity, before I get sued for defamation or whatever, by saying that she was admitted as an "unclassified" student; she would not receive any credits, nor was she eligible for any kind of degree. She was working only for a degree in "dilettantism," as she put it, although even that required some doing on the part of the family and friends in Omaha—if not in Nebraska—including (I once heard) some important person in the University of Nebraska, who knew Pres. Nicholas Murray Butler of C.U. (or Nicholas Miraculous Butless, as the socialist Eugene Debs used to call him). This may sound like a lot of hoopla intended solely for the purpose of enabling a young woman to forsake the corn belt for Broadway; but her family had a problem with her, which they were unable to solve. Exerting enough influence among the right people got them the qualified approval of Columbia admissions office; so, since nothing else was working, her parents yielded to her wishes and hoped for the best. When the spring term ended, she returned to Omaha.

A requirement of the sociology course we were taking was that each member working toward a degree was required to submit a term paper, dealing with some sociological subject. The best source for the raw data I required, I believed, would be the Statistician of the Metropolitan Life Insurance Company. Accordingly, I called the Met and was referred to the statistical division, where a Mr. Kopf suggested that I come to his office at One Madison Avenue; he would see what he could do for me. He was the number-two man in that division.

In no time at all he was able to give me the data I was looking for, and under ordinary circumstances the interview would have ended there; but not in this case. Instead, he began a lecture, which, if given a title, would be called "The Metropolitan Life Insurance Company, One of the Most Beneficent, Altruistic, Salutary Organizations Ever Developed for the Good of Man." The Met not only rendered salubrious services to working men and women in the United States and Canada, he opined, but it took equally good care of its employees (10,000 of whom toiled in the home office at One Madison Avenue alone), virtually from the cradle to the grave. Yes: there were free lunches, accident and health insurance, life insurance, annual medical examinations, annual vacations, pensions, and job security. ("No one ever quits this company," I was told. "Somewhere in the organization there is always a job to match one's makeup.")

Referring to the paper I was writing for the sociology course, he commented proudly that Mother Metropolitan put out pamphlets like that every day of the week, by the hundreds of thousands, or even millions; the company even had its own printing plant. I couldn't avoid becoming impressed.

Then, the punch line: what was I planning to do with my education? I hadn't thought too much about that, but in view of my interest in the intellectual life, I think I said that I probably would become a college professor after I got my doctor's degree.

"That is a long way off," he said. "*We* are interested in social engineering here and now, every day of the week. This is a sociological institution. Mother Metropolitan is doing more to improve the health and welfare of working people in America than are all the college professors in captivity. You should go downstairs and talk to our personnel people. They will confirm everything I have said about this public-service company. We are the largest insurance company in the world because we work for the public welfare. We have no stockholders; we have only policyholders, and *they* are our primary beneficiaries. If we reduce mortality we don't pocket the savings, we return them to the policyholders in the form of reduced premiums. We are a mutual company: our policyholders are our partners. We love them and they love us. You will, too, when you get to know us."

I was unavoidably impressed by this description of one of the largest corporations in the United States. But I didn't make a commitment at that time, mainly, I think, because I wanted to work on my master's degree.

Over the summer of 1923, the gal I'd met during the spring term evidently made clear to her parents that she intended to return to New York in September, and that she would want an apartment this time, not a room. She also told them that the student she'd met in the sociology class could find a suitable apartment if they would agree. They did, and so did I. I selected a small unit in a residential hotel in the west seventies or eighties that was called the Ransby.

During the fall term I found it desirable to keep in touch with Mr. Kopf of the Met in connection with the paper I was writing, and he continued to tell me what a desirable place One Madison Avenue would be for a person like me; me, penniless and without specific prospects for the future, but with interests that dovetailed nicely with those of the Met. Nevertheless, I continued to attend class.

Looking back, it appears to me that the successful people in the company, from the top executive in the home office to the field man (no women) on the debit, all had what it takes in the life insurance business—sales ability. The home office people "sold" the company as assiduously as the agents sold insurance. They had become believers by association.

Meanwhile, one of the things my girlfriend did on Sunday was to go to an Episcopal church on Forty-sixth Street, a block or two east of Times Square. Rather than say no to her every Sunday, I occasionally went along. Strangely enough, I detected an unexpected resemblance between what I had been hearing Mr. Kopf say and what the preacher at this church was saying. The only practical difference was that, whereas Mr. Kopf was offering a place here on earth that took care of everything from the cradle to the grave, the parson promised the same thing, but in a future life; provided, that is, that we walked the ecclesiastical chalk line in *this* life. On balance, I felt Kopf's deal was better than the parson's, mainly because Kopf was offering present value; the parson, futures. My girlfriend, though able to get into a graduate school without credentials, didn't quite get the point when I asked her if a bird in the hand wasn't worth two in the bush. She *said* she did, but I don't think she realized that Kopf was talking about a bird in the hand, while the parson's deal was strictly a bird in the bush, capable of flying away at any time without notice.

Regardless of who understood what, I felt that I had to make a decision. Should I take Mr. Kopf's advice, and go to the personnel office at the end of the school term and offer my services in exchange for the incomparable benefits provided by the largest life insurance company in the world? Should I grab an opportunity to work for this company if the employment officer considered me as acceptable a candidate as Mr. Kopf apparently did? After all, there was no assurance that I would be offered a faculty appointment in some university after I got the doctor's degree; maybe the only appointments available at that time would be at second-rate freshwater colleges, out in the hinterland. Was *that* the kind of risk I should take in preference to taking a job at the Met and staying in New York?

The decision seemed compelling: I would go to the Personnel Division. When I got there, I found that I had already been introduced by telephone by Mr. Kopf. Before I realized it, I was in. But in what?

Chapter 20
Getting in Deeper

After a medical examination (the first of what would become thereafter an annual event), I was admitted. I felt a bit flattered, in a way, that this big magnificent company was willing to take me into its family and share its largess. At this point the record becomes a bit blurred, if not altogether blank. If I were a Freudian (and I guess I am, in theory), I would say that the reason I don't remember precisely what happened next is because it turned out to be a minor disaster.

The mystery is, Why did I land in the correspondence section of the Group Insurance Division, instead of in some department where the loftier activities of the company were handled? When I made the decision to leave the university, I didn't feel that I was changing my vocation; I was only changing the way I would live it. I take some of the blame, for not asking a few intelligent questions; Kopf shares some of the blame, for not telling the personnel people how I happened to be there and how the company could best use my services; and the Personnel Division bears blame for making no effort to fit me somewhere in the company where my aptitude and that of the company Kopf described were in harmony. If they didn't have some kind of psychological test, they should have.

Evidently, the Personnel Department had an urgent request from the Group Insurance Division for a person capable of writing intelligible letters to presidents of corporations praising the virtues of group insurance; and, like the personnel manager of the Corn Exchange Bank a year or so before, when a greenhorn with my background came in they grabbed him and sent him to the Group Insurance Division, where a body was needed at once. That was a feather in the cap of the personnel officer, but a pain in the neck to me.

The duties of us three letter writers in the Group Insurance Division were to read the weekly reports from the company's group insurance agents in the field relative to the "prospects" they had canvassed during the week. We would then write a letter to the prospect amplifying and explaining this form of insurance, thus relieving the field man of the necessity of spending time writing letters.

We had dictaphones, which, in those days, used wax cylinders. These were collected from hour to hour and taken to the stenographers. In due course, letters would come back for signature—unless the office boy dropped the cylinders, in which event our valuable contributions would be lost and we would have to recollect our persuasive palaver and impregnate another cylinder. (Probably the main difference between what happened when the office boy dropped a cylinder and what the prospect did with a letter was in the timing of the two events.) All a person could do in a job of this kind was to keep an eye on the clock and hope to find something intellectually stimulating to do after office hours.

While this was going on my girlfriend from Omaha was attending classes at Columbia, her second year of dilettantism. We had dinner together two or three times a week; on Sundays, she attended services at the Episcopal Church of Saint Mary the Virgin (so called), on Forty-Sixth Street east of Times Square, and I was urged to go with her. I was about as much interested in spending a Sunday morning in this way as I was in dictating sales letters. But I went along on the assumption that it might widen my psychological and social experience, i.e., get acquainted with WASPs.

My first reaction was that someone had made a mistake: this was not a Protestant congregation; this was a Roman Catholic outfit—the kind I used to belong to. But the celebrant used English, not Latin. That was confusing. Then I noticed something about confessions in the handout offered by the ushers; and before the service began, the celebrant walked up and down the aisle, aided by two acolytes, one of whom held his vestment so as to free his arm (the right one, unless he was a southpaw) while the other carried a bucket of water (hopefully holy), which the priest carelessly and inconsiderately sprinkled on the people who had come to the service. If the water spotted someone's blouse or starched collar, that didn't seem to bother the Reverend. Catholic priests behaved the same way, I recalled.

After that the service began at the altar, and I'll be damned if they didn't go about it in precisely the same way Catholics do. After a certain amount of ritual the celebrant retired to a bench (to take a little rest?), while one of his associates went to the pulpit and proceeded to do the same thing that the priests I used to listen to did: he told us to believe, and be good. It apparently hadn't occurred to him that the people who were there didn't have to be told that—they knew it, that's why they were there in the first place. What he should have been doing was hollering his head off at the nonbelievers in Times Square, in the hope of bringing those godless people past the pigeons and into the church.

After the sermon the offering was taken. Ordinarily, this would be a nonevent. But this time, I almost fell out of the pew—not because I wanted to dodge the man in the morning coat and grey trousers who was taking up the offering, but because the head man this time was—brace yourself—the president of none other than the Metropolitan Life Insurance Company! Now I'm more confused than ever. Surely, he, an ex-Britisher, was not a Roman Catholic, so what was going on here? In my bewilderment I alternately sat, knelt, and stood (but did not respond verbally, as the rest of the congregation did routinely, in English) until the ceremony ended, when the priest and his helpers left the altar and hid somewhere behind it, as the priests in my boyhood days did. Except that, in this case, one of the ministers returned in a cassock and shook hands with parishioners, including my girlfriend, whom he embraced (very circumspectly), which I thought indicated either that she was a good friend, a generous (sinful) contributor, or both. That left me even more bewildered, which I tried to conceal. She later told me that the priests of this congregation practiced celibacy—which, however, didn't surprise me, considering all of the other similarities to the Church of Rome— (but I didn't ask why).

After dodging the product of the pigeons who perch disrespectfully on the statues of various saints adorning the facade of this church (even more productively than they do at a certain Presbyterian church I mention elsewhere), we decided that, in addition to the spiritual food we were supposed to have received in the service, we should now partake of something more solid and immediately satisfying.

There was a restaurant, of sorts, across the street that was owned and operated by emigrants from India. It was open, inasmuch as the proprietors apparently considered Sunday nothing more than the first day of the week. So in we went. We were practically the only ones there; evidently after a typical Saturday night Times Square people aren't up and about at that hour. Not only was the management glad to see us, they were also quite agreeable to our staying there as long as we liked (perhaps to attract others?). At least we probably gave the impression that the food was edible and the consequence of eating it less than lethal.

We started with soup and salad, as we watched the pigeons across the street sit on the saints and wait patiently for penitent parishioners to pass through the portals. Eventually I took the step of asking her what she thought had been accomplished by the morning's ceremony, and why didn't she call it a Roman Catholic service? Apparently she had been asked that question before and was ready for it.

She started off by saying that, in my fascination with sociology and population control, I had paid too little attention to British history. The church we had attended, she said, *was* a Catholic church—an Anglo-Catholic church. "We have everything the Roman Catholics have, in addition to which we don't have to put up with a pope, who, in reality, is no more than the bishop of Rome." The Catholic church in Great Britain had been in disagreement with the hierarchy in Rome for many years before Henry VIII came to the throne, she wanted me to know. Nor did he "found" the Anglican church. Indeed, he was glad that the break with Rome came during his reign because, as Catherine of Aragon, his wife, had been unable during her child-bearing years to present him with a male heir, he was becoming desperate. If he could divorce Catherine and marry, say, Anne Boleyn, maybe she could deliver a son. But the pope would not grant the divorce. "Please note," she reminded me, "Henry was a moral man: he could have taken a mistress, but he didn't. He took a wife."

By this time she had finished the main course, which was a Tandoori (even though she had done most of the talking or lecturing), and I had polished off a bit of curry. In spite of the fact that it was after two o'clock, I made it clear that I had no interest in hanging around that pigeon-polluted area until it was time for vespers (yes, the Anglo-Catholic congregation had this Roman ceremony, too). So we began the long walk to her apartment.

When we arrived her roommate, a gal her age named Fran Roberts (whose divorced mother owned a section of corn-producing land in Nebraska), said that her father had called from Omaha and would like to talk to her.

What was happening, apparently, was that her family had come to the conclusion that their unpredictable daughter might be "up to" something again; her father, therefore, had found it "necessary" to make a "business" trip to New York without delay. In other words, daughter's letters to the family, plus, perhaps, comments Fran Roberts may have made from time to time to her mother about the fact that Elizabeth (Libby, for short) appeared to be romantically involved with that fellow she'd met last year at Columbia, were sufficient reason for father Barker to come to New York and look things over—especially that young fellow from Columbia.

I didn't know, at the time, that her father had rather strong feelings about certain matters. One of them was religion. When Libby once casually remarked that I had been a Roman, his reaction, I later learned had been, "Once a Catholic, always a Catholic." (Note that he, like many Episcopalians, considered himself to be a member of the *Protestant* Episcopal church, but their Protestantism is primarily against the primacy of the pope, not against the theology of Catholicism. Episcopal priests, the better-informed members will tell you, have the same authority vouchsafed by Jesus to the apostles as Roman Catholic priests have, i.e., the powers that go with Apostolic succession.)

So, in a real sense her father was the Catholic, but I don't think he saw it that way; in fact, I know he didn't. Another of his attitudes (I won't call it a prejudice) was that college professors, or teachers in general, either do not wish to work, or are unwilling to take the hard knocks one encounters in the business world. Consequently, if his daughter married one, she could expect to live on a middle-class income all her life.

Although I had become identified with the insurance company, he seemed to have a lingering suspicion that I preferred the academic life; and, in this respect, he should be given credit for having had a better psychoanalytic profile of this unknown character, who was pursuing his daughter, than the subject himself had. Otherwise, why did the subject wind up in a clerical job where he wrote sales letters all day long?

So now I seemed to have three strikes against me. Was I out on strikes? As a matter of fact, I wouldn't have been too adversely affected if the whole thing had come to an abrupt end at that point, for, to tell the truth, I didn't feel that I was ready to marry. Among other things, I, in my conservative way, began to wonder how I would cope with a situation where there seemed to be such a wide gap between my impecunious way of life and the kind of life to which this girl was accustomed. This disparity tended to show up, for example, if we went to dinner together. If alone, I would not be totally averse to dropping in to one of those uncivilized Automat places where one put nickels into slots, following which, in a few minutes, I could be on my way to something more important. But when we were together, her uncompromising preference would be for a place like Rubin's—at that time, a chain of first-class steak houses—where she would have no compunction about spending as much for one meal as I, if left to my own devices, would spend in several days. But that was one of the eating places her parents favored when they were in town, and she was only behaving like a Barker.

Now, as to her father's telephone call. He told her that he would be in New York Wednesday, staying at the Plaza; he wanted to have dinner with her, alone, on Wednesday night, and with both of us on Thursday night. A brief conversation, but loaded with significance!

That capped a rather eventful day. It was now after five o'clock, time for me to go home—which, at this time, was a settlement house on Sutton Place that was owned and operated by a Fifth Avenue Methodist church. I was an evening "counsellor," so-called, having been recommended by the faculty of Columbia. The clientele of the house consisted of East Side immigrants and their children. We provided classes in the English language, instruction in civics and other subjects, and game rooms, which gave children an alternative to playing in streets and unsupervised playgrounds. This activity did not interfere in any way with my work schedule at the Met, while providing living quarters, breakfast, and dinner, during the week, and all meals on weekends. My take-home pay in those days was net, no discount, and my living expenses practically nil. So (although by now I probably don't have to tell you), my account at the Bank for Savings, just around the corner from the Met, was growing by leaps and bounds. My salary was $35 per week, plus a bonus of 10 percent of weekly salary ($3.50) if I was at my desk by nine o'clock every day of the month, as I usually was; plus lunch at the expense of the policy-holders. What a deal!

On Thursday I got the message that Father not only wanted me for dinner that night but that we would have it at the Plaza, and go to the theater afterwards. If I couldn't round up a tuxedo I would be irremediably embarrassed, and Father Barker would be vindicated in his premature devaluation of this nobody his problem child had picked up.

Nowadays renting evening clothes doesn't seem to be declassé, but in those days it did. How I managed to obtain a tuxedo on such short notice escapes me, except that I do remember a tailor I contacted on West Twenty-third Street had a tux he said had been made for "a baseball player," who'd declined to take delivery of it because, he said, "it didn't fit." (If that is a valid reason for not buying a suit, then I shouldn't have bought this one either.) But I had bigger fish to fry, and besides, I had to get back to my desk or I might find that, although I had found a tux, I had lost a job.

At the appointed hour I appeared in the lobby of the Plaza, which was only a stone's throw from Fifty-ninth and Sutton Place to the hotel at Fifty-ninth and Fifth. Walking the streets at night in those days was not a hazardous undertaking. Libby was in the lobby, as was her eleven-year-old brother, who was writing a letter to his mother. Years later I was told that the boy, who had seen me for the first time only a few minutes before, had said in the letter, "He's not bad looking and seems *willing to work*" (emphasis supplied). (Undoubtedly the youngster had overheard his father express the opinion that academicians choose their vocation because they don't want to work and face the rigors of competition with other adults.) Mr. Barker deserves a lot of credit for being able to see through the outward signs, understanding intuitively that here's a man who is basically doing what he doesn't want to be doing. (And who, consequently could be unstable—in which case he would add another dimension to his daughter's instability, with the result that the family would have two problems to deal with, instead of one. Horrible thought.)

Libby was sitting on a couch in the lobby, dressed in her finest attire. She said that her father was in his room putting on his evening clothes, and wanted me to come up as soon as I arrived. So up I went.

That was not the most enjoyable trip on an elevator that I had ever taken: and what's more, I wasn't even sure why I was taking it. I was not about to make a commitment; on the contrary, I probably would have been more comfortable in the reading room of the New York Public Library, seventeen blocks to the south, than I was here in this pulchritudinous palace of the prosperous, where I was about to be measured relative to a set of values that were in a category entirely different from mine.

When I arrived, father Barker was putting some diamond studs into his starched-bosom shirt. (My shirt, at least, was white, though not starched, with buttons sewed on—except where they had come off in the laundry.) He greeted me most warmly, as if he had known me from his prep school days at Saint Paul's, Concord. He didn't seem to be interested in my ill-fitting suit and the fact that my shoes, though black (thank God) were not pumps or patent leather. Indeed, he smiled and made me feel really comfortable, as I suppose one who was to the manor born would do.

He didn't ask me if I was interested in his daughter. He didn't ask me if I preferred academia to group insurance; he didn't ask me anything about my personal life. He did ask me if I would prefer to go to the Follies after dinner and see, in addition to the chorus girls, Will Rogers, who was part of the cast. (And of course I would, never before having taken in this kind of eye- and ear-opening entertainment.)

Dressed now, fit to kill, he suggested that we go to the dining room where I saw him slip a "fiver" (as the British say) to the headwaiter, which guaranteed that we would have the choicest table in the house and a waiter who'd undoubtedly gotten the sign from the headwaiter that here was a guest who should be given the best. If I still had any lingering doubts as to whether I had allowed myself to get beyond my depth, they certainly should now have been dispelled.

I managed to be very punctilious about my table manners, as Mother required; not even the Automat had erased them from memory. Everything about the dinner was top-notch, as it should have been, considering the numbers in the right-hand column of the menu and father Barker's fabulous fees to the flunkies.

The next day he really did devote to business, and in the evening the three of them had dinner alone. On Friday, he and his son left on the Twentieth Century Limited for Chicago and home.

At the end of the spring term in June 1924, Libby returned to Omaha. We had continued our friendly relationship but our behavior was not too different, I would say, from that of the Reverend Father of the Church of Saint Mary the you-know-what.

Early in the summer of 1924 I was summoned to the office of the vice president of the Met, who was the boss of the Group Insurance Division. He told me that he was going to establish a group-sales correspondence section in the head office in Canada, and that I could have the job if I wished.

Offering a New Yorker an opportunity to move to Ottawa in the summer seemed, to me, almost to be the equivalent of releasing an otherwise pledged-for-life tenant from an eternity in hell. Indeed, I'd never liked New York in the summertime, so my answer was an instant "yes"; besides which, it was a promotion. And also, it's never a good idea to decline an offer from the boss. Consequently, within a matter of days I was off, with all of my possessions in two or three handbags to Ottawa, which was then, and, I hope, still is, a relatively small, beautiful city.

In my new location I had a private office, a private secretary—no dictaphone with its wax cylinders—and a salary of $75 Canadian per week.

When the fall semester began my girlfriend did not return to New York. Our connection, therefore, was by mail, and occasionally by telephone. Under these circumstances, it should come as no surprise that she sensed our relationship was cooling—and I did nothing to offset it. At this point, enter mother Barker. She urgently suggested that I come to Omaha at Christmastime for a series of parties that would be given in my honor. In my honor! Holy Mackerel. (Or the equivalent thereof!)

Chapter 21

Just Say *No* If You Can and Oh . . . If You Can't—Then Make the Most of It

There was little to do in my new assignment, because there were no group sales representatives west of Ottawa; and the only person working Quebec to the east was Capt. Jack Jones (a pal of Mr. A.F.C. Fiske, president of the Canadian head office) and son of Haley Fiske, president of the parent company, M.L.I. Co. Captain Jones had not only all the secretarial help he needed but other perquisites, including Canadian Scotch, that A.F.C. conveniently kept available for their mutual benefit. There also seemed to be some question as to who my boss really was.

In a nutshell, I wasn't keeping Mrs. Johnson, my secretary, busy, because I wasn't busy; instead, I was becoming bored. So, without consulting anyone, I began canvassing employers myself. The market in Ottawa was rather limited for group insurance, the main industrial center in the west being Toronto. I kept making trips there and using space in the office of the manager of a district office, with his approval. I am sure the home office found out that something unusual was going on in Canada, as a result of which, Mr. Kavanagh, the head of the whole group Insurance Division, finding suddenly he had "urgent" business in Canada, came to see me one day when I was in Toronto.

Quite innocently and routinely I brought out my notebook, which contained the names and addresses of companies I had called on and the prospects of doing business with them.

This surprised him. Office employees in the Met did not normally get out of their cushioned desk chairs and go to work, for if they did, they would have to get back in time to have lunch in the company cafeteria: and after lunch the time would be too short to make calls and still be able to go home at four-thirty. He didn't tell me I should or should not continue what I was doing; all I remember is that I did continue, and he acted as if I, like everybody else in the company, would be there until retirement age—on a pension!

I might also add that he did not find any corkscrews, empty bottles, drinking glasses, or any other alcohol-related paraphernalia. While Americans at that time were drinking Prohibition "hooch" and bathtub gin, and the Canadians were downing the real stuff, I was not interested in it in the least, in which I differed from the attitude in the upper echelon of Ottawa office personnel.

Mr. Kavanagh was a sincere and ardent Presbyterian, and although my teetotalism was a point in my favor, he was not too happy about the fact that, at the age of twenty-six, I was not married; which probably explains why he mentioned that "Everyone who works for the Metropolitan gets married." That kind of thinking harmonizes with the mentality of a person in the life insurance business, where the ideal is a family protected by life insurance. It was also a hint, I thought, that if I wanted to advance in the company I would do so more rapidly as a married man. At that time, as I look back, I evidently thought that I would stay with the company; consequently I did not brush off the hint as mere conversation.

As the Christmas season approached I began to get more urgent suggestions from Omaha that I come out during the holidays, which is a dull period in the insurance business; nobody thinks of insurance policies as Christmas gifts. If the home office objected, I could take it as one week of my vacation.

Somehow or other I also got the idea that "someone" in Omaha thought it would be appropriate for us to announce our engagement at that time. (Again, enter Dr. Freud, and help me explain this rather rapid pace of events; my memory is not sufficient.)

What I *do* remember is that I had begun to feel somewhat discouraged inasmuch as the correspondence job turned out to be a dud—although that was management's problem, not mine. But the outside selling or agency work was also failing. For the first time in my life I felt, not lonely, but alone. In an office job progress depended on doing day-to-day chores, and that would be easy in comparison with canvassing and selling. There was no one with whom I could share my concerns, although I think my letters to Omaha must have revealed something of the sort. Added to that was Mr. Kavanagh's bias in favor of married men. So the result was that I did go to Omaha for the Christmas holidays in 1924; I did take a diamond ring with me; we did announce our engagement; and we were fêted in party after party, in the sumptuous manner of the best of Omaha society.

On my way back to Toronto, however, I began to be bothered more than ever about the wide disparity between the lifestyle to which my fiancée was accustomed and the way of life she would have to put up with if she lived with me, unless my fortunes with the Met improved greatly—at best, a speculative hope.

I also saw evidence during this visit of some of the characteristics of her youth—unwillingness to cooperate, a demand for attention, self-centeredness, and something of the superiority complex with which she'd been driving her sister Virginia up the wall, and which had made it impossible for the psychiatrist to work with her when she was a teenager.

It was also becoming increasingly clear that she had no interest in being a housewife. The only time she'd ever made a bed was when she had volunteered to work in a hospital as a Junior League girl. She knew where the kitchen was in her home because, if the chauffeur, for whatever reason, had not brought one of the cars to the porte-cochere, the most expeditious way to get to a car was via the kitchen, which, to her, was only a passage way to the garage. She was accustomed to saying, as if it was of no consequence, that she knew how to perform two culinary operations: one was making muffins (which she said were usually tough and full of tunnels because she beat the hell out of the mixture); the other was using a pastry tube. So housework or housewifery was foreign to her, as a result of her having been brought up to do nothing of that kind. Her mother had a cook, a downstairs maid who was also the waitress, an upstairs maid, a laundress, a man who was a combination gardener, chauffeur, and handyman, and a seamstress subject to call.

I didn't sleep much the night I left Omaha by train after the week of parties. Instead, I tried to figure out what kind of new situation I had gotten myself into. As the train left Chicago the next day, headed for Toronto and the real world, my thoughts grew progressively more troubled. What have I done? Have I really made a commitment? If so, was it a prudent decision? Or have I been swept off my feet? Should a $75-a-week-inexperienced novice in a strange business, with an uncertain future, become involved in a socio-economic stratum of society in which the male members made as much money in sixty minutes as I made in a week; and where their wives spent it as if it grew on trees in the backyard?

I agonized over this situation for about a week. Finally I laid it all out in a letter to the young lady to whom I had given the diamond ring about two weeks before. What the letter boiled down to was an expression of my feeling that it would be in the interest of both of us to terminate our relationship, or at least put it on hold. (What a shocker! Was I a cad at heart? Even today, more than sixty-six years later, I wonder how I managed to do it.)

The response I received was a telephone call from her mother; she asked me if I would meet her at the Blackstone Hotel in Chicago two days later. I could have said no, but I didn't, because I had the naive hope that she might have a solution that would avoid embarrassment for her daughter and afford some measure of relief to me. I met her after breakfast on the appointed day and we talked—or, more accurately I listened—for about two hours. The sum and substance of her message was that I was overemphasizing the differences that were disturbing me; that questions of this nature are present in many marriages, and are usually resolved; and that the "perfect" mate and completely trouble-free marriage are storybook figments of the imagination. By the conclusion of our meeting I had agreed to stop fretting, and start thinking positively about our courtship. The word marriage was not mentioned; but as I sat in one of the swivel chairs in the Pullman lounge car on the way back to Toronto that day, early in January 1925, I had to concede that it was now only a question of when, not whether, we would be united in holy matrimony "until death us do part," according to the wording of the Episcopal ceremony, in the presence of all the "best people" of Omaha, plus my parents and my bride's-maid sister.

As I look back on this episode I feel that mother Barker believed sincerely that I would benefit, in more ways than one, by becoming a member of the family, and that this could, or would, compensate for at least some of the incompatibility I foresaw. *I* was anything but certain about that, however.

I also blamed myself for having allowed the relationship to reach the point where turning back would amount to a breach of confidence and distress—not for me, but for her. About three years later her maternal grandmother told me that, when all other efforts on the part of the family had failed to alter her teenage behavior pattern, they'd decided that marriage, the only therapy that had not been tried, was really the only option left, and as a result should be given a chance at the earliest opportunity. When she'd met that young fellow at Columbia, therefore, although he had not, from their point of view, been an ideal solution, he did nevertheless seem to have some possibility and might well be the "opportunity" they'd been hoping for. The meeting at the Blackstone was thus an unavoidable step in that direction.

When I got back to my totally different, spartan way of life, I put my evening clothes away and tried to pick up where I had left off some two weeks, which now seemed like two months, before. Selling an American contract in Canada was difficult, to say the least. In fact, Henry Frey, who was the most successful group salesman in the company, had given up Canada in despair several years before. Therefore, when I got back from my eventful two weeks in Omaha and Chicago and found a letter from the Imperial Reed and Rattan Company of Kitchener, Ontario, accepting the group-insurance plan I had presented to them early in December, I was elated—as I had a right to be. This was the only group-insurance policy that had been sold in western Canada by our company in many, many months, if not in years.

It may also have contributed to the fact that, after further reflection on the events that had taken place in the previous fortnight, I concluded that I might as well carry them to their logical conclusion—i.e., go through with the marriage as soon as practicable and hope for the best. This decision met with instant approval in Omaha.

But it also involved a problem of a different, minor, short-range kind. That is, if you happen to be among those who set the social standards, you will have nothing but the best when it comes to the wedding of your daughter. But this takes time. Dresses have to be made; invitations have to be engraved, addressed, and sent out; patterns of flat silver must be selected, and caterers engaged, to mention but a few of the more obvious items.

Under ordinary circumstances a date is selected that will allow ample time for these preparations. However, in the year 1925 Lent came early. Lent? What, you might rightly ask, does Lent have to do with what we are talking about? This is where more religious irony comes in: Lent is a period during which faithful Christians deny themselves pleasure; the more they sacrifice, the greater their sanctification. It is a sort of additional penance, or mortification, for one's sins; a method of empathizing, in a small way, with the suffering Jesus endured before and at the time of his crucifixion. The more sincerely one believes the account of Jesus' last days on earth, the more assiduously one voluntarily undergoes deprivation of one kind or another during the Lenten season.

One of the pleasurable activities that is proscribed in Lent by the Catholic church, or was at that time, was marriage, (which, asks he sarcastically, is supposed to afford pleasure?). As I have said, the word "Protestant," when followed by the word "Episcopal," merely indicates that the Church of England protests the primacy of the pope. The liturgy, the creed, the articles of faith of the two religious bodies are substantially the same, including the mutual adherence to such practices as Lenten abstinence—at least among the so-called high-church Episcopalians, which included my in-laws to be. Thus they did not look with favor upon a wedding in Lent. The trouble was that, in 1925, Lent started on the twenty-fifth of February; it was now about mid-January. That left only about five weeks to prepare for the event bearing in mind that in those days dresses for the bride and bride's maids weren't instantly available.

The irony of this scenario is that when I first came into the picture, one of the objections to me was that I had been born a Catholic; an "irreversible" condition, unfortunately. Actually, I had not the slightest compunction about getting married in Lent; but ironically, here were my parents-in-law-to-be paying homage to a rule that was common to Roman Catholic and Anglo-Catholics alike. Indeed, in the last analysis it was they who were the true Catholics, not I.

Technically, therefore, the marriage date had to be some time before February 25th. At this point, enter the ghost (not the holy one) of the late George Washington. It was customary, in those days, to commemorate the birthday of an illustrious person such as the first president of the United States on the date of his birth, not on a day which would facilitate a three-day weekend enabling millions of people to clutter highways, create traffic jams, indulge in unaccustomed and strenuous exercise, and get heart attacks.

In 1925, Mr. Washington's birthday came on Sunday; and since this high-church, high-society family wanted an elaborate church wedding in the morning, it could not conveniently be held on Sunday, because that would interfere with the regular morning service. But in those days, if the twenty-second of February came on Sunday, the following day would be declared a holiday in honor of Washington's birthday. So that was the date set for the nuptials; Monday, February 23, 1925. (A day which has been noted sixty-seven times since then, and counting!)

Here again we see a bit of ironic inconsistency. If Lent is to be a period of self-denial and abstinence, how does a marriage on the eve of Lent, instead of during Lent, meet the requirement? Nothing was said, as far as I can recall, about how this bride and groom should behave during the next forty days. If they were old-fashioned they had refrained, up to this point, from doing anything physically together, preferring to wait until the sacrament of holy matrimony gave them the moral and spiritual privilege to do so. Is it reasonable to suppose they would sacrifice their urge to merge for forty more days, in spite of the fact that finding a suitable place and time would now no longer be a deterrent? Instead of eliminating a problem presented by the confluence of religious dogma and reasonable desire, solemnizing a marriage on the eve of Lent basically had the effect of complicating it—for believers. I am not going to relieve your curiosity by going into detail about how we adjusted to the situation, or whether I suggested to the bride that she forget the humbug, since I saw no relationship between Lent, license, and libido. Nor should the fact that our one and only child was not born until three years later lead you to the assumption that we might have voluntarily adopted the Lenten restrictions as a way of life.

Chapter 22
From Pillar to Post
(with a Happy Ending)

After the wedding there was an elaborate "breakfast," although it was noon, at the home of the bride's parents, where there were also an unbelievable number of wedding gifts on display. The only hitch I can remember was that the maids—who had not gotten over the excitement of having been permitted to attend the church service along with the rich people of the city whom they, up till then, had only served at parties—forgot to put the champagne on ice; and as it was then too late for the caterer to do so, the bubbly was served at room temperature. It was also served in contravention of the law of Prohibition; evidently, the Volstead Act carried less weight than canon law.

The Union Pacific, on its way from the West Coast to Chicago, picked us up early that evening. The next morning we registered at, yes, the Blackstone Hotel. That evening we had dinner at the home of a friend of Libby's from childhood, whose father was the retired president of the Boston and Main Railroad. I remember his comment when I asked him how he passed the time in retirement. He said he devoted half the day to his investments and the other half to "hating Roosevelt." We listened during a part of the evening to marital disagreements between the hostess and her husband, who divorced not long thereafter, which I referred to subsequently as our home-study course on "How to Be Unhappy though Married." (I don't recall having gotten any kudos for that.) A day in Chicago was enough; Toronto was the next stop.

Before I'd left Toronto, I'd engaged a room at what I considered a respectable private home, so that on my return we would have a place to land until better accommodations could be found. When we arrived the landlady showed us a room, which was not the one I'd chosen but one on the top floor, more accurately describable as an attic made over with a skylight in the roof. That brought back memories of my escape from those carnivorous creatures in Margaret Casey's apartment to the inside room in Hartley Hall at C.U., where the skylight had been, to me, a symbol of freedom from blood-sucking parasites. But my bride's attitude toward the skylight differed from mine. (I soon realized that there would be more examples of Skylight Syndrome.)

The reason for the switch, the landlady said, was that she had not heard from me for some time and thought I might have changed my mind; when she got a cash customer, she'd let him have the room. (Naturally. She knew a bird in hand is worth two in the bush.)

I probably need not say that this sudden descent from the affluence of Omaha to a modest little rooming house in Toronto came as something of a shock. Indeed, I think I remember hearing the poor girl saying something to the effect that "this is the kind of accommodation we provide for the maids where I come from."

In self-defense I should say that I intended it as nothing more than a roof over our heads until we, or she, could find more suitable quarters, which, to my amazement she did almost immediately. How she accomplished this feat in so short a time I do not recall, precisely, but I think it came about as a result of her connection with an Episcopal church, the rector of which put her in touch with one of his affluent members (aren't all of them affluent?). This particular parishioner was about to leave for a vacation in Florida and was quite willing to let us have her attractive apartment, which was furnished with antiques, Royal Dolton china and Persian rugs, for the nominal amount of $125 per month. (Damned decent of her, I said to myself.) Money managers and budgeteers tell us that shelter rent should not exceed one-fourth of one's income; so, on my $75 per week we were already over our heads. Instead of going to the savings bank on payday to put money in, as I used to do, I went to draw it out. Don't forget my upbringing; my parents always had funds set aside for emergencies, although I knew this was not one. But I couldn't start educating the girl so soon.

The going was rough: spring came and went without my closing a single group-insurance contract. At home things were not much better: the bride didn't know how to cook and wasn't interested in learning, because basically, she did not want to be a housewife. But having had no formal education, and with no professional credentials, she was in a functional no-man's land. This not only contributed to her restlessness but increased the frequency and severity of her migraine headaches—which it had been hoped, was one symptom of hers that marriage would ameliorate. Instead, they got worse.

The kind of culinary confusion that complicates a bride's attempt to adjust to a new way of life, for which she had never been trained, is exemplified by the perturbation of pie-making—which, I am willing to admit, may have been made even more confusing by a husband who tries to inject a bit of humor into practically all of life's problems, large and small. But why brides try to make desserts before they learn how to cook meat and vegetables and make salad dressing, I don't know. At any rate, for some unknown reason my young spouse decided one day to make a pie. The recipe she found called for a nine-inch pie tin; but all she could find was a seven-and-a-half-inch pie tin in the kitchen of the apartment we couldn't afford.

So she called my office. She wanted to know how much she should reduce a nine-inch recipe to make it right for a seven-and-a-half-inch pie tin. I tell her to calculate the area of the two pie tins and reduce the amount of the difference between the two. To get the area of the two tins I tell her to multiply Pi by the square of the radius.

"But I haven't made the pie yet; and furthermore, how in hell am I going to multiply a pie by that other thing, that square? This is supposed to be a round pie," she reminded me.

"Okay," I say. "Let's start over. The Pi you use is not the one you will put into the oven. This Pi is a Greek symbol for a value amounting to 3.1416."

"But I'm not interested in Greek symbols. If I were, I would be a member of the Greek Orthodox church instead of the Anglican version. And what in the name of common sense, does your Pi have to do with my pie anyway?"

"It has a lot to do with it: it is the ratio of the circumference of your pie tins to their respective radii."

"But that's irrelevant. I'm not interested in what's on the circumference of the pie, but rather what's *in* it. Why don't you tell me, in plain English, how much I should reduce a nine-inch recipe to get one that will be right for a seven-and-a-half-inch pie tin? That was my original only question. I didn't ask for a diatribe in Greek."

"Okay, honey. It's very simple, as I said at the outset. All you have to do is calculate, first, the area of each pie tin, and then the difference between the two; that will tell you how much you should reduce the ingredients in the recipe."

"When I was in one of the schools I went to (no comments, please), one of the things I learned was never to use the word being defined, in the definition. You defy this rule by persisting in telling me to use the pie before I make it—and a square one, at that. And finally, don't try to tell me that Simple Simon, who made pies long before you were born, either knew or cared about your Pi's, squares, or ratios." When I got home that night I found a batch of flour and shortening in the garbage pail.

Although I couldn't do much about her problems, I decided to take up my business problems with the home office. As I have said, throwing in the group insurance towel in Canada had been the rule, not the exception. Therefore, when I asked Mr. Kavanagh for a solution, he asked me what *I* would suggest. My answer was that, if I could carry on my group insurance work in the southwest territory, which included Nebraska, some of the problems we newlyweds were having might be solved.

He said he would look into it. A few days later he called me in Toronto and told me to report to our agent, Mr. C. E. Seese, in Kansas City. Mr. Seese and his son canvassed employers; if they sold a contributory plan, the employees would have to be persuaded to pay their share of the cost of the insurance. It would be my job to sell it to the employees, at least 75 percent of whom would have to sign up so as to avoid adverse selection against the insurance company. (No medical examination was given in group insurance; to offset this risk, a high percentage of participation is required.)

I would be able to make Omaha my home, but I would have to go wherever necessary in Iowa, Kansas, Missouri, and Arkansas. The result was that I was away from home most of the time, "home" being the family domicile where the wedding breakfast and luke-warm champagne had been served scarcely seven or eight months before. Not surprisingly, questions began to arise in the family as to what kind of marriage this was. (Nobody said openly "Maybe the bridegroom was right when he said he wasn't ready for this.")

Travel is not my cup of tea, at best. Pullman cars at night and in whatever kind of hotel might be available (in a place like Womble, Arkansas) can be tiring and intellectually numbing.

After about seven months of this knocking about in the southwestern part of the United States and spending a few days occasionally in Omaha between assignments, I decided again to test the company's ability to fit the company to the employee, rather than the other way around. With some embarrassment, I approached Mr. Kavanagh yet another time. This time I drew upon the lesson I'd learned in Dr. Kitson's psychology class on the rather seductive subject of "The Mind Of The Buyer," in which the recommended strategy was to find the buyer's point of vulnerability and then work it into your sales pitch, so that in signing on the dotted line he would feel as though he was doing as much for himself as he was for you. Not a very uplifting subject for a course in liberal arts, obviously, but there it was.

However, I drew upon this "educational" experience: Mr. Kavanagh's point of vulnerability, as I have said, was his hide-bound Presbyterianism and his advocacy of family life. Therefore I told him that it was becoming difficult for me to be a satisfactory husband and family man and, at the same time, cover four states.

Whereupon, sure enough, he had a solution—which was that I should go to the manager of one of the Metropolitan District offices in Omaha; he would put me to work as an agent. As such, I could sell weekly and annual premium policies and annuities, and I could have dinner at home every night, if I didn't have an appointment with a "prospect." (He didn't know that my wife still couldn't cook.)

The transition from the traveling job to the city job in Omaha went smoothly. Almost before you could say Jack Rosenblatt, the district manager had assigned me to an area, called a "Debit," in which I would be responsible for the collection of weekly premiums on insurance policies in force on residents in that area. As I collected premiums, I was expected to place additional coverage (insurance) on anyone I might contact. Under ordinary circumstances one could expect lapses from time to time, due to someone's loss of job, temporary unemployment, or some other emergency; therefore, the sale of new policies was necessary to keep from showing a declining volume of insurance in force in one's assigned district (debit). When a policy lapsed in his area, the commission originally paid to the agent who'd sold that policy, no matter how long ago, was charged against the earnings of the agent then responsible for the debit.

The commission on a twenty-five cent per week policy, for example, was $7.50. That amount would be deducted from my earnings if the policy lapsed. If I sold no more insurance than the amount lapsed during a given period, my earnings would be zero for that period. An agent who was able to maintain a *net* increase of a dollar a week (equivalent to four policies at twenty-five cents per week, or ten policies at ten cents-per-week) over a sustained period of time was considered a successful ambassador of good will, someone who offered peace of mind and security for pennies per week.

When I got into the guts of the business, however, I found that inasmuch as the breadwinner usually was not at home when the agent called, the wife and children were the ones on whom the agent concentrated. And if he outlasted the "prospect"—that is, if he persisted long enough—his "listener" was likely to say yes to get rid of the pest, and hope to squirm out of the deal later, when it came time to pay the weekly dues. Not infrequently, if the husband and wife were covered, the agent would suggest that an endowment policy should be placed on one or more of the children. These were often referred to as "educational" policies, which would mature at about the time junior would be ready for high school or college. Frequently when the husband heard about these shenanigans he would protest, and urge his wife to decline the policy, when it was delivered, on the (defensible) grounds that it had been sold under duress. I soon concluded that I would have to either pressure people who happened to be in my orbit to sign on the dotted line, regardless, or admit this business was not for me. High-pressure salesmanship and I had absolutely nothing in common. The successful men in the business had such thick skins they were impervious to the fact that many of the people who knew them shunned them. But not always. One of the agents in our office liked to say that when he went to a certain house in his debit, the children would say, "Mommy, the insurance man is here; are you going to pay him, or do you want us to go out and play?"

Agents reported in at the district office at 8:00 A.M., turned in the cash they'd collected the day before, and then responded when the manager called on each of them to report how many policies he had sold in the last twenty-four hours. Agent Marks always led the list; I was usually at or close to the bottom. Then the manager would deliver a pep talk. He would praise the producers and belittle the laggards. The final act of the convocation consisted of our singing the company song, a hymn in praise of Mother Metropolitan. Then, our enthusiasm adequately aroused, we went forth, like missionaries, to offer Mother Metropolitan's aid, comfort, and security for two bits or less a week. This psycho-stimulation by the manager was similar to the kind of harangue a football team gets from the coach at half time if the team is losing. The most successful managers were either the most blatant bulldozers or the most persuasive preachers.

Everything about this early-morning prayer meeting—this synthetic reverence for the company, this preparation for another day of evangelical endeavor to help innocent, uninformed people achieve the "security," which we offered for nickels and dimes that otherwise might be frittered away—was repulsive. The pep session, the inspirational company song, the pressure to sell—"everybody needs insurance and the Met has the best"—everybody is a prospect—this must have been good business training for the kind of agency force the company employed, but for me, in terms of monetary returns, it was a waste of time comparable to, though different from, what I'd gone through at the parochial school years before. The experience, however, was a first-class, laboratory example of the effectiveness of behaviorist psychology.

Wholly apart from the pros and cons of industrial or weekly premium insurance, the overriding question I kept asking myself was, How in God's name did I get myself into this situation? Why am I spending my days, and some nights, messing into the private lives of families who happen to live in an area of the city that Mother Metropolitan calls a debit? Have I forsaken my preference for the academic life? Am I not wasting my time in a business in which I could never rise to the top, because I am incapable of delivering pep talks to a sales force and singing the reverential refrain to the goddess Mother Metropolitan? Haven't I practically duplicated the error I made when I walked into the Corn Exchange bank a few years previously?

The answer came, eventually and painfully; but I kept it to myself, because I was too embarrassed to admit that, once again, I didn't seem to know what I was doing. Whatever had happened to the intelligence that was considered worthy of a scholarship to Columbia and honors at graduation? Had my judgment become impaired?

Or was I right when I'd bared the thoughts which had led to that morning meeting at the Blackstone early in January? Did I have, in the background of my mind, a gnawing conviction that I would be maladjusted to anything other than an intellectual career? Was that the true reason for my hesitation regarding marriage? Is that basically why I'd felt frustrated in Canada, bored with sales pitches to factory workers during their lunch hour in the southwest territory, and then the moronic morning preface to an equally wasteful day on the debit?

It soon became obvious that there was nothing else for me to do but lay all the cards on the table, starting with the table of the district manager, who was my superior at the time. He must have known it was coming. He had praise for the condition of my debit, i.e., the low rate of delinquency and lapses, but agreed that my "industrial increase" (the net gain of new premium income over lapses), was below par. His suggestion was that, in view of the social position of my in-laws and the entree that that should give me to the wealthy people of the town, perhaps I ought to give up the debit and concentrate on ordinary annual premium, insurance.

My answer was that while I believed I was psychologically unsuited to the agency part of the business, I could see myself in some phase of the financial or investment end. Although he did not know Mr. Kavanagh, he agreed with me that if Mr. K.'s patience was not yet exhausted, it would be a good idea for me to have at least one more chat with him.

In view of the fact that I had, in effect, resigned, I paid my own way back to New York. When I arrived at the home office at One Madison Avenue I had mixed feelings of guilt, defeat, and inferiority. I avoided the Sales Correspondence Division and my former colleagues, some of whom were still there. And I felt even more humble as I ventured into Mr. Kavanagh's inner sanctum; but it was a step I had to take.

After a brief review of my experience in five phases of the company's operation and my interest in economics and sociology, I asked him if he thought the company might be interested in creating a small department that would do research in those fields, either as a unit of the statistical department or on its own. He didn't know, but he referred me to another vice president, Mr. Henry Bruere, head of the Policyholders' Service Bureau.

Mr. Bruere proved to be quite interested in the idea; so much so, he said, that only a few days previously the company had hired Dr. William A. Berridge of Brown University to do economic research. However, he thought I might find it worthwhile to talk to him, which I did.

As I was now practically unemployed, I couldn't be too choosey. So, despite the fact that in some respects I considered myself better qualified for his job than he was, due to my broad experience in the company, I was willing to eat humble pie—at least until I could find something better. The job Dr. Berridge suggested I undertake involved interviewing employers in the New England states, to learn what was motivating so many of them to move their manufacturing operations to locations below the Mason-Dixon line. I finished the job and submitted my report in late August 1927. By this time it was apparent that there was no room in his department for both of us, in light of which I began considering my options. One I eliminated without further thought: I would not try to find another spot in the company, regardless of Mother Metropolitan's fecund facility at finding suitable work-stations within the company for eccentric employees.

By now my wife had joined me and we were living in a small hotel in the east thirties. She lent support to my longing for the academic life, and as a result, after more soul-searching and considering all aspects, we decided that I should go up to Columbia and talk it over with department heads and deans, if I could find anyone who remembered me after five years' absence.

So, the next morning I put my nickel into the IRT turnstile at Thirty-fourth and Lex for a run up to the university. I couldn't find the dean of the college, Dean Hawkes; so I walked over to the School of Business, where I found the amiable Dean Roswell C. McCrea. Much to my surprise and gratification, he had not forgotten me.

I briefly told him what I had been doing since graduation and how I missed the mental challenges and intellectual freedom of the academic life, where one's loyalty was only to the truth. His first comment, as I remember it, was that I should not apologize for what I'd called my mistakes in judgment and my amenability to the persuasions of others. In fact, he said, my experience, due to its broad nature, better qualified me to become a teacher. A *teacher*? Yes, he used the word before I did. My level of confidence rose 100 percent.

So now that the ice had been broken, I asked if he thought he might find a place for me on the economics faculty. His response was that he would look things over and get in touch with me later.

Meanwhile, my wife was registering at employment agencies. When the interviewer began asking questions about her educational background, the usual consternation and incredulity beclouded the interview. Employment agencies have to deal with all kinds of crackpots and impostors, and up to this point she'd looked a bit like one. But she was a good saleswoman: in fact, I sometimes said in jest that she could sell a pot with a hole in it. (That was before she became a casualty of Alzheimer's.)

She also had a keen sense of humor, which sometimes went awry, as when the person taking her application asked her what degree she'd gotten at Columbia. She said she'd gotten her "Mrs." there.

What you will not believe, however, is that this young woman, who you could say had virtually no formal education, was accepted a few days after registering at employment agencies by the mistress of a private school for girls in the east sixties, just off Fifth Avenue, as a teacher of English literature. This she was well qualified to do, because she was an inveterate reader of the classics. (It was later learned one of the main reasons she had been selected was her membership in the Junior League; and one of the features this little school advertised was its snob appeal.)

This gave us an anchor to windward. The next step was to find a place to live—which, once again, she did in short order. But this time her selection proved worse than the attic room in Toronto. On Twenty-first Street between Ninth and Tenth Avenues, across the street from the General Theological (Episcopal) Seminary, the *New Republic* magazine owned an old four story house. In the basement lived Lucy and Etienne (late of Italy). The editorial department was on the main floor; on the second floor there was a one-room rear "apartment," which consisted of a kitchenette (with emphasis on the ette) and a bath (I was going to say bathroom, but a room is a place in which one can take a step or two, if necessary, which was somewhat difficult in this case). There was also space for one twin bed, a chair, and a table, if it could be folded to a width of, say, six inches, so as to make room for a roll-away bed at night. The rent was something like $100 per month (which made the furnished apartment in Toronto at $125 per month look like a giveaway). In spite of it all, this gal, whose servants back home lived in far better accommodations, rented this cubicle. (But they didn't have an Episcopal seminary and chapel across the street!)

Little did we know when we signed for it, however, how many bonus items went with it. The biggest bonus was Lucy. When she discovered that Libby didn't know how to do much beyond boiling water and toasting bread, Lucy voluntarily offered a free course in cooking, Italian style. She also introduced madam to Berta, the butcher and greengrocer on Eighth Avenue; and what Lucy didn't tell madam about cooking, Berta and his wife did. The result was that we began having some of the best Italian meals this side of Palermo.

The neighborhood was quiet at night, and we had no bugs of any kind. Perhaps this statement should not be so allinclusive. Sometimes one can be disturbed at night, not by bugs or mosquitos, but by a mouse or two. However, one of the things I discovered was that, although Berta was right in saying we should include nuts in our diet, he didn't say we should be careful about where we kept them.

More specifically, we began hearing strange noises in or on the floor of the room at night, inasmuch as there was no carpet. (We'd left ours in Omaha.) So I'd just assumed that in Chelsea they have one kind of pest and in Morningside Heights, in Margaret Casey's place, they have another kind. That's New York. The remedy for noise may be ear stopples; for mosquitos, who knows? But the stopples didn't block out this nocturnal nuisance.

Okay, damn it all, I decide to get up and investigate the source of this tantalizing torment. What I discovered was (1) if you want to have nuts in a bedroom and there are no carpets on the floor, don't choose round nuts; (2) if you must have round nuts, hide them in some sort of container, preferably one made of metal, with a lid; and (3) if you can't find one, you can at least avoid some of the risk by not leaving said nuts on a table that is close to a curtain that reaches the floor.

If you are in doubt as to what these findings have to do with the interruption of sleep, be advised that when I turned on a light, I found an English walnut was being pushed along the floor to his lair by a mouse with amazing intelligence, which he must have acquired by osmosis as a result of living in the same house with the gifted editors of the *New Republic* magazine.

I reasoned (trying to be as smart as the mouse) he must have gotten to the top of the table by climbing up the curtain, just to look things over when he'd spotted those round things. "There's probably something good inside them," he said to himself, "otherwise this guy who says he's an economist wouldn't buy them. So I think I'll try to steal one.

"But first I've got to get one out of the dish and over to the edge of the table," said he to himself, "then gravity will help me get it down to the floor, after which I can putt it over to the 'front door' of our house, in the wall near the hole in the floor, and push it in, as I did with the other stuff last night."

When I observed the ingenuity of this little family man I concluded that he must be happy in his work: happily married, probably self-employed, not required to sell something he didn't believe in, and obviously willing to work the night shift.

Inevitably, my anger changed to admiration. The last thing in the world I could conceive of doing to a little fellow with so many good points would be to take his life. He had probably heard from his grandparents that a high reward awaits the two-legged creature on this earth who invents a better mousetrap; he therefore, must have feared the very sight of me.

But I could not harm him; I could only help him because he deserved it—not only because of his ingenuity, but also because of his devotion to duty as a family man. Then, as I was about to turn out the light and go back to bed, Pyotr Ilich Tchaikovsky and the *Nutcracker Suite* came to mind; even if the little fellow managed to get the nut through the portal to his dining room, I thought to myself, he might not be able to crack it open; his jaws can't be compared with those of his rat cousins. So why don't I help in the preparation of the next meal by using a nutcracker to break open the nut, extract the kernels, and put them on his door step, thus enabling the family to have Thanksgiving dinner early this year (it was then September). But that will be okay; smart mice know that a kernel in the hand is worth two in the shell.

In a way, however, my kindheartedness toward this little fellow was inconsistent with my bias against population growth. I knew that mice, like men, don't practice birth control sufficiently; consequently, he wouldn't have had to risk his life for food if he didn't have a lot of kids; mice, like people, never seem to learn some of the most important lessons of living. But respect, more than retribution, dominated me and saved the lives of this little fellow and his oversized family.

Chapter 23
Back Where I Belong

A few days after Libby got her appointment I got a call from Dean McCrea who offered me an instructorship at Columbia to conduct classes in the principles of economics in late afternoon and evening and the students would be primarily employees of banks, brokerage houses, and other businesses that encouraged their employees to take educational courses, for which the employer would pay part or all of the tuition fees. My salary would be $2,200 for the approximately eight-month school year.

There aren't sufficiently expressive words in the English language adequately to convey the feeling of satisfaction I derived from this turn of events. Yes, I know that those who can, do, and those who can't, teach, but I was convinced that I had been wasting time since graduation in 1922. I had made one mistake after another; I had put too much confidence in the opinions of others, and not enough in my own. Now I felt as if I was where I belonged; and, strange though it may seem, my wife agreed—so much so that, without giving it a second thought, she was willing to forsake eight barrels of china, an unbelievable (and unnecessary) amount of solid silver (which would require at least 10 percent of the time of a household servant and half a jar of silver polish from time to time to keep polished), and numerous similar items, for a life of plain living and high thinking. The metamorphosis, in her case, was nothing short of phenomenal: it marked the abandonment of her family background and the acceptance of mine.

This was in September 1927. Any respectable instructor in the field of economics is not worth his salt if he doesn't relate the basic principles to current conditions of the economy. Thus, in 1927 we were in a period of vigorous economic expansion, which followed the brief post-war recession of 1921–22. A "New Era" economic syndrome was developing in the psyche of Americans, to the effect that research in economics had taught us, finally, how to limit if not control business cycles—the 1921-22 experience being a case in point. One of the reasons, in other words, why the university was able to find a place for me, despite the fact that I had not yet received a master's degree, was that the business community was hiring economists hand-over-fist—thus depleting university faculties. Brokerage houses, trade organizations, foundations, and individual companies, if large enough, were setting up departments of economic research.

If a company or organization did not have a research department but needed a study of some sort, it would be inclined to call up a university and ask for someone who could do the study and then make a report. I was frequently recommended for work of this kind, which supplemented my "munificent" salary.

The university also had a Home-Study Department in those days in which a student would sign up for a course, study the texts at home, submit responses to questions and problems, and receive a reply in writing from an instructor, for which the latter received a fee of one dollar per lesson. I was an instructor in this department also. Thus, I had three sources of income: teaching, home study, and occasional research jobs downtown. (When time permitted, I prepared for the doctor's degree—an essential credential in research and teaching.)

If a doctoral candidate is a student and he fails one or more of the examinations he can keep trying; but if a lowly instructor-member of the faculty flunks he has several options: he can become a panhandler; or, if his hobby is woodworking, he can apply for admission to the carpenters' union; or, if he has neither hobbies nor hope, the George Washington Bridge across the Hudson is not far from the university—and might be considered as a convenient jumping-off place.

As far as I was concerned, this Ph.D. risk was a part of the resolution of my vocational problem and I would take it. Like everyone else, I had to prove a reading ability in two foreign languages; take and pass at least three courses offered by the faculty; qualify in at least three additional subjects, and, when confident, ask for a date for an oral general examination by a committee of the faculty.

A while back I suggested, as an alternative to the gas chamber, that a convict be required instead to sit for twenty-four hours in one of those converted cattle cars used in the early 1920s by American railroads for LCL human cargo, otherwise known as passengers. It has since occurred to me that the requirements for a Ph.D. degree might also be substituted for the gas chamber, so long as it is not declared cruel and unusual punishment.

If the candidate is still alive after the oral ordeal, he is required to write an original dissertation and publish it (or was, at least in my day). However, the Federal Power Commission published mine. If you can find a copy you might consider buying it; it will be cheaper than sleeping pills, and definitely non-addictive.

Although I had been sent downtown by the faculty to do temporary research jobs from time to time, they became more frequent after the faculty found they could not bump me off in the torture chamber. The first one of these had fabulous possibilities. You may recall that when F.D.R. took office in 1933, he professed to be a "hard money" man; but when the economy failed to respond to the New Deal remedies propounded by the "Brain Trust" (my colleagues from the Columbia faculty), Mr. John Maynard Keynes came from England with his solution: reduced spending by the private sector should be offset by massive government spending. The government would obtain the funds by selling bonds to the public. The public would borrow funds from the banking system, whose lending power would be increased by the Federal Reserve System. After the economy began to recover, the government would impose taxes that would bring in enough money to enable it to retire some if not all of the increased government debt.

The trouble with the "solution" was that although tax rates were increased, they didn't bring in much additional revenue because neither employment nor income (national and personal) was responding to the measures of the New Deal managers of the economy. Hitler, not the New Deal, brought about full employment. Keynes didn't. He induced us to try his new drug; we did and became addicted. It is now a $4 trillion disease and is increasing year after year with no cure in sight.

A few members of the Roosevelt team felt the futility and feared the fatality of adopting the Keynesian program; it was too easy and would lead to inflation if not offset by taxation, and to economic stagnation if it was offset by taxation. Among the most vehement opponents was secretary of the treasury, Mr. Mariner Eccles, who, unable to persuade the president to pursue a sounder policy, resigned.

Among other things, Mr. Eccles was a trustee of the Duke endowment. Like most such charitable foundations, its assets consisted largely of bonds; if deficit financing were to continue, he said, the fixed-dollar income from its bondholdings would decline in purchasing power due to inflation and to that extent decrease if not decimate its activities as a welfare organization.

Information of this kind should be made available to the public, with concrete evidence to back it up, said he, and one of the best illustrations would be the German experience after the First World War. It will be recalled that the Treaty of Versailles imposed a reparations liability on Germany in proportion to the enormous devastation the German army had wrought in Belgium and France. The debt was so large that even after gold reserves had been exhausted, enormous amounts had to be paid, although in paper currency (no longer backed by gold). Since the German mark then began losing value because it was being printed in quantity (not in relation to a gold reserve or in response to economic requirements), it was being exchanged for goods as soon as possible by the public, thus increasing the velocity of its circulation (equivalent to a further increase in quantity) and accelerating a decline in value of each unit (or increasing prices—two sides of the same thing). Hyperinflation, in other words, was underway.

This is the sorry tale the Duke endowment trustees said should be told to the American people. Accordingly, early in 1934, Dr. Philip G. Wright was commissioned by the foundation to go to Germany and Austria to review the records of various foundations and report how they'd fared as a result of the inflation.

Shortly after Dr. Wright returned to the United States with a volume of data he became ill and was unable to write a report. At this point, the Trustees requested Columbia University to recommend someone to put Dr. Wright's material into pamphlet form;

yours truly was so appointed. The booklet consisted of sixty-six pages and was widely distributed. It is now out of print, but may be found in various public libraries.

When the job was finished I assumed I was, too. Instead, the New York representative of the foundation told me that "they" were considering setting up a tax foundation, whose purpose would be to analyze tax and fiscal proposals emanating from Washington from time to time and publicize the findings in the public interest. I would be permitted to keep my Columbia connection if I so chose.

But I turned it down, for one reason: I was afraid I would lose my independence. There undoubtedly would be a Board of Directors and an Editorial Committee. If they wanted to promoted one system or kind of taxation and I, from an impartial standpoint, found myself unable to agree with it, I would either have to accept and promote it or resign. I would not have peace of mind; I would have forfeited intellectual freedom. (Incidentally, the organization was subsequently set up and still exists today.)

Thus, somewhat like a bird that has just been let out of a cage, I returned to the free-but-less-affluent atmosphere of the university, where I began to work on the doctoral dissertation—the rate-making plan of a public utility company. Six months later I was awarded the coveted degree, eight years after I'd conducted my first class—much too long a period, but one rich in experiences that were valuable to me as a professor in the field of economics.

As I have noted, my classes consisted largely of adults. Two young married women, Mrs. Green and Mrs. Lubetkin, waylaid me after class one evening. Mrs. Lubetkin was the wife of a man who owned a wholesale bread business. The customers of wholesale bakers are restaurants and some hotels. Among these baking companies at that time, competition was cutthroat.

We were still in the throes of the Great Depression. New Deal "remedies" were not providing sufficient employment opportunities, and wages were not rising. Employers responded by saying they could not pay higher wages unless the prices of their products rose. It was a vicious circle.

To break out of it, the self-appointed "managers" of the national economy—the brain trust—finding there were still enough letters in the alphabet to enable them to set up another alphabetical agency in

Washington, promptly started one called the NRA (for the National Recovery Act).

The scheme required each trade organization to set a minimum price for its product, a price that would enable it to pay higher wages to its employees. In the wholesale baking industry, the minimum price for bread was fixed at seven cents per pound. The trade association was then required, under the law, to have an independent enforcement officer or agent whose job it was to see to it that all members obeyed the law; which, in the wholesale business, meant that no baker would be allowed to sell bread at less than seven cents per pound. (If the baker did not then raise the wages of his employees, they were free to strike—a weapon that was not only approved, but actively encouraged by the "managers" of the economy in Washington, D.C.)

The reason the Green and Lubetkin women stopped me that evening was to ask if I would consider becoming the outside impartial enforcement agent for the wholesale baking business of New York City. When I pleaded that I knew nothing about the business, their response was that nobody knew anything about this New Deal gimmick; so, if I had no objections, Mrs. Lubetkin would put a bug into her husband's ear and maybe the association would decide to offer me the job.

Well, I thought to myself, it probably couldn't be any worse than peddling ten-, twenty-five-, and fifty-cent weekly premium policies; it could also be interesting and productive from an economist's point of view. The result was that I was hired by the association at $100 per week.

When I got into it I found it to be a hornet's nest, if not a can of worms. (Yes, I know you are going to say that that Bussing fellow is some kind of nut, a misfit; everybody can't be wrong and he always right. Can it be that, like his wife, he always undertakes something he doesn't know how to do?) Well, here is what I found: competition was so keen that, if Baker A learned that Freddie's Fast Food was going to open a sandwich shop on Second Avenue, he would try to get to Freddie before Bakers B, C, and D, and make a pitch for his business. So what's wrong with that? Nothing, up to this point.

But Freddie is no newcomer to the business. He owned and operated Carrie's Cake and Cookie Company before it went belly up, and he knew that if he waited he would be able to play one bread company against another. If one offered to buy a display case for him, another might buy him a mixing machine. Still another would suggest that every time he delivered, say one hundred pounds of bread (at seven cents per pound, per invoice), he would have a cup of coffee and forget to pick up the change for a one-dollar bill. That would make the price six cents per pound. Buying equipment for lunchrooms and restaurants was a common competitive device, and was decried in the trade as "banking, not baking." But everyone in the business did it, and everyone denied it; and I, as the "enforcing" agent, was caught in the middle. They didn't need an enforcer: they needed a private eye, a detective agency, a system for setting traps and obtaining evidence. That was outside the scope and purpose of the NRA, and beyond the capacity of a college professor, with the result that the situation under the NRA was no different from what it had been before. Consequently the whole NRA humbug came to a sudden end about eighteen months after it began when the U.S. Supreme Court killed it in the famous Schechter chicken case. The only one who liked the act was the federal administrator, who had an attractive secretary he simply had to take along on his numerous business trips.

So now I am back again in the academic world, not part-time but full-time. But don't forget—I am still reading lessons sent in by home-study students; and by this time, most of my students were in the "Principles of Investment" course. Before the Great Crash of 1929, the motive of most of these students was to learn the fundamentals of investment; after the 1929 debacle, their primary purpose was to find out, if possible, why they had lost money in the stock market.

Our presentation, however, was the so-called fundamental approach, i.e., the balance sheet and income-account analysis; no suggestions were ever made with reference to individual securities.

I received many letters from students, in addition to the regular lessons. One such letter came from a woman pupil who lived in Michigan. She told me that I was the cause of her divorcing her husband, the background for which was that as she'd progressed through the course, she'd become curious as to how her assets were being handled by her husband, who was vice president of a local bank. One of the little facts of life she'd learned was that bonds may be either bearer bonds or registered bonds. Bearer bonds may be sold by whoever possesses them. What she discovered was that some of her bearer bonds had been sold by her husband, but the whereabouts of the proceeds was a mystery. The upshot of it was that he lost a wife and a job. The ripoff, however, did not leave her destitute—far from it. In addition to whatever other assets she had, she owned a beautiful spread on the Island of Vinalhaven in Penobscot Bay, off the coast of Maine.

The reason for telling this tale is that, since our innocent little course on the principles of investment had led to such unexpected consequences in her life, she wondered if the Bussing family would like to come to Vinalhaven and occupy one of the cottages on her estate during June and July that year.

It had now been about ten years since I'd spent my first summer in New York in the care and comfort of Margaret Casey and her nightly visitors; and, as I regret to say that my opinion of New York in the summer had not improved much in the interim, you need not be told my answer. Her instructions were for us to proceed to a little jumping-off fishing village on the Maine coast, opposite Vinalhaven, and inquire for one Bill Winkapaugh, who operated an aerial ferry service to islands in the bay. (Our car would come by boat later.) Bill would be expecting us. Indeed, in less than five minutes we deplaned at Abby's dock.

The place was incredibly beautiful, bedecked with glistening pines and hemlocks. Our cottage was in a cove at the end of a short walk from the main house on a cushion of pine needles. We had dinner at the mansion, where lobster and lobster bisque were served daily, likewise soft shell clams and fish of all kinds—all of which had come not more than a few hours previously from the richly productive waters of the North Atlantic. We prepared our own breakfasts and evening meals in our cottage, which was called, not inappropriately, "The Ritz."

In the morning I would sit down with our hostess and discuss investment principles; the rest of the day was free, and I had time to do the kind of reading and research I usually did during the summer recess. (The more work of this kind I could do in the summer, the less I would have to do during the school year. On average I spent about two hours in preparation for an hour in the classroom.) During this particular summer much of my time was devoted to preparing for the doctor's examinations.

In my humble opinion a home-study program, with an arrangement for properly supervised examinations, could be a partial answer to many of the problems facing higher education today, and I daresay someone is going to confirm this one of these days. For some courses television would be a valuable adjunct to textbooks, although separate arrangements would have to be made where laboratory facilities are necessary. Home study makes it possible to carry on an income-producing occupation, live at home, and cut the cost of higher education.

Chapter 24
Falling into the Jackpot

If there is any doubt in your mind about the importance of a doctor's degree in the academic world, hear this: for nine years I was on the teaching staff as an instructor, during which time no one so much as suggested that I be considered for an appointment to a higher rank, either at C.U. or any other university. But as soon as I had passed the oral examination for the doctorate, and even before I had published the necessary dissertation, I was recommended and accepted for an assistant professorship at Connecticut Wesleyan University, where I met my first class in September 1935.

Enter now a little family problem. Columbia owned several luxury apartment buildings on Claremont Avenue in which the individual units, which consisted of eight rooms and two baths, were priced out of reach of 80 percent of the Columbia faculty; and due to the depressed state of Mr. Roosevelt's not-so-well-managed economy, they were not in demand by the lay public either. I therefore addressed a letter to President Butler, suggesting that these large eight-room units be broken up into two four-room units, and that a playroom on the ground floor and an area on the roof, adequately fenced, be reserved for children of the tenants. The mothers of the children would be able to rotate in supervising. Toys could be handed down as children outgrew them—recycled, as it were. Although I'd written the letter I handed it to my restless wife, who was still not interested in the "brainless" activities of housewifery and motherhood, suggesting that she sign and deliver it to President Butler herself and offer to be the coordinator of the undertaking, without compensation if necessary.

As I have said, Libby could sell a pot with a hole in it if she was interested. Result? She had an appointment with His Honor (which is more than I ever accomplished. The closest I ever got to him was when he handed me my diplomas—three of them). And what did His Honor say? He said, "Good idea. Go to see Mr.—— who handles our real estate, show him the letter, and tell him I sent you."

Mr. —— somewhat grudgingly gave the matter his attention (probably wondering why he had not thought of it first), while also apparently trying to think of a fly in the ointment, i.e., why the idea was unworkable. Evidently, the only drawback he could think of was that if the idea was to be pursued my wife could not be the one to pursue it, because she had no real estate license. Whereupon she, never having completed anything academically, read the rule book, took the examination, passed it, and became a licensed real estate agent.

Next problem: Mr. —— "couldn't afford" to pay her a salary. "Very simple," says she. "Let us occupy one of the eight-room apartments free of rent." That was agreed to. The project was started immediately, became instantly popular, and was economically successful; and we had a luxurious eight-room apartment for three years.

After this project was completed, she went after Mr. Lawrence Orton, who was then in charge of the Office of City Planning for Manhattan. How she managed to persuade him that she was competent in that field, I'll never know. Nor did Larry, who liked to say that she always did what she didn't know how to do; and, as I had my hands full in my new assignment at Wesleyan, I couldn't be of any help. But it does bring me to the little family problem I have referred to. Libby didn't want to give up her work and come to Middletown; she was now a professional woman. Coming to Wesleyan would only put her back in the lurch from which she had escaped in New York. Therefore, not being able to find an immediate solution—one of which would be satisfactory to both of us—I took seven-year-old Jack with me and hired a housekeeper, while she rattled around in the eight-room apartment and joined us on weekends.

At Christmastime I took the housekeeper and Jack in my Model A Ford to join her for the holidays. When we arrived at the apartment, Beatrice, the middle-aged housekeeper, said she wanted to go to the drugstore and would be back momentarily. The afternoon and then the evening came and went—but no Beatrice.

We alerted the police, to no avail. Days later we found that she had returned to Middletown, gone to the store where she purchased our food, and where she had somehow managed to establish a good credit rating for herself, cashed her personal check for something like $200, if I remember correctly, and then simply disappeared. She was later picked up by police in Florida.

The question now was, What was I going to do for a housekeeper? A dear friend in New York had an answer—a girl about eighteen years old, who wanted to get away from the little town of Coxsackie in upstate New York. When I arrived, on January 2, there she was: not particularly good-looking (she said about herself, "they never look twice"), but I needed someone who would be there when Jack was not in school, and I couldn't be too choosey. Besides, her physical appearance was irrelevant, wasn't it? It certainly should have been for me, imbued as I had been with the behavioral restraints imposed upon us by Messrs. Bryan and Mott, and Father Dickman of the church school.

She was quiet, sedate, and somewhat subdued for her age, as if she might have had an unhappy experience in her hometown. Maybe that was why she wanted to get away from it—even to the extent of taking up residence with a stranger, a married man, under unusual circumstances. There were two bedrooms, a living room–dining room, kitchen, and bath in this apartment. Son Jack and I had one bedroom and she the other. On weekends when mother Bussing was with us we rolled out the folding bed that we'd had on Twenty-first Street (along with the mouse). For reasons unknown, I treated her like a sister. From January until July I showed about as much interest in her as I did in one of the few pieces of furniture in the apartment. Some evenings she went out to take voice lessons; other evenings she sat in her room and, I believe, did needlework.

Spring vacation came, and the three of us again joined mother Bussing in New York. One day during the week, while downtown, I walked into the Bowery Savings Bank for the purpose of congratulating Mr. Henry Bruere (formerly a vice president of Metropolitan Life Insurance Company), who was now president of the Bowery.

He remembered my interest in economics and economic research, in connection with which he told me what was going on in the New York Savings Bank Association. The problem they were wrestling with was whether or not they should join the commercial banks in the Federal Deposit Insurance Corporation. The savings banks of New York State had an impeccable record of safety. For them to pay a yearly deposit-insurance premium based on the loss experience of commercial banks would, many savings bankers believed, be an unjustifiable charge against their earnings. For a century, not a dollar had been lost by depositors in the savings banks of New York State.

With this in mind, he told me, all but a few of them had decided to set up their own insurance fund. Each member bank would deposit an amount, based on size, into the Savings Banks Insurance Fund, and would deposit annual amounts thereafter depending on loss experience, if any. This fund would be administered by a wholly owned Savings Banks Trust Company.

The operating officers of the trust company were men who formerly had been bank examiners supervised by the New York State superintendent of banks. They were, therefore, familiar with procedures necessary to determine whether a bank was being operated as soundly as it should be. By taking steps immediately, losses could be prevented and charges to the MSBF kept much lower than the premiums of the FDIC.

Having given me this background, he said he thought the trust company should have a research economist and asked me if I would be interested in considering such a job. If so, he would call Mr. Ihlefeld, president of the trust company, and ask him to see me. I assured him that I would be interested.

Now if you think that the rite of apostolic succession endows a priest with supernatural powers, be advised that presidency of what, at that time, was the largest savings bank in the world carried practically equal weight in the temporal world. As a result, when he told Mr. Ihlefeld what he had in mind I was, in effect, employed—at three times the salary I was receiving at Wesleyan, plus an assistant who would do the donkey and secretarial work for me, plus an expense account and a private office, at Fourteen Wall Street. (And, biggest bonus of all, Madam Bussing wouldn't have to leave New York.) June arrived; I moved our few sticks of furniture, including the folding bed, and Marian to the Claremont Avenue apartment.

In July my wife went on a business trip and son John was in a summer camp. Marian and I were alone. However, a strange thing happened a day or two before Libby left on her trip. It seems that Marian chose to tell her about some sort of experience she had had, either in high school or thereafter, which caused her to lose her virginity. What was even more strange, however, was that my wife related the story to me. Next scene: my wife is gone, we are alone, and now, for the first time in seven months, I begin to think of the girl quite differently than at any time before. Under these circumstances, why not take a peek into her bedroom to see if she is managing to keep comfortable in spite of the heat and humidity?

I found her sitting in her bedside chair, clad in a diaphanous, tantalizingly transparent nightie, apparently reading. Maybe I suggested an alternative form of recreation, or I may simply have put out my hands in the hope that she would take them, which she did. Then, with little effort on my part, and with her cooperation, an embrace inevitably followed. But her gown and my pajamas only seemed to make the evening warmer, whereupon, when she lifted her arms, I was able to make her more comfortable by removing her gown. Reciprocally, she quite amiably assisted me in getting rid of the impediment of my pajamas.

I found it much more difficult in the weeks following for us to duplicate the delightful duplicity of that evening in July; we did manage it occasionally. Maybe we were not as successful in concealing our activity as we'd thought, however, for in September Libby suddenly decided, without explanation, that Marian would have to go. I did not see her after that except for one Sunday afternoon in November, when I was doing some work in the New York Public Library, where we ran into each other entirely spontaneously. Nothing came of this; but through a strange coincidence, she told me, she was living in a rented room with a girl who was employed by a close friend of ours. She seemed depressed, and I felt sorry for her, but as a practical matter there wasn't much I could do. Evidently she had encountered hardship and disappointment before but had never talked about it. Her finding us, I am sorry to say, probably did not make life any easier for her in the long run.

This was not my first encounter. The first one was with a war bride. After the First World War, French girls would marry doughboys, as we called GIs then, so they could come to the United States. They would agree to let the soldier off the hook, if that seemed desirable, when they arrived in this country.

Through my wife's socializing I'd met one of these war brides in 1932, and although she was still married to her ex-soldier, she felt that she and I should shack up together—if not permanently, at least sporadically—which we did. Our trysting place was an apartment occupied by her friend Miriam in Brooklyn Heights. (Miriam also had more than one partner.) But I was too busy with Ph.D. problems at that time, and I squirmed out of this connection as soon as possible.

After I started working for Savings Banks Trust Company, in 1936, we gave up the apartment on Claremont Avenue and bought a five-story house on Grace Court in Brooklyn Heights. It took ten minutes or less to walk to the subway, five minutes on the train, and five minutes more to get to Fourteen Wall. In good weather I would walk to and from the office via the Brooklyn Bridge; this took about forty-five minutes.

My first offering on the job was a study in which I showed that most of the railroads, which were then in receivership, could have avoided financial failure had they retired debt by means of sinking funds instead of paying off maturing debt by offering new bonds. (This is the same phenomenon I referred to above regarding the growing debt of the U.S. Treasury.) What got me into a bit of hot water, however, was the fact that the savings banks, which were heavily represented on the railroad reorganizing committees, were already committed to reorganization plans that were based on the old system of fixed maturities without the provision of funds for redemption.

The next problem was a bit more troublesome. The Nazis were beginning to threaten the peace of Europe, and by 1938 the savings banks began to have doubts as to whether the Mutual Savings Banks Deposit Insurance Fund would be able to provide enough liquidity to the savings banks in case depositors became apprehensive and started a run or two, which might then spread to other savings banks. Under the Federal umbrella, the FDIC may call upon the U.S. Treasury for funds to meet an emergency and, if necessary, the treasury can cause the government printing press to meet the demand. Paper is cheap; when the right symbols are printed on it, it becomes (funny) money (or phony money), but nevertheless circulates at "par" or face value so long as the public has confidence in it. However, the mutual savings banks had no such unlimited source of funds, and their insurance system had been in existence too short a time to have built up a sufficiently large reserve; even if it had, it would have had to depend on the securities markets to convert bonds to cash. In a time of crisis the market might not absorb the fund's bonds, except at substantial discounts, and that could become disastrous. (Some of their assets would probably be railroad bonds in default, because there weren't any of "Bussing's sinking funds" to support them!)

There was a wide difference of opinion; finally a suggestion was made by the daddy of all savings banks, Mr. Bruere, that the board turn the problem over to young Dr. Bussing with instructions to study the matter and report back to the board.

This came as a shocker. If I concluded that the MSB Fund was adequate, some would say that I was biased and trying to save my job (and that of the other officers). If I found that the MSBF was inadequate, my associates would say that I lacked the ingenuity to find a solution, or that not having been brought up in the savings bank business, I did not appreciate its strength.

My belief was that self-insurance via the MSBF was impractical under the circumstances, but I didn't say so; instead, I made a comprehensive study of the loss experience of the 135 savings banks in New York State during the preceding one hundred years. The losses were insignificant; there were no failures, although there had been mergers. Concluding what should be done was left up to the banks themselves, which was where the responsibility rested before the job was dumped into my lap.

When the war started, debate stopped; most savings banks in New York State joined the FDIC; the others, the FSLIC. During the war, however, the trust company offered service to member banks in subscribing to treasury bond offerings and providing research into other avenues of investment, including mortgages, but its future was in doubt.

Due to the moratorium on housing construction during the war savings banks were not able to do much mortgage-loan business in their home territories, unless they were defense areas, where housing might be required. I and a number of others therefore recommended that loans be made in defense areas, wherever they might be. This kind of thinking probably was responsible for a few cases of apoplexy among trustees and operating officers, who customarily made mortgage loans only in familiar, home territory, although I was never accused of manslaughter. But something had to be done to increase income. Most new deposits were being invested in 2 percent government bonds; but mortgages in defense areas were insured by the Federal Housing Administration (FHA) and bore 4 percent.

In order to reduce the "mortality rate" among these ultraconservative savings bank managers, who were likely to begin hemorrhaging at the mere mention of so outlandish an idea as investing precious savings bank funds in totally unfamiliar areas of the country, an arrangement was made whereby a bank that decided to "risk" the depositors's savings in 4 percent FHA loans in faraway places like Houston, New Orleans, Atlanta, and others, would not have to do it directly, but could instead place their trustee funds in the hands of their wholly owned subsidiary, Institutional Securities Corporation (a companion to the Savings Banks Trust Company), with one limiting restriction: assurance that any defense housing they financed would have post-war usefulness.

That's where I came in. It was my job to select defense areas, and industries in them, that would fulfill this requirement of long-term economic soundness, thus converting my work from a desk job to one of travel—under the trying conditions of wartime. I had a low priority when it came to transportation; as a result, trips usually had to be made at night in DC3s. A flight to New Orleans, for example, would leave LaGuardia at 9:00 P.M. and arrive at 6:00 A.M. Sometimes my hotel would be ready; at other times it wouldn't be. In many cases a room would only be available for the purpose of "freshening up," my night's rest having consisted of catnaps on a DC3 interrupted by several stops. Not to worry; often the sheets on the hotel bed had not been changed anyhow—and besides, had I been a few years younger I might have been in a jungle in Southeast Asia, where an unclean bed would have looked like deliverance from imminent death.

Clean sheets or no, it would be daytime and a broker or builder would be waiting to show us the houses he was building and the locations where he intended to build more housing, which were usually miles away. At the end of such a day I was ready to hit the sack, twenty-four hours after leaving New York.

Usually this was made difficult by Southern hospitality, however, which could also be called tax-deductible entertainment, consisting of a sumptuous dinner followed, if there was any interest, by a friendly rest-of-the-night rendezvous with a person engaged in practicing the world's oldest profession. In some instances the visiting investor would become so involved with this "side line" of defense work that he wouldn't find time to make field trips to the projects he came to inspect. However, the investment would be insured, regardless, by the FHA; which made an inspection practically a waste of time, but which was ordered to pacify the old fogies on his Board of Directors, who didn't value anything, like the FHA, produced by those New Deal clowns in Washington.

I don't know why brokers and builders never offered to provide me with this kind of relaxation, to lighten my burden of determining the postwar value of the housing we considered financing. That left them only two other "courtesies" to offer me—booze and beef steak. But again, I was no more interested in booze than I was in babes in the bed. (Gee—what's the matter with this guy?) Eventually I would get to bed.

I ran into a bit of a problem in Knoxville, Tennessee. There was a need for an enormous number of houses near several huge plants that had just been constructed. Trainloads of rock were being hauled into the plants day and night; smoke billowed out of tall smokestacks. Obviously, something big was going on, but nothing was coming out of the plants other than what appeared to be the same old rock that had gone in at the other end—except now it had been pulverized.

Nobody would talk to me. All that a chap who seemed to be a kind of superintendent would say was that, if I wanted to get any information, I would have to see Maj. Gen. Leslie Groves in Washington. So on my way back to New York, I stopped at his office. The only thing they didn't do there was fingerprint and handcuff me. They were armed and prepared to shoot if I made the wrong movement.

"Could I see Major General Groves?"

"Why do you want to see him?"

"Because I want to know if what they're doing down there will require the continued use of the new housing my investors are planning to finance."

"The operation will continue after the war."

"May I quote you on that?"

"No comment."

"May I talk to someone who will answer a few more questions?"

"No one is authorized to talk to you or anyone else about that operation."

With that bit of elucidation I prepared my report for the mortgage committee, recommending they buy a piece of this mysterious undertaking in Knoxville.

A number of months before my trip to Knoxville a research man at the Bell Laboratory, Leroy MacColl, asked me, at a dinner at our house, why economists were not giving more attention to the atom as a source of energy. He then proceeded to give me an elementary explanation of the potentialities inherent in splitting the atom—getting energy-providing material out of rocks, of all things. Very interesting, I'd thought; but, as it was only remotely related to my immediate problems, it went immediately into my subconscious.

Several months later another friend of ours, Douglas Howard, an Englishman and member of the British Purchasing Commission, was a dinner guest at our house, along with several other couples. In making dinner conversation I talked about my trips to defense areas, and how I had run up against one wartime activity I couldn't understand. Shipbuilding, airplane construction, tanks, parachutes—such operations I could understand. "But in Knoxville," I said, "they produce a lot of smoke; carloads of rock go into the plants, but nothing of value comes out," which, I said, "made me think of a science-fiction story a friend told me recently, about getting energy out of rocks by splitting them."

When we left the dinner table Douglas Howard took me aside. Although we were not yet in the war, he said that in Europe "loose talk," such as I had just indulged in would be enough to put me into solitary confinement for the duration. He advised me to keep my mouth shut. Good advice, no doubt; but I had already told the mortgage committee that it looked as if, in Knoxville, "they might be doing something like splitting the atom."

Of course you now know that I was looking at a part of the Manhattan Project, the best-kept secret of the war and the origin of one of the most important ingredients of the atom bomb.

Chapter 25
Milk, Migraine, and Monkey Business

In the summer of 1943, my wife and I had the use of a house in rural Connecticut. I was on a two-week vacation in this delightful place when Libby got a telephone call from a woman in New York who ran something like an employment agency and who had heard one of her broadcasts on the local radio station—a program Libby had devised herself, without any guidance or assistance from anyone in the radio business, and which she called "The Food of Our Allies." It dealt with recipes and menus of our European partners in the war effort. Generally speaking, the rank-and-file population of Europe had less meat, even in peacetime, than did we Americans; they therefore knew how to stretch it. So now, since there was less meat available to us on the home-front and what there was was rationed, methods for getting the most out of what we had were of considerable interest.

The federal government was also looking for ways to keep the American diet as close to par as possible (while simultaneously supplying vast amounts of food to the armed services). Consequently, two questions asked by officials in the Department of Agriculture were, Why, if milk powder is good for pigs, wouldn't it be good for people? And why not put it on the market in small packages? Nutritionists agreed; it *should* be done, not only as a part of the war effort, but generally for the benefit of the consumer, and as a less expensive way to obtain milk. So the Borden Company was persuaded to offer powdered milk to the public in pound packages; they called it "Starlac," and food stores featured it.

Merchandising is a mysterious business; I guess that's one of the reasons why we have advertising agencies (in spite of the fact that there may be other even better reasons for *not* having them). In this instance, however, although a substantial amount of money was spent on advertising and promotion, the product didn't sell. Young and Rubicam was the advertising agency that handled this part of the Borden account at that time; the woman who heard my wife's radio program had a connection with Y & R. It therefore occurred to her, and she duly passed the suggestion on to Y & R, that they should get in touch with Mrs. Bussing. Y & R said, "Go ahead."

"Going ahead" meant going back to town, for us, forsaking the comfort of rural Connecticut in the hot month of August, 1943. (The attempt to assassinate Hitler shortly before had failed, and the war was destined to go on.)

The next morning Libby saw the woman, Mrs. Millard, who told her the Starlac story and asked her if she would care to go to work at Y & R for a few weeks to see if she could put some life into the Borden Starlac account, provided Y & R agreed after seeing her. She said she would; Y & R did; and the "few weeks" turned into eleven years. When Larry Orton heard about her taking this job his comment was, "There she goes again, doing something she doesn't know anything about." Whether she did or not, the fact is that sales picked up immediately and, before she'd finished the job, she had managed to introduce the product in all forty-eight states. I don't know what advertising agencies normally do when they no longer need an employee; but when her work came to an end the agency presented her with a sterling silver fruit bowl, suitably engraved in recognition of her success. And the Borden executive who was responsible for Starlac is still alive today, living in Connecticut, and calls her every year on her birthday. Also, the last time he was in San Francisco he took her to dinner at the Fleur De Lys, which, in case you have forgotten, is one of the city's best restaurants.

I have mentioned that Libby was a victim of migraine headaches; I can now tell you that during the eleven Starlac years, she had very few of them; and, when one did occur, it was short-lived and less severe. In my opinion, those eleven years at Y & R were the only period in her life when she was truly contented. At no other time was she in a situation where she could use her creative energy to the extent that was possible in that job.

Both of us were traveling far and wide during this period, and occasionally our paths would cross. On one occasion we happened to be in Houston at the same time; the new Shamrock Hotel was *the* place to stay, so we shared a room. When Libby got back to the office in New York, a woman employee of Y & R said that she'd seen her having breakfast with "a man" in the Shamrock dining room one morning. Libby said, "How interesting. Why didn't you come to our table and join us?"

"Oh," she said, "I didn't want to embarrass you. I thought you wouldn't want anyone from the home office to know that you were with a man on a business trip." We hoped she believed it when she was told that "the man" was Libby's husband.

I have three reasons for telling you this tale, one being to promote dry skim milk, because it is less expensive than fluid milk, with a long shelf life; two, to relate what I think is an unusual kind of success story; and three, to lead up to a tale of a totally different kind.

One afternoon Ruth, one of the girls in the trust company, came to my desk. She had nothing to do with my work, so that her sudden appearance was unusual. I have often wondered what my associates, who were more worldly wise than I, thought her purpose was—if they noticed it, as I am sure some of them did. In fact, some of the men paid too much attention to certain of the girls, with what the girls themselves knew to be ulterior motives, Ruth told me; and I, she said, paid too *little* attention to them.

Here I have a memory lapse. What I can't understand is how I am able to recall names and episodes ad infinitum, but when I try to recall what Ruth said at this tête-à-tête, I draw a blank. No explanation fits any psychoanalytical theory I learned in college psychology courses. In any case, whatever she said, the net effect was to communicate that she wanted to see more of me. And, inasmuch as my wife was busy promoting Starlac out of town, I had considerable freedom. Across a dinner table a few days later, she said that she had been married but that it had turned out to be a brief, painful, and disastrous experience. I gathered that she was interested in finding out if all men are brutes. I offered the opinion that not all of us are. Although one "demonstration" in this respect might have been sufficient, we had, as it turned out, a number of repeat performances. On one of these occasions she introduced me to her mother, following which I found, to my astonishment, this most accommodating parent had actually made suitable preparations for us in one of the bedrooms. (I was learning the ways of the world.)

Some time after I left the trust company, I saw her on Forty-second Street. On this occasion, she told me how she'd happened to be the one to approach me at my desk. The four good-looking girls in the office (and there were only four out of fifteen) were apparently feeling that life was rather dull while so many men their age were in the armed services, under which circumstances even an old goat like me would be found preferable to nothing (although she refrained from implying that I resembled one of those hollow-horned ruminants).

The other girls knew that her marriage had been a disaster, and that she would like to find out if all men act like gorillas when they become aroused, and that is why they agreed that she should try me out first; and if her report was favorable, the others might subsequently decide to take a chance with me.

Her report, she said, indicated that I did not behave like a beast, and that, in fact, I had been anything but aggressive.

When I heard this scenario I began to understand several incidents that had occurred before I left the trust company. While I had received hints, and other subliminal indications, now and then from the other three girls, I had been too naive to suspect that these might be actual messages rather than simple greetings—that is, until Jennifer had one day made the proposition outright, in plain English. On a hot afternoon, as we passed each other in an outer corridor where we would not be heard, she said something quite explicit (again I cannot quote exactly) which added up to an outright offer. My response—"It's too hot." Her reply—"The hotter, the better. You know that."

That's as far as I went with Jenny, and I didn't get that far with the other two, simply because I didn't know when I was being propositioned. If that doesn't convince you that you are reading about a romantic moron, then you may be as innocent and naive as I was.

Chapter 26
Partners: Are They Worth the Pain?

The war was over. Financing the construction of housing in defense areas came to an end. Likewise the outlook for the trust company was dismal, because the savings banks had abandoned their self-insurance fund, of which the trust company was trustee. Consequently, I began to look for greener pastures.

Four factors loomed large in my thinking: (1) the savings banks were heavily invested in high-grade, low-interest bonds yielding, on average, little more than two percent; (2) this condition could be remedied by making mortgage loans elsewhere in the United States, provided they were insured by the FHA or guaranteed by the Veteran's Administration; (3) I was familiar with the national market as a result of my work during the war; and (4) savings bank managers knew me and had confidence in me. So I joined my friend, Connie Lowell, who three years before had quit his job as president of another company (ISC, wholly owned by the savings banks of New York State) to set up his own company, Lowell, Smith & Evers, Inc. At that time, Connie was originating and servicing only conventional loans in the New York City area for upstate savings banks; branching out into the national market was, therefore, a logical next step for us and for the banks.

One of the obstacles to entering the national market by a New York savings bank at the time was that although lending money on mortgages in other states was not considered "doing business," collecting monthly mortgage installments would be, for which they were not qualified.

That's where we came in: we could sell mortgages to them and collect monthly payments of interest, principal, and hazard insurance premiums, i.e., "service" such investments, provided we were considered as reliable and dependable as they and worthy of a servicing contract.

As a result of my wartime exploration of the national mortgage market for the trust company, my conclusion was that the most desirable states from the standpoint of demand for mortgage money were Florida, Texas, and California. We chose California.

While we were busy making these plans and decisions, which amounted practically to embarking on a new venture that required more capital and more risk, we began to notice that the most important member of our company, Connie, frequently was unable to calculate yields on a mortgage transaction. He also was troubled by a persistent cough, which, he said, probably resulted from his "hollering" at Russ Smith, who, although a good appraiser, was not qualified temperamentally or otherwise to work in the national market, besides which private appraisals were unnecessary since the only kind of loans our investors could make outside New York State were FHAs and these were appraised by the federal government, whose valuation was final. And on the personal side, Smitty had what seemed to be a superiority complex, was unwilling to play second fiddle to anybody, refused to adapt to our new and expanded way of doing business and to top it all off, secretly objected to my having joined the company because I had a handle on the national market and was likely to be more productive than he.

Meanwhile, Connie's coughing and confusion became worse, as a result of which we suggested to his wife that he switch from the doctor who was treating him with cough drops to one who had hospital connections. This he did. The diagnosis was cancer of the throat, which had metastasized into the brain. The solution? Surgery. The verdict? Inoperable. The ultimate result? Death within about six weeks.

That left me in another pickle—worse than either the Corn Exchange Bank or Mother Metropolitan—because I had capital tied up here; also, if the investors with whom we had servicing agreements sensed that there was disharmony in the company, they could withdraw their contracts and we would be left with little more than the shell of a company. There was really not much to do but try to make the most of a bad situation, which I did for about twenty-five years, that is until he, not like me, had no plans to stay here in three centuries and departed this life.

One of my business undertakings on behalf of our company was working well until the rug was pulled out from under me. ("Here he goes again" you are saying. "That Bussing fellow either is accident prone or exceedingly stupid. Nobody could get into as much hot water in one lifetime unless he has less common sense than God gives most people and lives long enough to allow all of his short-comings to come out.") Well, frankly, my friend, I've begun to think that way myself. Nevertheless, I've got to tell you two more tales, both of which were troublesome enough to drive me up the wall; but I managed to survive while the perpetrators have either died or disappeared.

In the mortgage banking business, companies like ours usually borrow money and make it available to builders, who in turn agree to let the mortgage company have the mortgages that come into existence when the builder sells his houses. These are the stock in trade that a mortgage company offers to its investors.

If a mortgage company such as ours has a stockholder who, like my partner, is too "chicken" to take the business risk of borrowing to finance a builder in order to acquire an inventory of loans (to sell), it is necessary to become a panhandler and pass the corporate cup among one's competitors who do finance builders in the hope that they will sell us a few loans so we can fill a commitment to one of our investors.

Under those circumstances, what kinds of loans do you think these competitors are likely to drop into our corporate cup? You guessed it. Stuff nobody else wants because of substandard credit of the mortgagors, proximity of the dwellings to an overhead power line and its electromagnetic field, irregular payment records that may portend foreclosures, or various other possible reasons.

"Junk" loans increase the cost of servicing and reflect badly on the servicer. Consequently, since I was unable to induce my partner to originate loans in our own name, I decided to risk my own capital and take in other California venture capitalists as stockholders.

Without going into the technical reasons, suffice it to say that it was necessary for me to pay my branch managers a quarter of 1 percent commission on each loan they processed, and my friend in

New York agreed to provide that amount out of our first year's servicing fee since we were being relieved of the necessity of begging for loans from others or risking our capital.

I soon had five branch offices in the state, and we seemed to have found a solution, except that one day, out of a blue sky, my amiable partner either forgot his agreement or his superstitious imagination suggested that I might be outsmarting him somehow. Whether for these or for some other Machiavellian reasons, he reneged on the quarter of 1 percent.

When I passed this word on to my producing staff, they called me a double-crosser. Some began to dip into the till; the manager of the San Jose office managed to steal enough from the trust funds to buy a Porsche automobile, which, with his girlfriend, he proceeded to drive to New York, where he was about to board ship to Europe when I got wind of it. I then called our New York attorney and asked if I could make a citizen's arrest. He told me that I would need evidence, which I was unable to document on such short notice, and that without it I would put myself in jeopardy. So this trusted employee got away, and I have not heard of him since. (If you run across a person who says his name is Barry Silver, please tell him I would like to see him.)

In short, my whole apparatus fell apart. The undertaking cost me many thousands of dollars, and I am still, voluntarily, indemnifying one of my stockholders in installments for his loss. This was the most expensive and disturbing mistake of my entire career.

This returned us to the *status quo antebellum* of selling loans we didn't have and then scrambling about to find them. The New York office didn't feel the pressure of this way of doing business as much as I, because I was on the firing line and they were not.

More or less in desperation, therefore, I established a working relationship with the owner of another mortgage company. He would deliver loans out of his warehouse to our investors, in exchange for my signing with him as co-obligor on bank loans advanced to builders; when the builder sold a house, the mortgage company I was now working with would receive the mortgage, which would be offered to my investor, if I had one, and if purchased the proceeds would liquidate the loan at the California bank that had advanced the funds on the strength of my guarantee.

All seemed to be working satisfactorily, until someone began to suspect the buyers' credit reports. An extensive investigation disclosed that the owner of my "cooperating" mortgage company had offered an employee of a credit-rating service a job—presumably at a larger salary, or possibly with enhanced fringe benefits or other inducements—in which she was to take home, adequately concealed over a period of time, a supply of pads of blank credit-rating forms, making them available to her new employer (the man I was working with in this new venture) so he could then fill them out (i.e. forge them) himself.

In this manner my co-partner was able to "qualify" home buyers who had weak or unsatisfactory credit. The chickens would come home to roost after such a loan was delivered to one of our investors: monthly installments would become delinquent and foreclosure would follow—but only after considerable expense to regain possession of the property, refurbish and resell it to a qualified buyer, all of which reflected badly on our reputation.

To make matters worse, shortly after this skulduggery was discovered, interest rates began rising and the market value of all loans, good and bad, funded under my guarantee at the lower rate of interest, but which were still in warehouse, became worth less than the amount necessary to liquidate the bank loan against them. The difference had to be made up by the guarantors, which in this case was I. That's what guarantors are for. You either make good, or get sued, lose *your* credit rating, and go out of business.

Hal Menden, vice president of the United California Bank, said that I had a way of getting into business with the wrong people. He was a good friend, but he was powerless to relieve me of my obligations to the bank and I never asked him to. What finally happened to my perfidious partner, the forger? He was killed in an automobile accident shortly after his credit-report shenanigans were discovered.

Meanwhile, my fine-feathered friend in New York was coming into the office as usual, at about 9:30 in the morning, when the first order of business was to go over to Stouffers at 60 East Forty-second (one of Helmsley's buildings—Harry's, not yet Leona's) for coffee. By 11:30 the *Wall Street Journal* would have been read, and it would now be time to think about lunch—usually at the Commodore across the street, where we were friendly with the head waiter, who flattered us by giving us a good table. Afternoons were usually dull, partly as a consequence of the excessive consumption of the liquid part of the menu (Johnny Walker and his Black Label, primarily) at lunch, the "other" food being of secondary importance. So, a little after three it was time to consider going home, an impulse that was acted upon positively at 4:00 p.m.

If this sort of handicap was not enough, how about adding a little superstition to the business? We didn't have to add it: we had it. My partner knew it was nonsense; he admitted he was "stupidstitious," but he was not about to discard his personal voodoo; that would be the ultimate defiance and an invitation to disaster! For example, we needed more space in our building at Forty-second and Madison. The building manager offered us newly renovated quarters on the floor below, which would have met our needs and would have cost us nothing for redecoration; there was also some space on an upper floor, but we would have to pay to have it renovated. So which floor did we take? The upper floor, of course, despite the cost of renovating it. Why? Because it's bad luck to move down. Can you imagine the bad luck that would plague us if we moved our New York office to California?

Russ used to say to me, "Doc, stop worrying. Take it easy. There'll be enough income from our servicing to take care of you and me as long as we live. That's all that matters." (I didn't tell him I intended to outlast him by a quarter century.) But I had been bitten by the California bug. When I pulled up anchor in New York in 1957 and came to San Francisco at age fifty-nine, I shed my New York conservatism and became a small-time venture capitalist. I went into undertakings I wouldn't have considered before. And yes, I made many mistakes but also some fabulous conquests. My net worth is twenty-five times greater today than it was when I left Forty-second and Madison in 1957. My greatest shortcoming has always been that I believed what people told me; I put too much confidence in others. Considering my fascination with psychology, including abnormal psychology, I should have been a better judge of human behavior.

One of my ventures was particularly interesting. I can't recall how I met William A. Burkett, superintendent of banks in California in the administration of Gov. Goodwin Knight. One day at lunch he told me that he intended to buy Security State Bank in Pacific Grove, which had been founded in 1889 (Charter 17); if I was interested, he and I could become the sole stockholders. Of course I was interested, and he was right. When the sole remaining stockholder died, the executor of the estate gave Bill the option to buy and Bill gave me the privilege of taking 49 percent of the stock, while he took 51 percent. The bank prospered under his leadership as president, while I, as chairman of the board, minded my own business in San Francisco. It was not long, however, before the big banks began knocking on our door with offers to buy. It was difficult for us to turn a deaf ear, because we knew that if we did not take them seriously they could become more aggressive. And since we were operating in an ultra conservative manner, investing only in highest grade low-earning assets, we didn't have enough earning power to use the same tactics they threatened to use against us. The result was that in time, United California Bank came through with an offer that made sense and we accepted it, at a respectable profit.

Chapter 27

Tax Shelters: Are They Worth the Price?

In spite of the ups and downs our business survived, although, in 1972, my son gave it up; he said life was too short to try to carry on forever with those New York nitwits. So he sold his sixty-foot yacht, drove to Florida, bought another sixty-footer, and sailed away in the direction of the Virgin Islands in the Caribbean. Although I think he intended to wind up in the Mediterranean, his passage from Lauderdale to Saint Thomas was so rough that he confined his sea-faring thereafter to the Caribbean as far south as Venezuela. Soon he tired of being a bachelor playboy, met and married a woman from New York, who was living in Saint Thomas, and suddenly found that the Bank of America, in need of a man with mortgage-banking experience, wanted him for the job. So now, for the first time in his life, he was on the other side of the market—making loans for a commercial bank instead of buying them for a savings bank.

Not long after he'd taken the job, a real estate developer came to the bank with an armful of blue prints, a fat prospectus, and an application for a construction loan amounting to seven figures—the biggest proposition ever to darken the doorway of this branch of the B of A; so big, in fact, that Jack had to take it to the head office in San Francisco before he could give the developer an answer.

The loan was approved, and the project started. Later on, at a social gathering, the developer and Jack got into a conversation, in the course of which he asked Jack why, since he seemed to be well versed in finance, wasn't he in the business for himself? In fact, he said, the project needed a man who could handle financial relations with its creditors (the bank and individuals); and as financial vice president, this person would become one of the founder-owners of the project.

Having considered the undertaking from the standpoint of a lender, he now looked at it as a developer; he liked what he saw. A short time later he resigned from the bank, although when he tendered his resignation, the B of A offered him the job of mortgage-loan coordinator for the entire Caribbean region. As this would have entailed island-hopping and absence from home much of the time, he declined and joined the developer. This was in the late 1970s. Having the curiosity of a cat, my wife and I took a combination vacation and inspection trip to get a first-hand view of the undertaking. I may have shown too much enthusiasm, because not only was it suggested that we buy a condo, which we did, but also that I become a mortgage lender to individuals who were making down payments on other condominiums, which were being built on the hilltops surrounding the golf course. Having emancipated myself from the narrow thinking of my pre-California days, I said, okay.

Everything was going according to plan until the credit crunch of the early 1980s caused interest rates to rise to a prohibitive level in mainland U.S.A. and still higher in offshore areas like the Virgin Islands, with the result that the project managers couldn't obtain construction funds at rates that would enable them to deliver condos at contract prices. That left my money tied up in finished and partly finished properties, and no one could say when I might get it out. It was a good thing that it was my money and not someone else's I was lending. You might ask the embarrassing question, "Why didn't an ex-college professor of economics have enough insight to foresee a rise in interest rates?" (Confidentially, economists, stockbrokers, business consultants—all have a miserable record as forecasters. The economic system is simply too complex, the variables too numerous, and human behavior too erratic. It is difficult enough to make predictions in a free-market economy; and now that practically all national economies are, to one degree or another, "managed," the complexities are even further magnified. That's my excuse for not anticipating one of the most disastrous credit-crunches of modern times.)

After about two years of uneasiness a large investor from New York took over the project and I was paid in full, including accrued interest. So you see, while I tried to make another mistake I didn't quite succeed. However, I still have four 360-degree-view lots on hilltops, which I hereby offer at $25,000 each; they are inaccessible at present, however, because a street has not yet been put in. Why don't you try to make a mistake and take them off my hands? If not all four, how about one?

We have now come to the latter half of the 1980s—the expansionist era, when greed and graft infected otherwise respectable business transactions. It was the period when limited-partnership interests were offered by individuals and corporations who originated the deals as general partners. Many of these partnerships were heavily leveraged. That is, if the partnership bought, say, a mainframe computer for a telephone or insurance company (good credit risks), only 10 or 15 percent of the cost of the equipment would have to be paid for by the limited partners; the rest of the cost would be funded by bank loans. The limited partner was allocated, in the economics of this setup, his proportionate share of the depreciation of the equipment, and likewise, his credit for interest paid on the borrowed funds. These tax write-offs could be so large that a limited partner could have enough tax credits to reduce his taxes on other income. And it was all done in compliance with the current revenue code and IRS and SEC regulations.

Elaborate prospectuses accompanied every offering, calling attention to the possibilities and pitfalls so that the investor knew what he was getting into (if he bothered to read the several pounds of boilerplate). In most cases, though, he relied on statements made by the general partner—someone he knew, usually, and trusted as a finder or broker. That confidence, all too often, turned out to be misplaced.

Such partnerships were formed to drill for oil; to purchase expensive machinery, equipment, airplanes, apartment houses, warehouses, disposable nail-polish applicators, delivery trucks, restaurants, racehorse breeding farms, office buildings, shopping malls—the list is long, because the program had enormous possibilities for stimulating the economy, and indeed is one of the reasons for the economic expansion of the 1980s.

But the IRS found that the tax-avoidance feature was so seriously depleting tax revenue that it was necessary to go before Congress and recommend the law be changed, which the latter agreed to do—with a vengeance: Congress changed the rules in the middle of the game. Partnerships that were legal when formed became illegal overnight; tax-deductible items were now taxable retroactively. Limited partners sued general partners, but this was a waste of time and money, because it was the change in the law that was turning everything upside down. It proved that "the power to tax is the power to destroy." It was probably one of the least-justifiable uses of the taxing power in the horrible history of the income tax.

I had invested in a number of such partnerships, which were offered by my bank to preferred customers. I went to court on only one, a partnership that had purchased an IBM mainframe computer and leased it to an insurance company. After the law was changed, the IRS had levied a heavy tax.

My attorney (who had written the prospectus) believed that the ruling was unjust, and we appealed. The case went to the tax court, and I had to go to New York to testify. Result: I was assessed $102,000 by the IRS; my legal fees were $35,000. (This is the Sutton case, if you care to look it up.) There were five other limited partners in this deal, but the IRS never got around to four of them; the fifth got off with a small assessment, probably because the IRS agent didn't understand the complicated setup of the partnership. (I had trouble understanding it myself.)

Partnerships can also be used with nefarious efficacy by a general partner if he has larceny in his heart. For example, Jim, a real-estate broker, sets up a partnership with himself as general partner and you and four or five others as limiteds. He then pays the seller a little more than the asking price, on the understanding that the overage will find its way back to Jim. The property, meanwhile, has gone into the partnership at the inflated cost, but the limited partners are not aware of it.

If the general partner is still hungry, he may write a letter to the limiteds, telling them that previously unobserved items of deferred maintenance, such as a leaking roof, a back-up in the plumbing system, or overloaded electrical circuits require immediate correction, to pay for which a capital contribution is required. You either kick in your share or have your interest in the asset proportionately reduced. Usually, the limiteds are too busy with their own affairs to check out these matters; and besides, they trust the general partner, otherwise they wouldn't have gone into partnership with him. But how much of this special assessment goes into his pocket is hard to say without an audit.

Like hundreds of thousands of other venture capitalists, I also looked with favor at oil- and gas-drilling partnerships. In self-defense, I can say that I did so only after receiving an offering from a newly formed department in one of California's largest banks. None of the oil and gas ventures has lived up to its projected potential although the write-offs, while they lasted, were substantial.

Another highly touted tax-shelter partnership offered by the same bank was a cattle-ranch feedlot. It was a flop. Then came real estate; these offers were successful. The department was suddenly closed down, however, when the board of directors of the bank decided it might be exposing itself to undue risk. Therefore, each partnership it had offered was turned over to its general partner; most of them came to an end through sale of the assets, for whatever they would bring, but a few were retained and these were, or are, profitable.

I became interested in another group, before the IRS and Congress killed this goose that was supposed to be laying golden eggs, which had developed a disposable nail-polish product that would be spillproof and preferable to the bottle and brush. It was approved by a nationwide retailer, but our machine proved to be incapable of turning out the volume required. Improving the machinery costs money, and the money must come primarily from the limited partners; that means a capital call. We shall each either pay our respective share or accept a smaller proportionate interest in what still looks like a reasonable gamble. What would you do? (P.S. If you see such an item on a cosmetic counter one of these days it may be ours.)

Another "friendly" venture capitalist came to me with a corking good idea. (Aren't they all sleeping beauties?) You may recall that some people died as a result of inhaling the acrid fumes given off by burning styrofoam upholstery in a hotel fire in Las Vegas a few years ago. Obviously, said my enterprising capitalist friend, we should set up a partnership, hire some chemists, and produce a type of styrofoam that would not smolder and produce harmful fumes if subject to fire. A maker of fire-resistant materials has made some progress but requires additional capital. Wouldn't I like to get in on the undertaking as a limited partner, considering the enormous market that would exist if, hereafter, all styrofoam-stuffed furniture in public buildings had to use our fireproof product? Of course I would, and thanks for the opportunity. (It pays to know the right people.)

Today, five years later, a styrofoam material has been produced that has passed the fire test. It will not give off acrid fumes if subjected to flame. But there's one little difficulty: it is useless in upholstery (which is the only place where it was supposed to be used), because, if you sit on it, you flatten it. Unlike a cushion, which is what it is supposed to be, this material is not resilient and spongy. The limited partners, therefore, have exchanged the patent rights for shares in the developing company. These shares have a par value of one cent each; the market value is a little less than that!

Brief reference has been made to racehorse-breeding partnerships. Knowing me as you now do, I am sure you are ready to believe that I would fall for one of these. The fact is, however, that when a broker friend, in whom I had more confidence than he deserved, recommended I take an interest in one such venture, I demurred, saying that it was so far afield I felt incompetent to evaluate it. He was a CPA, however, and assured me he had exercised due diligence in researching the venture, and was confident it would be a profitable investment for me, considering the substantial tax shelter it would provide (under the original legislation, which was then still in effect). So I plunked down a sizable bit of cash.

From the outset, the foals didn't come forth as forecast; were the mares frigid, or the stallions stupid? Or was the general partner unqualified for his new undertaking? He had been a stockbroker; he knew, or thought he knew what to do in bull and bear markets, but did he know what to do in the horse market?

About a dozen of these partnerships had been formed by the same general partner to take care of the demand by baseball and football players, among others, who found themselves at enormously high salary levels during the relatively few years of their prime, as well as by others who were, perhaps temporarily, in the top tax bracket. To meet this demand, the general partner might have bitten off more cud than he or his horses could chew. In fact, the partnerships were faltering—some more than others. Was the GP juggling the accounting? Whether or not he was, one day, out of a blue sky, all several hundred of us limiteds received a huge document of hundreds of pages proposing a "roll-up" of all of the partnerships, good and bad, and requiring our approval in something like fourteen days, if I remember correctly.

Not unlike a corral full of stallions next to another corral of ready, able, and willing mares, the limited partners raised holy hell. They figuratively kicked down the fences, hired attorneys, and proceeded to go after the general partner.

The case went to court, and after about three years the decision went against the limiteds and in favor of the general. Don't ask me to explain; the reasoning is too legalistic and technical for an old goat like me who is still more interested in sociology and population control than in accounting. The experience cost me about $170,000 in cash, plus legal and accounting fees, accrued interest, and peace of mind. On the plus side, however, I was entitled, at least, to some tax deductions.

Although we lost the case, I understand that the general partner didn't win it: he is said to be bankrupt. Therefore, the only ones who may be better off today than before this stillborn attempt by a stockbroker to breed racehorses are certain members of the legal profession—not to mention the stationers, who sold uncounted reams of paper for numberless interminable briefs; "briefs" being a legal euphemism for the hundreds of pages of opinions, decisions, and citations, which were printed on both sides of the paper and were no more comprehensible on one side than the other.

I also made reference above to real-estate partnerships. Here the story is entirely different. These, with a few exceptions, have been quite successful. We apparently managed to avoid the excesses of the 1980s, which is quite the opposite of what was happening nationally.

Indeed, much of the debacle that befell the savings and loan companies during the 1980s, and to a lesser extent the banking system and life insurance companies can be traced to the excesses made possible by the liberal partnership legislation before it was amended and abridged. We overbuilt office buildings, hotels, apartment houses, golf-club and tennis-club condominium projects, and even undertook economically unproductive activities such as horse breeding, all of which involved substantial borrowing. If a period of prosperity is a time when we go into debt, and a depression a time when we work off our debt, then two conclusions stare us in the face: one is that in the '90s, we are busy settling, in one way of another, the excessive debts we incurred in the '80s to sweeten the returns on our highly leveraged partnerships; the other is that the length of time it is requiring to compensate for the excesses of the '80s is in direct proportion to the amount of debt we incurred. We are witnessing a classic verification of one partial explanation of business cycles.

At the bottom of it all is our mental makeup. Most of us are content to play simple games of chance like tossing coins or lotto at a church party; but others, in order to satisfy their avarice, grab at opportunities afforded by the kind of liberalizing legislation we have been talking about, and then go to extremes. This group evidently grew through spontaneous incubation or by cell division during the decade of the 1980s and we and they are paying the price for it in the 1990s, which payment now goes by the names "unemployment" and "depression."

Chapter 28
What Price Success?

Toward the end of the 1970s I began to go to the office later; then, less frequently. I had two able employees: one, a young man who studied for the bar at night and passed the exam the first time, and the other a Chinese woman my son hired in 1952. The young man left to practice law. I then decided to retire Margaret on a pension and transfer all operations to the Los Angeles office, which was, and is, operated by Roger Norton, who joined our company after college forty years ago. His number-two man is Bill Sullivan, the son of one of the two New York officers. So I can't say when I actually retired; rather I seem simply to have tapered off.

At about the same time, Russ, the first of my New York associates, died. Not too long after that the second associate died, and that enabled Roger, with my wholehearted agreement, to do to the New York office what I couldn't do—namely, terminate it. The company then took on a new life: it has since grown from a staff of some eighteen employees to about fifty, and now does a nationwide business. While many mortgage-banking companies have shrunk or gone out of business in recent years, ours has grown. It is a great tribute to these younger men, who had been held in leash so long by misguided management.

In many respects I was relieved to back out of the business; and, although the internal conflict I had inherited as a result of the untimely death of Connie Lowell many years before had now been removed in the same inevitable way, I still had the same noticeable lack of enthusiasm for the business. If this somehow leads you to the conclusion that the old man is about to confess to making another unwise decision, your opinion would not be too far removed from the truth. If you will think about it for a moment, you will see the inconsistencies between what a mortgage banker does and what my personal philosophy was and is.

Our business is to make available more land for more housing for more people. If the land selected by a builder for "development" was useless, or inappropriate for any other purpose, there might be no objection to its use as building sites; but, all too often, it is land adjacent to or near a city that is either productive crop land or a green belt. When I first began coming to California, San Mateo and Santa Clara Counties, for example, which adjoin San Francisco County to the south, consisted largely of orchards producing plums, apricots, and other fruits and truck gardens producing berries, vegetables, and melons. Now there are houses, factories, office buildings, schools, highways, parking lots, water rationing, and inadequate sewage-treatment plants.

"Naturally," say you, "this was necessary to accommodate a growing population. That's progress." "Yes," say I. "But it's not progress, it's regress. If we had kept our numbers stable, that area would still be a garden spot (rivaling the Garden of Eden, in fact), and the only housing we would have had to provide would have been, for the most part, replacements. And manufacturing plants? They should have been built on land unsuitable for agriculture. Wouldn't we all be better off it that had been the case? Not only in San Mateo and Santa Clara counties, but everywhere?"

My problem is that I am one of the gang of marauders who raped fertile soil; I imported bank funds from New York and made them available to builders so they could buy precious cropland, emasculate it, cut down and burn fruit and nut trees, and pour concrete and asphalt on the rich soil Mother Nature had produced for us in centuries past. Silicon Valley's housing value exceeded its value for horticulture in terms of dollars but not sense.

Some housing construction was justifiable, because of the war moratorium except in defense areas, but more was made necessary by the growth of population. If you want to exhaust natural resources, continue to use valuable cropland, and bring about urban sprawl, just let human procreation and immigration continue.

Another natural resource we are doing our utmost to consume faster than it can be replaced is lumber. Originally, a large portion of the earth's surface was covered with trees; they are now becoming an endangered species. The denuding of forests adversely affects our entire ecosystem, in addition to raising the price of lumber and the cost of housing.

Our failure to control the growth of population, including immigration, has adversely affected our lives in countless ways, not the least of which is the spreading out of cities, or urban sprawl, which we in the mortgage-banking business have aided and abetted. In doing so, we have contributed to the decay of central-city areas; to the time it takes and the money it costs to travel from home to work; to atmospheric pollution, since adequate public transportation is unavailable in single-family subdivisions and private automobile transportation is usually necessary. (The automobile has, in fact, been as much a cause as a consequence of urban sprawl.)

Thus my problem was basically that I found myself in a line of business with which I was not comfortable or sympathetic; and this, added to the internal personality conflicts in our company, made life less than enjoyable.

We might fantasize for a moment as to what it would be like to live in a society in which births merely offset deaths after an "optimum" level of population has been reached. First of all, it would not be necessary to increase the number of living units year after year, only to compensate for the number destroyed or rendered uninhabitable in one way or another. Replacements could be built where the former dwellings were—including sewer, water, gas, electricity, transportation facilities, stores, schools, churches, and other amenities. The amount of lumber required for replacement housing would be trifling compared to new growth. Forests would increase, which would be ecologically desirable inasmuch as woodland prevents soil erosion, enriches the soil, adds water to underground aquifers, and improves the quality of the atmosphere.

In addition to replacements, there would undoubtedly be some custom-built units for those who wanted more "modern" design; but the volume would not compare with typical subdivisions of recent years.

Cities need not be Manhattanized. A city with a relatively stable population can be planned and developed in ways that will avoid congestion. Buildings need not abut each other. Proper planning and intelligent use of land can provide light, air, trees, and other greenery between building blocks. Land can be "condominiumized," as well as buildings, with the result that all owners of lots on a block could receive increased income from more intensive use, via high rises, whether one's particular plot was built on, or preserved as, a landscaped area to provide light, air, and openness.

We are a society seemingly unable to distinguish between short-run practices and long-run consequences. Are we unable to learn from China, India, Mexico, and many other countries of the world what happens when human beings procreate indiscriminately, without regard for their own welfare?

A well-ordered society would offer inducements to men who would consent to vasectomy after the second child was born; and to women who would favor tubal ligation or other preventive measures. Whatever the cost to the community, it would be more than made up in reduced costs of welfare, child care, and other public-assistance programs. If any additional justification is needed, it is that the welfare of mankind as a whole transcends that of the individual. Failure to accept this viewpoint lies at the bottom of our resistance to otherwise perfectly justifiable measures of social control, which sometimes seem to encroach on individual liberty. But the group comes first.

When you were in high school you learned, as I did in the composition class, that an acceptable essay should have unity, coherence, and emphasis. So how come, in telling you about my business experience, I drag in the inchoherent subject of overpopulation?

Quite simple. As I have said before, it is difficult to consider practically any sociological, environmental, ecological, political or economic question in this world without first taking into account the population factor. There simply are more people in the world than is good for us; our allowing population to continue increasing year after year literally amounts to genital genocide, or sentimental suicide. But since everybody, even if he is supernumerary, needs a place in which to live, and since I was in the business of providing such dwelling places, the coherence of the two must be obvious.

Chapter 29
Is There a Monetary Cycle?

One of the dialectical diseases of the twentieth century is the notion that whatever we may have failed to do for ourselves should somehow be done for us by the government. As time goes on this attitude grows in volume and vitality, as we do less by and for ourselves and demand more. When one of life's vicissitudes arises for which we have not provided we call it an "emergency," rather than negligence; an urgent appeal for help goes out to the government and, to avoid losing votes, the party in power comes to the rescue.

Only a few courageous people in Washington will then call a spade a spade and deliver a lecture in elementary economics, to the effect that the only way Uncle Sam can come to their aid is to take from Peter and give to Paul; then, when Peter begins to squeal, the quick-fix, uneconomic printing-press method has to be applied—political quackery. Only one public servant in recent years has been willing to suggest that we should "ask not what your country can do for you, but what you can do for your country." Unfortunately, President Kennedy was removed from office before he could implement this policy.

The trouble is, we have allowed our priorities to become disarrayed. We have forgotten that we should not buy optional goods until we have purchased the necessary ones, such as insurance against more of the potential tragedies of life that may strike at any time. Of course, if we followed this rule it would tend to lower our current standard of living, but financing emergencies with printing-press money, i.e., government debt, will lower it eventually, in the long run, by way of inflation; or sooner, if we retire the debt by means of taxation. The only question is, whose ox is to be gored—and how soon?

Meanwhile, when hurricanes, floods, conflagrations, earthquakes, and periods of widespread unemployment occur, ethical considerations and economic logic are put aside in a compassionate society, and financial assistance is provided to cope with the immediate problem. But when the emergency has passed, will this painful experience have persuaded or induced us, as individuals, to provide insurance against future occurrences of this nature? So far it has not. Having found what the public thinks is a hidden "reserve for contingencies" in the U.S. Treasury, (which, in reality, is only a loan to be repaid in the future), the necessity for us to begin, as individuals, to do something more constructive here and now—like rearranging our priorities, putting first things first and providing for future emergencies—is put on the back burner, if not filed away and forgotten.

Our reluctance to buy insurance against emergencies stems from the fact that it involves giving up present goods, which offer immediate gratification, for protection against events that may not happen. However, the cost of such foresight could be kept at a reasonable level if something along the line of universal all-risk catastrophic group insurance policies were developed by the casualty insurance industry. They need not be compulsory; but anyone so shortsighted as to decline to buy them would become his own underwriter, and responsible for his loss if one occurred.

Until some such arrangement is substituted for our failure to prepare for emergencies (catastrophies, sickness, unemployment, old age, and welfare generally), we shall probably continue our present policy, which, in some respects, is no policy at all—i.e., the policy of going to the well, i.e., the printing press—thus shifting the cost to the next generation, which will then have to pay not only for our losses, but also for their own: double trouble. Incidentally, we will leave them very little money and even less inclination than they have at present to erect statues and memorials in praise of our statesmen.

This "benevolent" political, suicidal, monetary solicitude on the part of a democratic government for its citizens (in exchange for their votes) is the essence of the welfare state. Like drug addiction, public demand for welfare grows, intensively and extensively; but, unlike drugs, the supply, in the form of cash, can easily be adjusted to demand by creating it *ad libitum* out of thin air and the photosynthetic product of trees, more briefly called paper. This is what leads to what I choose to call a monetary cycle.

Economists, politicians, investment advisers, stock and bond brokers and dealers—practically all of us look at questions of this sort from a short-run viewpoint. The monetary cycle, on the other hand, is usually a long-run phenomenon, although, in Germany after 1918, a cycle ran its course in about six years. Some wag said that it ended when the Germans ran out of wheelbarrows. Wheelbarrows? Yes, because on payday the amount of paper money one received was so great that a wheelbarrow, or something with a wheel, was required to transport it to the next place, where it would be traded for something physical, that would also be more conveniently transportable in a device with a wheel, which minimizes friction. But, wags or no wags, the causes and consequences of fiscal and monetary disaster were present in Germany as that episode unfolded. The only difference is that, in Germany between 1918 and about 1924, the cause was not spontaneous but deliberate; it developed, not in response to an unfunded system of social security and public welfare, but as a means of nullifying the demands imposed on Germany by the Treaty of Versailles.

A monetary malady usually begins to affect a nation when expenditures or outlays by the central government exceed income. This cannot happen unless the government has the power to issue paper currency and declare it legal tender. If it has this authority, the party in power, unless it is willing to put responsibility ahead of reelection, is tempted to issue paper money to various and sundry citizens enabling them to satisfy "needs" they either do not or cannot pay for themselves. The system appears so simple and yet so successful in enabling a "generous" or "sympathetic" party to remain in power that the opposition party has to offer even more largess, public assistance, and welfare in its effort to win the next election.

Any candidate who so much as mentions that welfare and giveaway programs should be financed by taxation is sure to be defeated by the candidate who vows not to tax. Government, whose proper function is to protect human liberty and maintain law, order, and justice, begins to take on the characteristics of a charitable organization with a supernatural capacity to produce something (money) out of nothing, which it is then free to distribute to various and sundry individuals, from the farmer in the field to the drifter on drugs, the unmarried teenage mother or any other unmarried mother in proportion to the number of children she has been able to produce, to the unemployed gun-toting high school dropout, to families with more than two children (a subsidy for each additional child), to immigrants from overpopulated countries that have a worse population policy than we—in short, to anyone or anything that a representative of the people finds "necessary" or desirable (to assure him his re-election).

Sooner or later, increasing the supply of money willy-nilly causes it to lose value, just as donuts do if we produce more of them than the market will absorb. If it now takes twelve units of money to buy a widget where only ten were required before, more units of money will be created; otherwise, our welfare recipients will begin to suffer hardship: they won't be able to buy as many donuts or other goodies, and we might not be reelected. So we "accommodate" our needy constituents; they are entitled to it. The trouble is that it is a self-perpetuating process: higher prices require more money; more money brings about higher prices—a vicious circle.

If the velocity of circulation increases, as it is likely to in an inflationary environment, and if the volume of goods and services is not increased as rapidly as demand, except at higher unit cost, this adds more fuel to the fire of inflation, as the malady feeds on itself, growing by geometric progression.

Longer-lasting physical commodities, such as real estate, are preferable to ephemeral goods, because they rise in value roughly equivalent to the cost of reproduction. But even income-producing real estate fails to keep up with inflation unless rents are increased correspondingly—which puts landlords in the category of benefici- aries or profiteers in the minds of tenants. During the German inflationary period following the First World War, for example, intelligent entrepreneurs, including many farsighted Jewish inves- tors, understood the value of real estate as a hedge against inflation and invested heavily in income-producing property; but, as rents were increased to keep up with inflation, these property owners incurred the enmity of the German people, which Hitler was later able to capitalize on, giving him an excuse, if he needed one, not only to persecute the owners but also to seize their property and put it into the hands of the Nazi party.

Der Herr Gutenberg probably rolled over in his fifteenth-century coffin when he heard that his invention, the printing press, had degenerated from printing Bibles to turning out fiat currency—stuff that would have to be accepted as money if some dictator said so. He would probably be equally embarrassed if he thought the story in Mark 6:30 gave politicians and dictators the idea that, if Jesus was able to stretch five loaves and two fishes far enough to feed five-thousand people, a government could do the same thing on an even larger scale, by printing money, passing it out to the people, and thus staying in power indefinitely.

Or could they? Money, which came into use because barter was so cumbersome, had to be a universally desirable store of value not subject to sudden changes in quantity. Precious metals, primarily gold, satisfied most of the basic requirements.

In time, the inconvenience of carrying metal was replaced by printed certificates backed by gold. Instead of carrying one-hundred gold ducats about town in a bag, one could carry a slip of paper bearing the certification that one-hundred gold ducats were being held as security and could be had on demand by the holder of the printed certificate.

Monetary history is too long a story to be told here, except to say that in 1933, when the New Deal government took charge in this country, the amount of gold behind our currency had to be at least 40 percent. But that created a problem: the amount of gold we had put a limit on the amount of money the administration could spend, and you can't run a welfare state without spending a lot of money. You could "soak the rich," as some of the Washington insiders recommended, and this was done to a degree; but to do it on a large scale takes time, and unemployed people can't wait. Besides which, the prevailing thinking of the bureaucracy at the time was that private enterprise had failed and only a "managed" economy, with the government free to spend public funds, would create full employment. (Maybe the Russians were right?)

So we went off the gold standard; der Herr Gutenberg's invention was then equipped with a cooling system, put on a three-shift, twenty-four hour work schedule, and has been turning out fiat money ever since. It has to; how else could our government pay out a *billion* dollars more than it takes in every day?

Increasing the supply of "money" independently of the volume of production causes prices to rise eventually. Rising prices increase the velocity of circulation of money, because the consumers prefer to exchange cash, which is declining in value, in favor of goods, which are increasing in value. Beneficiaries of the welfare state (unemployed, unmarried teenage mothers, residents of public housing, parents who have more children than they can afford [and society needs], and a hundred other classes of recipients) need more funds to cope with rising prices. It becomes a vicious circle, and a larger one as time goes on.

Ultimately, confusion turns into chaos as a critical mass of the circulating medium is reached and it is generally realized that the would-be benefactors in the government are, in reality, unrealistic charlatans and quacks, and it is time for a change. At this point another quack, a dictator, usually rises out of nowhere and, either by force of arms or popular acclaim, manages to take over the government. He declares the old currency worthless and issues a new monetary unit, in a ratio of one new for hundreds or thousands of the old.

The public, so disillusioned by the impractical idealism of the former welfare state, usually allows the new leader to continue to exercise dictatorial powers. But if power corrupts, absolute power corrupts absolutely, and in time the new ruler tends to become as undesirable as his predecessors; as a result he is overthrown by, yes, you guessed it, a leader who promises to be more considerate of the needs of the public.

And how will the new democratic government do that? First, by taxing the rich and giving to the poor. But that will soon prove to be insufficiently productive. S-o-o-o, it will be "necessary" to incur a little deficit, which will, of course, be kept under control, and is only a "temporary" or "emergency" measure.

Financing such situations by the obsequious but convenient method of "creating" the funds through the use of paper and printer's ink tends to continue, accelerate, feed on itself, and thus repeat the monetary cycle. My immediate reason for including such a tale of woe here is that there is an element of similarity between it and the fiscal policies we are following in this country today.

"If so," you say, "why don't we have more inflation? We have been living off deficits for the last sixty years, during which time the annual rate of inflation has averaged only about 3.5 or 4 percent—bad enough, but not nearly as large as our more than $4 trillion debt would warrant, according to your theory." The answer is probably our enormous capacity to produce goods, which has kept up with our production of (paper) purchasing power. But faith is fickle; and mass psychology, unpredictable. So long as the public has confidence that the dollar is not likely to lose a substantial amount of its purchasing power, investors will continue to buy government bonds and consumers will not rush to exchange currency for commodities. But if something occurs to shake confidence, bondholders will decline to accept refunding issues and demand cash, thus monetizing public debt to that extent. Interest rates will rise, the vicious circle will have begun, and mass psychology will shift from confidence to concern. The fluidity of public opinion or mass psychology is exemplified by the sudden and significant change in our attitude toward sex, which has, so to speak, occurred in the last few minutes of man's existence. Public opinion can shift as suddenly and decisively with respect to the value of the dollar.

Financial turmoil and monetary upheaval seem unreal and unlikely in this prosperous land; but that is precisely why they should not be ruled out as possibilities some time in the future.

Chapter 30
Pigeon Pollution

When granddaughter Cindy read the preceding chapter, she reminded me that her sister Beth had recommended I "juice up" the discussion, and what I had just written did anything but that. Accordingly, she offered the following suggestion: "Since you had a lot to say about the pigeons that penalize the parishioners who patronize the Episcopal church on West Forty-sixth Street in New York, and I have heard you compare the behavior of the pigeons who produce the same kind of punishment on the faithful when they patronize the Presbyterian church around the corner from where you are sitting, why not show your ecumenism by reporting how Presbyterian pigeons conduct themselves and what that congregation does about it?"

"Good idea, Cindy," said I. So here's the tale. However, before derogating a member of the family of Columbidae (pigeons), we should admit that they are remarkable birds. Their eyesight is so good that they can spot, from a rooftop, a tiny morsel of food on the sidewalk or in the gutter. You and I can't even see what they are picking up; but it must be nutritious, otherwise their feathers would not be so beautiful. Indeed, they always appear as meticulously groomed as if they had just been coiffured by their favorite feather stylist, despite the fact that they are practically homeless and spend every night in inhospitable sleeping quarters, like windswept ledges of buildings, in the rain, sleet or snow. They also put nutritionists to shame: if you think they find a balanced diet in dumpsters and gutters, then you and I have a different opinion of what constitutes a balanced diet. And yet, they not only survive; they thrive. We tend to look askance at them because they don't provide their own bathrooms but then neither does your cat, so who's to blame?

Although they have been able to survive in spite of the hardships to which the human family has subjected them for countless centuries, our mistreatment has not been accepted lightheartedly. In fact, if we could understand pidgin English, we would probably find that one of the first things a squab is taught is to drop whatever might be available on people, especially churchgoers, who ought to be more charitable toward God's other creatures.

The minister in the situation referred to here has tried in various ways to appease the congregation; in one of his sermons he reminded the faithful, citing Scripture, (Tob. 2:10-12), that Tobias, weary from work, lay down by a wall and slept. "And as he was sleeping, hot dung out of a swallow's nest fell upon his eyes, and he was made blind."

This was probably intended to comfort those in the church who had nothing more serious to complain about than a washable stain on an Easter bonnet, droppings on a dress, or a nuisance on a necktie.

Solutions, however, not sermons, were what the congregation wanted, but some proposals were so outlandish that they were dubbed heretical rather than helpful. One such suggestion was made by a member of the congregation who had recently switched from popism to Calvinism. He told his fellow worshippers that in the Catholic church, the priest sprinkles holy water on the congregation before the service begins, which is supposed to drive out any evil spirits that might be hiding either in their minds, their bodies or their clothing. The ceremony is called the Asperges, from the Latin verb meaning "to sprinkle." He asked why Calvinists couldn't take one of the buckets used by the sexton, call it an aspersorium, if necessary, put some water into it, find a stick with a bit of a knob on one end (call it an aspergillum, as the other people do), and sprinkle the pigeons. Wouldn't that cause them to fly away, as the evil spirits do when they get aspergated?

This brought deafening cries of "heresy!" from some, and equally loud shouts of disbelief from others, while those who were grasping at straws attempting to get rid of the menace liked the idea, but couldn't figure out how to make holy water.

"We can't make water holy, can we?" asked a little old lady.

"I guess we could if we wanted to," said an old timer.

"How do we know it becomes holy water?" said a doubting

Thomas. "All we really know is that somebody dressed in thirteenth-century clothing says it's holy after he makes a ceremonial gesture."

By this time the coffee hour had arrived, and although caffeine may be an addictive, habit forming substance, it has not been outlawed by the Presbytery. It is also a stimulant; and the questions it invariably stimulated were, Why were the pigeons in such an inappropriate location in the first place? and Why couldn't anyone find a way of persuading them to take up residence elsewhere?

One of the more analytical members of the congregation said that the problem started with the architectural design of the portico. The architect had been more interested in erecting a replica of an ancient Greek temple than a pigeon-proof, monotheistic assembly hall, he said.

Some others of the congregation, who were more accusatory than analytical, took the view that the architect was probably a Roman Catholic who had deliberately provided resting places for the birds above the entrance to the sanctuary as a form of punishment for these defectors from the original church; pigeon pollution visited on the parishioners would be one of the penalties of their Protestantism. For his good work, the architect could expect some kind of reward or indulgence, either here and now or in the hereafter, from the mother church, the only one from which all blessings flow.

But pigeons are nothing if not ecumenical. There are instances, though rare, in which Protestant architects have been commissioned to draw plans for Catholic churches; then they delight in placing statues of saints directly above the portals, and so arranging their halos and arms as to provide comfortable perches for the birds, thus enabling them to combine catharsis with Catholicism. Although the architect may have done his best in such cases to pester the parishioners, even experienced pigeons sometimes found it a challenge to make a direct hit on a worshiper, who would make a mad dash through the entrance to protect an Easter bonnet or bald head.

Since the Presbyterian congregation didn't believe in the possibility of aspergising the pesky pigeons, and reconstructing the facade was as impractical as the holy-water humbug was heretical, other possible solutions had to be considered; such as the one proposed by a member of the congregation who was in the business of manufacturing detergents.

He proposed that the number of ushers be considerably increased, each of whom would be equipped with a bottle of his brand of liquid detergent. The ushers would stand inside the church doors and be ready to give first aid to anyone who had been bombed. In exchange for this accommodation, parishioners would look with favor upon the stuff and buy a bottle. Others might not buy it, but would probably follow the example of the pigeons and drop something almost as filthy, such as lucre into a collection plate, which would be in plain view and that no one could ignore without being caught in the act.

This promotion-minded Presbyterian additionally suggested to the minister that he approach the manufacturer, suggesting he make a tax-deductible contribution of the detergent to the church so that the church's profit would be 100 percent. If the manufacturer wavered he could be told, whether true or not, that another detergent company was ready to step in if he didn't. (The end justifies the [spurious] means even among ministers.)

If this strategy failed, the minister was advised to suggest that the bottles offered could be seconds, i.e., those whose spray devices, say, were defective but still usable; or whose labels were crooked; or some other specious reasons. The lack of truthfulness in the valuing of the seconds as first-quality for tax-deductible purposes would probably be forgiven, said the minister, who insisted that God was a Presbyterian at heart.

The congregation thought the idea was good except for the unethical part. But it was never tried; first, because ushers were unwilling to go into the dry-cleaning business under these circumstances, and second, because one of the elders said the scheme looked too much like an Ivan Boesky insider-trading deal, inasmuch as the member who'd proposed using the detergent was an employee of the company that produced it.

This left the congregation in a state of confusion. Some didn't know who Boesky was, while others thought he might be one of the cardinals behind the Vatican wall who never explained the failure of, or defalcation in, the Vatican bank a few years ago. One of the young female members of the congregation offered what she thought was a corking good idea, one that could not so easily be turned down. At the risk of revealing something of her lifestyle, she said, why not interrupt the breeding process?

"How?" asked a matron.

"Go to the bird store a few blocks south of here, near Fillmore and Pine, and buy a few of the birds known to be prejudiced against pigeons. There's more racial prejudice among birds than there is among people," she said. "These pigeon-haters will raid pigeon nests, break any eggs that may be there, and eat the embryos, hopefully before the end of the first trimester."

But this idea, too, didn't get very far. Loud protests were heard from the right-to-lifers, who were against the idea even if the resulting holocaust could be limited to the first trimester—which, of course, would be impossible. Furthermore, they said, such a policy could send the wrong signal to the younger members of the congregation, that of interrupting the birth process (as if they didn't know how to already). Good Presbyterians should have nothing to do with thoughts of this kind, it was said. So there the matter was left, unsolved, as it has been ever since the classical Greek columns became a part of the facade.

One bright Sunday morning (that is, after the indigenous San Francisco morning fog had given way to sunshine), I decided to take a walk. As I approached the church, I saw a group of men and women on the sidewalk singing, a cappella, the hymn "Onward Christian Soldiers."

Soon another walker came along with his dog. He listened for a moment as the dog, who apparently was well trained not to howl at hymns, sat patiently on the sidewalk, hoping that he would not have too long to wait for an opportunity to do in the gutter what the pigeons do anywhere. He showed signs of restlessness at the number of verses in the hymn, however, and apparently was about to do on the carollers' shoes what the pigeons do on others' heads.

When there was a pause in the singing, the dog's master asked in a whisper, "Is this a Salvation Army Chapel? Are they really trying to bring religion to people on the street? If so, isn't that a new wrinkle?"

"No," I said. "These people are holding a group therapy session to screw up enough courage to dash through that perilous portal up there, which is more benignly and less justifiably referred to by keepers of the faith as the 'entrance' to the sanctuary."

"Strange world," said the dog walker. "We dog walkers carry sanitation devices called scoopers; why don't they have something like that for churchgoers? In fact, as I think about it, why couldn't they have something like subway turnstiles at the door, so that in order to get in you would have to deposit a coin in a farebox, which would activate a device that would deflect the pigeons' deposits into a receptacle? When it was full the contents could be packaged and sold as fancy fertilizer, a Presbyterian compost; and what's even more important, the purchaser could call the cost a tax-deductible contribution to the church. The IRS wouldn't smell a rat because it would be unrelated to rats."

I had to admit that my dog-walking acquaintance was a man with original ideas, some of which, however, were not entirely in harmony with the principles that the church was supposed to be espousing. Notwithstanding, he offered another solution.

"There's another gimmick they could use," he said. "They could make the turnstiles operate only on tokens, and these could be sold for, say, two bits apiece, or even for a dollar. Then all you would have to do is set up some kind of lock-box control, so the users or the parson wouldn't be able to steal the money. Also, if you people could figure out a way to make water holy, the church could offer a bottle of it to go with a package of the fertilizer. Soon, pigeons would be as useful to you Protestants as saints in the Catholic church are to sinners."

I was amazed at the fertility of this man's mind. If I were a proselytizing member of the church I would have given him a sales talk about the advantages of membership, emphasizing especially the rewards occurring in the future—which, they say, is an eternity. As such it's one of the best, if not *the* best affiliation a person can make, I would have told him. At this point his dog reminded him emphatically that they should finish what they'd started out to do, which they did. I have no idea what, if anything, he has done about a religious affiliation.

At the next meeting of the church's Decontamination Committee, another member announced that he had a good substitute for the liquid-detergent proposal, which had been turned down because the ushers were not willing to combine washing with worship. This person reported that he had been approached by an enterprising individual, a Mr. Shapiro, who said he was in umbrellas; he had heard about the church's pigeon problem. It was his suggestion that the congregation give him a franchise to rent umbrellas to those who wanted only to get safely into and out of the holy place. He said he could always be on hand on Sunday, because he attended his place of worship on the Sabbath; holy days presented no problem, because in his congregation the holy days never seemed to occur at the same time as those in ours. He was agreeable to discussing compensation, either as a flat fee or a percentage of the gross. However, there was an administrative problem; either they would have to invest in as many umbrellas as there were members of the congregation, or they would have to re-use a smaller number of them at each service, regardless of how contaminated they had become—unless the ushers could be persuaded to do to parasols what they had previously refused to do to people. However, the ushers again respectfully declined to augment their worship to this extent. Mr. Shapiro had no immediate solution for this, and so the problem persisted.

It was inevitable, however, that sooner or later someone would say the pigeon problem had a positive side—it could be put to good use as a proselytizing public-relations ploy, somewhat as the monks at San Juan Capistrano make headlines every spring when the swallows are alleged to return. In spite of all the other places to which the birds could go, they prefer (or so it could be said) the hallowed nesting area of this holy Presbyterian place; the propaganda punch line could then be, "Wouldn't it be a good idea for you, too, to come to a closer relationship with God?" At least it seemed, to some members of the congregation, that a skillful public relations firm would be able to figure out how to get some positive result or advantage from these persistent poachers who perch above the porticos of this prestigious place of prayer. I don't know if a committee has been appointed, or a PR firm hired; but I do know that no productive proselytizing publicity has appeared—so far.

I also know that the congregation is continuing to rack its collective brain for a solution, the latest being a suggestion that the best way to coax the birds away from the church would be to lure them to a place where they could find a better diet—a balanced diet, rather than depending on contaminated garbage in gutters and on sidewalks, where at least 50 percent of what the birds pick up has to be expelled by them as being inedible, even by pigeons.

Probably the best way to lead the birds to this solution, one practical-minded parishioner suggested, would be to climb a ladder up to the nesting area at night, gently pick up several birds, place them in portable cages, and take them to the area around one of those restaurants that has a big M sign on it. After tasting the luscious morsels that would be found near the garbage cans and around one of those places, the birds would rush back to their brethren and sistern [sic] and tell them the promised land is here. Here—not in the hereafter, as they are told so often at the church. "There is manna from heaven at a Big M," they would say, "only a few blocks from here; real food, not that spiritual stuff; real meat and french fries, in quantity. You won't have to scrounge all day just to survive. You will have more leisure and you can have more babies, too, since there will be enough to feed them; your infant-mortality rate will also be much lower."

It sounded sensible and practical until one of the old-timers in the congregation said that, regrettably, this remedy had been tried in a slightly different form and had failed completely. Either the birds that came back to the church roosts, he said, couldn't convince their neighbors and relatives, legitimate and illegitimate, that there was a better way, or else they decided that feeding in the gutters around the church not only was more in harmony with their evolutionary development but also that garbage in gutters surrounding the church very likely contained leftover spiritual morsels, the bread of life, that were offered the faithful every Sunday. No restaurant or fast-food joint, franchised or not, could compete with that.

Therefore, in light of this evidence of avian intelligence and ecumenism it was recommended that at the next meeting of the Contamination Committee a resolution of reprieve in favor of the birds instead of one of rejection should be entered in the minutes.

This outcome was inevitable. Even the most bombed believer had to admit that any creature able to subsist on tiny bits of garbage often so vile as to be rejected by lower forms of life and yet still manage to keep its health, beauty, and agility is a unique and remarkable product of creation, blessed with more adaptive capability than the rest of us have acquired ontologically, inherited genetically, or received spiritually.

These birds were also fully prepared for the motor age long before it arrived; they can dodge an oncoming vehicle and pick up a snack at the same time. They are masters also in the conservation of energy. If you and a pigeon choose to be in the same place at the same time and you refuse to give the bird the right of way, he will move at the last split second, but only enough to let you go by; if you appear to be a bit aggressive he will levitate himself, but only enough to avoid a confrontation. They never complain or fight back: pigeons are far more pacific than people.

The homeless also could solve most of their problems if they would study pigeons, for they have been homeless ever since man came upon the face of the earth. The poor, too, could alleviate much of the anguish of their poverty if they could somehow adopt the attitude of these creatures who think nothing of going to bed hungry; they simply fly farther and work harder the next day, and invariably find something to eat; we never see a dead one.

In all probability, long after this church building and others like it will have crumbled to dust and blown away, these feathered foragers will be here, having adapted to the conditions of a new and entirely different environment as they have done, so successfully, to ours.

Chapter 31
Out of the Frying Pan

One morning in December 1985, a visitor at my front door asked me if I was Irvin Bussing. I told him that, to my best knowledge and belief, I was, and had been for eighty-seven years and counting. Whereupon he presented a large envelope containing papers of legal size.

Having just finished reading a series of horror stories (i.e., the morning newspaper), I returned to my easy chair. Although it was just two weeks before Christmas, I was still curious to see what someone was offering (and by special messenger, too). In a way I was already in a holiday mood, having received reminders as early as September from secular organizations such as Sears, Macy's, Penney, Tiffany, and many more, that I should not forget to celebrate commercially the advent of you-know-who, and that they were, as ever, ready to assist me in doing so.

But this package had no fancy wrapping, ribbons, or rosettes; it was a big, plain white envelope addressed to me with a return address, not of Santa Claus, but of an attorney I had never heard of in San Rafael, a city across the San Francisco Bay in Marin County.

All I knew about San Rafael was that, in 1961, I'd purchased a brand new twenty-two unit apartment house in that beautiful suburb. This particular property was attractive in that it was being built under supervision of the Federal Housing Administration, inasmuch as the FHA was insuring a thirty-year, 5.25 percent mortgage for 80 percent of the cost of the project.

Sound like a good deal? Yes, it was a good investment; that's the only kind I make. (Stop laughing.) I felt reasonably secure, in this case, because the FHA, at least up to that time, had been a valuable partner in the field of residential real estate; and, in making certain that its insurance of the mortgage was economically sound, it effectively assured a purchaser of the property that the project was sound.

When the building was finished, all the apartments rented in short order. But, as the leases expired, a seemingly large proportion of tenants decided to move out. That, in turn, involved not only the cost of renovation, but also the loss of rent for a month or more.

The cause, we soon decided, was not dissatisfaction but competition—the fact that a family could "buy" a new house in a new subdivision with a small down payment (or sometimes with no down payment), while the monthly installment on the mortgage, in place of rent, built up the owner's equity.

Not necessarily a bad idea from the tenant's point of view, but a headache for me; the project thus began taking up too much of my time, diverting attention away from my main business of mortgage banking—so much so that early in 1972 I decided to give the property outright to my son Jack.

It was also at about this time that we in California were having increasing difficulty with my partners in New York. For the reasons I mentioned earlier, however, I had decided to live with the problem rather than try to cure it—out of fear that, although I might win the battle, I could lose the war, which would have left us all in the soup. On the other hand, son Jack was in a more flexible position: he was a bachelor (the result of a divorce), with a modest income, and, like the rest of us, he was disgusted with the attitude of the New York partners. Besides, he had leukemia, and he was in the mood to make the most out of life while it lasted. Consequently, he had, at age 44, begun to look for a way out.

"So," he said to me, "why don't I mark up the price of the San Rafael apartment house and put it on the market?"

"And then what?" said I.

"Then that added to what I've got, if I can get enough for it, should enable me to take my sixty-foot sail boat to the Caribbean and start a charter service, or do something else I enjoy so long as it has to do with sailing."

I was basically in sympathy with the idea, although it meant that I would no longer be able to turn over chores to him (such as the apartment project). So he marked up the price; and, within a week or so, he had an all-cash buyer.

A month or two later, having wound up his affairs, Jack took off. (He didn't sail his yacht from San Francisco; he sold it, bought another in Florida, and sailed the new yacht to Saint Thomas, the Virgin Islands.)

That was in 1972; the large envelope from the lawyer in San Rafael was delivered in mid-December 1985. I opened it. Instead of a holiday greeting it was *in re: P. v Bussing* (P. being the first letter of the name of the plaintiff). In the thirty pages of this document, I found that I was being sued for having failed to disclose a defect in the apartment complex that P. had bought from son Jack thirteen years before. The "defect" showed up in the 1984-85 rain season when several ground-floor apartments were damaged; the catch basin had overflowed again.

The argument or logic of the suit was that, when flooding occurred in 1969, I had decided I would not be able to sell the property for as much as I'd paid for it if the drainage problem became known; if I gave the property to my son, on the other hand, he would be under less obligation to disclose, because he was not the owner in 1969, and indeed, might even plead ignorance. But if, in spite of this, it were to come down to a lawsuit, the plaintiff wouldn't be able to recover as much from him as from me, because his net worth was much less.

In any case, whether Mr. P. sought out the lawyer or the lawyer saw a lawsuit in the making, I do not know. Nor did I have the slightest notion of avoiding liability when I turned the property over to my son: I sincerely believed the FHA's drainage system was adequate, that the cause of the flooding in 1969 was our negligence, and that, if the catch basin and duct were to be kept free of debris in the future, there would be no more flooding. I'd gifted the property to Jack because I'd found it too time consuming. Although I had had a resident manager, the drainage system had been neglected, which is the sort of thing that I, as the owner, should have discovered.

If ever there was a case of plausible circumstantial evidence, this was it. All I could do was to deny the motives that were attributed to me. The plaintiff said that it was in my interest to do what they accused me of doing, and that is why I "did" it. What is worse, most juries would probably agree.

After wading through the brief I called my son, who was now

in Los Angeles, only to find that he, too, had been served. Regardless of how high your IQ may be, you can't plead your case; the plaintiff's lawyer draws the complaint and you have to engage an attorney to present your defense. The result? For the next eighteen months my son and I had to go to Marin County and give depositions, answer interrogatories, assist our attorney in preparing briefs, and lie awake at night.

Finally a date for trial was set; but as is usually the case, a pretrial conference of the attorneys and their clients is held in the judge's chambers for the purpose of seeing if a compromise is possible. After reading a statement given to the judge by the plaintiff's attorney, the judge made an extremely significant remark. He said, "Doesn't a buyer have to do anything?"

When the plaintiff's attorney heard that, it was obvious to him that the judge might be more inclined to take my side than the buyer's, and he saw therefore the possibility of losing the case. The two attorneys and the judge then conferred briefly, following which the meeting was adjourned. The next day the case was dropped. Mr. P. was awarded nothing and we paid nothing, *except* legal fees. These were substantial, as you can imagine, considering the fact that the altercation went on for about eighteen months. I was reminded again of my fellowship with M. Voltaire who, two centuries ago, said, "I was never ruined but twice: once when I lost a lawsuit, and once when I won one."

Some time after this experience, the broker who had offered that investment brought me another—a humdinger, as he put it. (Don't I ever learn?) This was a downtown building occupied by a very aggressive chain of men's clothing stores; this particular branch was destined to become the flagship store in the Bay Area. The current owner was an insurance company, which should have raised the question in my mind as to whether they had acquired the building in a foreclosure, but I didn't ask the question.

The deal called for a cash down payment and a fifteen-year amortizing mortgage. I soon discovered, however, the underlying lease that was due to expire in five years. That didn't seem to be too important at the time, first, because this was the only branch the company had in that city (Oakland); second, because the location was prime; and third, because the Bay Area rapid transit system (BART) was under construction, and this location was where the east-west and north-south subway lines crossed; that location would therefore be accessible from any point in the entire metropolitan area, and would probably become one of its hottest spots.

So having gotten rid of the headache in San Rafael, I was able to sleep at night. I hadn't yet reached the stage where I would fall asleep in my chair in the daytime. So I was ready to take on a new project.

But my tranquility was transient. The first disturbing development was a noticeable drop in store sales; upon inquiry, I found that in order to build an underground transportation system, you have to provide an underground right of way. (Startling revelation.) So you have to dig up the street; and, while you're at it, you might as well dig up the sidewalk, too, because it will be necessary to do so sooner or later. But construction people are nothing if not thoughtful; they put huge, thick, planks of wood over the trench that was Broadway, where our store was, and similar boards where the sidewalk was, thus making it possible for vehicles to navigate the street (slowly) and people perilously to pick their way along the planks where the sidewalk used to be, sometimes even managing to avoid turning heir ankles.

The only trouble was if John Doe lost his shirt in the stock market, or in a partnership, he would buy another at one of our competitor's stores where the sidewalk had not become a hazard to life and limb. In fact, the whole downtown hub of the system was becoming a no-man's land; evening store hours were discontinued, and sales declined. But optimists and the Chamber of Commerce assured us that, when the job was finished, downtown Oakland would be the hot spot of the Bay area.

The fact is, the area did not recover and my tenant served notice that he would vacate the building upon the expiration of the lease. That left me with a mortgage that had about ten years to run, plus taxes and upkeep. I put it on the market; no takers. There was, however, one bright spot: the city had a large-scale redevelopment plan for the area close to our property, and all buildings in the area to be redeveloped were condemned. The owner of one such building offered a price for our place, and although it was not enough to bail me out, it was the only offer I had; he assumed the mortgage and I walked away from the deal, a little poorer than I had been when I went in. One of the lessons I learned from this "investment" is so obvious that you already know it: never assume a long-term liability, like a fifteen-year mortgage, against a five-year lease.

My A-1 tenant—the dominant men's clothing retailer in the Bay Area, I might add—went out of business not long after vacating my building.

While I'm at it, I might as well tell you another true story. My broker friend, who was dedicated to helping me make good investments, subsequently interested me in a restaurant-franchise deal. He told me that a restaurateur had bought a fast-food franchise from a national steak-house chain, and had selected a location on a major freeway leading into Sacramento. All that was needed now was someone to build the restaurant. Under the contract, the landlord would be paid a base rent and a percentage of the gross.

When the building was finished, however, neither the franchisor, whose office was in Los Angeles, nor the franchisee could be found. If the franchisee had actually paid for the franchise, he, too, was left holding his bag, wherever he was. So the whole deal fell apart, and I, as a landlord, was now left holding not only a brand-new bag, but also a brand-new (and very empty) restaurant.

I have no time to take care of a problem like this (which is supposed to be a "net, net" deal), so I engage a Sacramento realtor to find me a tenant capable of running a restaurant. He soon comes up with a prospect. A "prospect," in this business, is usually somebody who knows how to boil water and scramble eggs, has little capital or not much more than is necessary to stock his refrigerator and either will not sign a lease or, if he did, would render it value-less—but, who, nevertheless, wants to occupy the place on a trial basis. If you have a choice between a vacancy and a possibility, however, you might as well take the latter and hope for the best.

I found that although applicants usually had no cash, they often had creative ideas; one of them, for example, had hopes of developing a chain of restaurants whose specialty would be "Yogi Bear" hamburger sandwiches that would be promoted by a person dressed in a bear suit, who would cavort in front of the restaurant with a

"Yogi Bear" sandwich sign. Franchisees would pay for a franchise to sell Yogi Bear sandwiches if the promotion succeeded, he hoped. The only trouble was that Yogi Bera, the ex-baseball player, got a court order preventing the use of a name so close to his, thus ending a venture that could have become a nationwide success rivaling that of what is now known as the Big M!

At length, after two years of trial and error, a bona fide restaurateur came along and paid enough for the building, parking lot, and large refrigerator (which was fortunately too large to be stolen); as far as I know, he has made a success of it. Without the able assistance of Paul Johnson, the realtor in Sacramento, I might still be in the restaurant business.

My broker friend who helped get me into the three foregoing "investments" (headaches) also persuaded me to buy the three-family house in which I am living today. I paid approximately $60,000 for it in 1960. For a time I had the same problem with tenant turnover that I'd had with the San Rafael apartment house—i.e., new housing in the suburbs, at a cost of little or nothing down and with 5.25 percent long-term mortgage loans. However, about eight or nine years ago the tide turned, and an MAI appraisal a year ago put a market value of a million dollars on the place. So my broker friend, who'd helped get me into so much trouble, insisted, before he died, that on balance he was the best investment "advisor" I'd ever had.

Chapter 32
Religion, Revolution, God, and Government

We take the separation of church and state for granted in this country; and there are good reasons for thinking that will continue. But it is amazing to see how the tendency of religious and government leaders to join hands is spreading in other parts of the world. It is most noticeable in countries where Islam is the dominant religion. Muslims, moreover, constitute about a fifth of the world population, and their proportion is increasing due to their birthrate, which is comparatively higher than that among most other religious denominations. In Israel, likewise, religious dogma and political decisions are closely articulated. The two do not mix well, and are usually unintelligible to nonbelievers.

Uprisings in communities where dogmatic religions, such as Islam, are sanctioned if not actively promoted by governments, tend to be excessively bloody and brutal, because they are undertaken "in the name of the Lord." Suicide missions are passports to heaven. Nonbelievers are infidels; the more of us the apostles of the "true" faith wipe off the face of the earth, the better: the millennium will not be realized until all such "infidels" are dead.

It is difficult to understand how, in this day and age, such imperious theocratic notions can not only survive, but spread unless the educational system is stripped of catholicity and slanted in favor of intolerance, fanaticism, and bigotry.

Even if a government is not totally theocratic, the existence of an orthodox party, if large enough, can influence government policy. We see evidence of this in the Middle East, where claims to parts of what we used to call Palestine are based on a literal interpretation of a book of folklore.

Orthodox Islamic communities place the dictates of the Koran above civil laws and regulations, even if these are promulgated by otherwise duly constituted legislative bodies. Indeed, to a follower of Muhammad, the Koran is the basic law of the land, the constitution of the nation. For was the Koran not communicated to Muhammad by a holy spirit, sometimes called by the name Gabriel? (Possibly our old friend, who, you may recall, previously served five or six centuries before as the heavenly messenger boy who broke the incomprehensible news to that girl in Judea, to the effect that she was about to become the virgin mother of Jesus.) If so, Gabriel's continued existence and apparent health and vigor should have some impact on you infidels, you skeptics, and convince you that in heaven "everlasting" isn't hogwash. (And unfortunately the same may well be true of the afterlife in hell.)

The Roman Catholic church must, as much as any other orthodox religion, accept blame for using biblical imperatives to ignore the population problem and override the United Nations Population Fund forecast, which states that if family planning is discouraged or outlawed, the world's population will increase from about 5.3 billion today to 6.25 billion in less than ten years, and, by the end of the next century, to an incredible 11.3 billion—more than double our present number. These children of God will be here as a consequence of their "right to life," (which also carries with it the right to die of disease and starvation). Even in the developed countries a growing population lowers the standard of living for all, not merely for families that have outgrown their capacity to survive. Meanwhile, we in the United States currently either withhold funds for family-planning organizations, or give them grudgingly and sparingly, because such agencies, when requested, may give helpful advice to a woman who may want to terminate a pregnancy. This holier-than-thou attitude helps no one and does not save lives; overpopulation is the greatest murderer of all.

What is the lack of a comprehensive population policy doing to the livability of this planet? It is destroying it. We are running short of the necessities of life even for the present inhabitants. We know that rain forests, arable land, potable water, clean air, and numerous other amenities of living are becoming scarce relative to the growing demand; to say nothing of the waste products with which we are gradually becoming inundated. The trouble, fundamentally, is that the cornucopians have all gone fishing (in increasingly polluted streams, lakes and oceans), and have neglected to help rescue us from our developing degradation.

Although a deteriorating physical condition is one of the most obvious consequences of an inadequate diet, a more serious consequence is the effect on the brain. A nutritionally deprived person is a mentally underdeveloped person. As such, is he or she likely to be able to cast a ballot intelligently? Can a nation where there is a substantial degree of mental retardation depend on its citizens to participate constructively in a democratic form of government? Or will they become fair game for dictators, despots, racketeers, drug lords, religious fanatics, or others who see a chance to seize power? Will they be able to understand and operate complex machinery and technologically advanced devices and systems, some of which are in the military?

P.S. It is now 10:00 P.M. on October 13, 1992—two years to the day since I started this combination of recollections, reactions, and regrets. At the rate I'm going, I can't say how much longer it is going to take to unburden my mind of the additional material it has accumulated during the last ninety-four years, but I am hoping to finish before I become incompetent to hear or understand how my friends feel about it—that is, if they do me the favor of reading it. With that in mind, I think I'll go to bed.

Chapter 33
The Government Will Do It for Us

"That government is best that governs least." Those who believe this, as the twentieth century draws to a close, are in the minority—a small minority. Can they be right, and the rest of us wrong? It is perhaps the most important difference between the major political parties in the United States today. Those who want the government to do more are in constant conflict with those who think that we would all be better off if it did less.

Those who favor more and bigger government believe that if the economy were only managed by a government agency made up of unselfish, public-spirited citizens, then prices, production, interest rates, wages, hours, welfare of workers, and practically all economic activities could be regulated to produce a more just, ethical, prosperous, and smooth-running economic system, free from periods of depression and unemployment.

This assumption—that we could provide the necessities of life by means of a centralized management organization better than individuals who pursue their own selfish interests—probably developed long ago as people found that by organizing themselves into a cooperative unit (such as an army) they could better defend themselves than if each person fought as an individual. But there are so many differences between the military and the monetary that what may be true in one case will not hold water in the other.

This fact, however, has never prevented well-intentioned groups from attempting to organize utopian societies, the most recent having been somewhat incorrectly called Communism. The main difference between this experiment and many previous utopian efforts along the same lines is that when the earlier attempts failed, the groups died out peacefully and were laid to rest. But when the twentieth-century brand of utopianism began to fail, almost immediately after it was set up, it was converted to a police state, One may say, therefore, that the Communist ideal—"From each according to his ability, to each according to his need"—failed, quite like all similar previous attempts; but, unlike the others, the twentieth century method of dealing with its demise was violent and genocidal toward its opponents. Which should raise questions in our minds as to how these murderers could be so violent in their failure, and yet were supposedly unselfish and self-sacrificing in their original motive, namely, producing for the benefit of all regardless of the cost to themselves.

There are at least two reasons why these efforts to "reform" the economic system have run into so much difficulty: one is the inherited urge to keep what one produces as a means of self-preservation; the other is the multifaceted complexity of the economic system. It is all one person can do, in most cases, to keep track of a single market in which one operates; one's responses sometimes have to be spontaneous as well as instantaneous—reactions that are not characteristic of bureaucratic employees, agencies or congressional committees, irrespective of how idealistic or concerned with public welfare they might be. One need only reflect on the way the Federal Savings and Loan Insurance Corporation handled its job—at a net cost to customers of the institutions and American taxpayers of hundreds of billions of dollars. Frauds were literally being perpetrated under their very noses.

The public leans more heavily toward the government in periods of unemployment or inflation; government responses tend to be of the quick-fix variety that often makes matters worse in the long run. As a "cure" for unemployment, for example, one of the procedures is likely to be a jawboning effort to bring interest rates down so consumers will borrow more, spend it, and thereby stimulate production and employment. The stupidity of this approach is that one of the principal reasons for a depression and unemployment is that consumers are already in debt, which they are trying to liquidate by curtailing consumption. It was too much borrowing that overstimulated the economy and helped to bring on a depression in the first place; more borrowing only compounds the felony.

What is the answer? In a system of private enterprise, its shortcomings and irregularities are self-correcting—in time. If the price of a commodity rises, consumption declines and its price comes down. If interest rates rise, borrowing will decline and they will fall. It requires time, patience, and a rainy-day reserve in order to let the process of readjustment work itself out during the time required. But where is the money coming from for these reserves?

This question keeps cropping up, and my answer is always the same: our personal budgetary priorities are not properly or closely enough related to the exigencies that occur in a monetary-exchange economy. We do not live in subsistence homesteads: we don't produce anything we consume. We depend entirely on a flow of cash; we are dependents on the uninterrupted flow of commerce—a risk of no small proportion. We could weather economic storms with less mental turmoil if we consumed less (or did so with more foresight), and saved more.

During the Second World War, I recall advertisements in the *New York Times* that offered one or two acres of land in Connecticut to be used as subsistence homesteads after the war. The ads showed drawings of a house, a stable, vegetable gardens, a few chickens, possibly a goat or cow. The sales pitch was that if a family had a place of this sort, it would be less dependent on continuous, uninterrupted employment and monetary income. Children could do many of the chores, some of the family's basic needs could be met without money, and unemployment would be less traumatic.

Sounds like a mild reversion to the Middle Ages, but does that degrade it? It would not be necessary to include the Black Death. But subsistence homesteads would combine domestic and commercial employment, and would provide more security than most families have today. Needless to say, the idea is far too sensible to ever take hold, but it serves to illustrate a point.

So now we still are on the same road to more and bigger government, along with the inevitable swings in the economy this course ensures. One thing we *have* learned, however, is that this bumpy road is not a FREEway.

Chapter 34
Horror in the Hospital

While writing the foregoing monologue in December 1991 on the economic disease of depressions, I began to feel some of the symptoms of human disorder myself, and by the twenty-first of the month I was abed with a cough and fever. This caused some anxiety on the part of my daughter-in-law and my wife's nurse, as a result of which they conferred with our internist (who makes no house calls). He advised that, in view of my age, I be taken to the hospital. Almost before you could say Jack Rosenzweig, a 911 ambulance and two paramedics arrived and saw to it that, according to doctor's orders, I was so delivered. Very soon the household's fears were confirmed: the diagnosis, pneumonia. Following this I was wheeled into a two-patient room. The other patient was not there at the time (and, as matters turned out, I would have been better off if he had never been returned).

When he was wheeled in he was quiet for a brief period, but he soon began to behave quite unlike patients in this sort of hospital; the rest of us were lying there, giving the various manufactured medications time to combine with our innate biochemical secretions and hopefully restore us to health. But he, evidently, was in perfectly good health, at least from the neck up; or looking at it from another angle, whatever his ailment was, it had not in the slightest diminished the vitality or capacity of his vocal cords.

Although I could not understand the language, he immediately began shouting; it was obvious that his lungs were in better shape than mine. I was able to identify a word now and then, which gave me the impression that he was in a heated argument with or against either Yeltsin, Gorbachev, or both; at least, he certainly was not trying to mediate the ideological differences that separated the two men; if anything, he was making them worse, judging from the rising crescendo of his recriminations, recommendations, or whatever they were, in the volume of a Bolshevik bravado, minus the finesse of a basso profundo, late of the Bolshoi.

At about daybreak he turned day into night and enabled the rest of us to get a little rest between occasional interruptions, not by a rebellious Russian, but by conscientious servants to the sick. By nightfall, however, he was full of energy again and ready to continue where he'd left off the night before; except that this time, his altercation was with Sascha.

If Boris was in Moscow and Gorby relaxing in his dacha outside Moscow the night before, then Sascha must have been in Siberia, and worse still, at the bottom of a coal or gold mine, judging from the decible count, which was louder the second night than it had been the night before, if that is possible—or so it seemed.

I know a few Russian words, but they are useful only in communicating with sane people on suitable subjects; I was therefore unable to relate to him verbally, and I was additionally handicapped by my current infirmity: fever and forcefulness don't go together. However, if I could have infected his vocal cords with the same virus that was affecting mine, I might have overcome him—peacefully. But I'm about as inept at getting rid of a virus in that way as I am at overcoming it without the assistance of two doctors, half a dozen nurses, several hundred dollars worth of pills, and ten days of treatment.

Evidently there is nothing in the nurses' rule book under the heading of raucous Russians and What to Do with Them or, for that matter, paranoid patients who wear down the patience of roommates and others and nullify the effect of sleeping pills. So finding that restlessness is not conducive to recovery, I decided to ask a nurse on the 6:00 A.M. shift if I might be moved to a room in which the occupant was less involved with high-ranking people in foreign countries or at least, with officials in a foreign country with which it was possible to communicate by phone, fax, or cable. Instead, she came back a few minutes later and said they would move the relentless Russian to another room and shut his door, since they couldn't shut his mouth. Good.

Shortly thereafter they rolled a new patient into my room. He turned out to be a ninety-three-year-old codger like me. After they got him into bed (he doesn't seem to be ambulatory), one nurse after another came in; then doctors came in. I heard them tell him it was a simple operation and that, like the characters in one of Gilbert and Sullivan's operettas, "They never will be missed." Although I was too tired to pay close attention, I was nevertheless too curious to ignore the proceedings. (*That must have been a surgeon who told the old man that "they never will be missed,"* I thought to myself; obviously, eyes, ears, hands, and lungs certainly "would be missed." So what were these bozos talking about? What else in the human body comes in pairs?)

Soon a crew of nurses came in and lifted the old man onto a mobile stretcher and took him to an elevator. At about the same time, one of the friendly nurses came to me and suggested that it would be a good idea if I had a shower, to which I agreed.

In the shower room I begin asking the nurse questions about what they were planning to do to the old gent that would involve removing parts of his anatomy that "never will be missed." She confided that they were going to castrate him.

"Oh," said I. "Is that to emasculate him so that he'll not have a loud voice, like that of the rapacious Russian?"

"No," said she. "It's merely a coincidence. He has cancer of the testicles."

"Remarkable coincidence," say I. "Why not do the same thing to the rattled, ravenous Russian?" (Logical question, but less inappropriate in a shower room, especially in today's world, where nothing is left to the imagination.)

Apparently trying to dodge the question, she said, "People don't age at one rate; some are old at seventy, while others don't become senile until their middle or late nineties. So when you get over your pneumonia you can tell anyone who asks that you don't have any parts that can be removed without being missed." (I felt flattered; wouldn't you, if you were a male?)

A few years ago I would have hesitated to mention this incident; but now, when "how-to" courses in sex, including paraphernalia, are offered (when necessary) to kindergarten children, there are no longer any inhibitions. If you don't fully understand what I am trying to explain, your grandchildren will be glad to help you.

I wonder how they handle sex education in parochial schools

today. In the first place, sex in any of its interesting aspects is sinful; at least when I was a youngster it was for all of us, clergy especially. More recently, however, a bishop, now and then, and lower ranking male members of the clergy have been known to have engaged in a little hanky-panky with members of the opposite sex (and maybe with each other) from time to time, much as they did in the Middle Ages. In the second place, how can nuns teach girl pupils about sex unless God forbid, they learned about it before taking the vow of chastity (poor things). How much longer this denial of sex as a way of earning eternal future benefits will continue, where it does, is a question. Like many other religious relics, the spiritual value of asceticism is being questioned by even the most dedicated believers in other details of the dogma. Something will have to give, but it will probably not happen officially until the present pope takes up residence in heaven, where, unlike the others up there, he will feel insufferable pain as he witnesses our continued relaxation of sexual inhibitions here on earth.

After ten days in the hospital (and an unbelievably large bill) I was able to come home. A few days later I was awakened by a loud outcry from my wife shortly after midnight. When I turned on the light I found her half conscious at the foot of the bed, her head in a pool of blood. Two granddaughters upstairs heard the commotion and came rushing down. One of them dialed 911, and soon madame was on a stretcher in an ambulance headed for the same emergency room I had entered a couple of weeks before.

She must have fainted or become disoriented and, in falling, struck the metal frame of the bed, which caused a concussion and a gash in the forehead, whence came the blood. After three days, however, she, amazingly, was back home, quite oblivious of where she had been—forgetfulness being one of the symptoms of Alzheimer's. In her ninety-third year she is half deaf, half blind, and half here, but not in need of skilled nursing care. She sleeps in her chair, eats without assistance, and soils her diaper—unless she took it off unbeknownst to her nurse or the rest of us, in which case the episode takes on much larger and more laborious implications, especially if the trouble includes the bowel in addition to the bladder. Although we have lived in this house thirty-three years, she tells me from time to time that she doesn't like it here and wants to "go back" to San Francisco.

I have digressed on the rather irrelevant subject of senile dementia because, like our national debt which continues to get bigger, the same thing is true of the relative number of partially or totally dependent so-called senior citizens; they are going to become one of our greatest social and economic problems in the next century due in part to the unavoidable demographic imbalance that is developing our society.

Here's the evidence: in 1945 there were approximately forty-two wage earners to bear the burden of caring for the aged, infirm, and dependent citizens to whatever extent they were unable, financially or physically or both, to take full care of themselves; in 1980 there were eight of these younger members of society to do this; last year there were three; and by the end of this century it is anticipated that there will be only one producer for one retiree. (What it will be in the twenty-first century I leave to your imagination.) This is a reflection of the demographic imbalance in the American population.

Concomitant with this demographic dilemma, one of the resources that used to be available to care for grandparents and other oldsters, namely the family, is disintegrating. Gone are the days when a husband and wife kept house and when the children became old enough to go to work, get married, or flee the coop, the space they vacated could be made available for Grandpa and Grandma as the wife continued to "keep house." She made jelly, cooked, did laundering, a little mending—in short, there used to be more relatively less expensive ways to take care at least some of so-called senior citizens than there are today. Today either a couple doesn't marry or if they do they can't conceive of its lasting sixty-nine years (as the one I am talking about has). More frequently it is thought of as a trial balloon rather than a total commitment or else there is no marriage at all—only a congenial liaison, which can be as easily ended as entered. In such situations both parties tend to employ themselves or be employed outside the home; and if there is a child or two, nursery schools and day-care centers fill the need. In short, homesteads where elders can be cared for by relatives are becoming fewer relative to the need as the need becomes greater due to the adverse trend in the demographic structure of the population. The end result is that there not only will be fewer youngsters to take care of more oldsters, but also less expensive family care will be replaced by more expensive professional care.

Getting back to the Alzheimer matter that started this digression, I should like to add that as an amateur diagnostician and pseudopsychologist, I have come to think that somewhat in the way that ontogeny recapitulates phylogeny in the biological world, an Alzheimer patient replicates his innate, inborn childhood behavior in his senile-demented, Alzheimer state because whatever inhibitions and self-control he may have adopted during his adult life become inoperative in his senilely demented state.

In my wife's case, for example, which is the only evidence I can point to, I think I see the same kind of attitude or behavior in her today that drove her parents and a psychiatrist up the wall when she was a teenager. During her adult life she managed to keep most of it under control most of the time; but now she acts like her original, adolescent self, verbally lambasting her nurse and anyone else who encounters her displeasure.

One swallow may not signal summer and one patient's behavior is not enough to justify a theory, but it would be interesting to know if other caretakers suspect a correlation between senile behavior and youthful deportment, since in both periods the individual does not suppress his inclinations. (I'm not sure what good will come of it if we find a correlation, but the psychological fraternity may derive a constructive conclusion of some sort and my curiosity will be alleviated, if that is worth anything.)

Chapter 35
Tapping the Till

One afternoon about four o'clock, I was in our Beverly Hills office talking to Roger (who was, incidentally, having nighttime convulsions at that time that were diagnosed as a reaction to the stress of dealing with the clowns [my partners] in New York, who continued to misunderstand the problems of servicing mortgages in California). While we were planning the next day's work, a telephone call came for me from the secretary to the manager of our San Francisco office.

She was disturbed, almost to the point of having the same kind of mental upset that afternoon that Roger was having at night. Between sobs, she asked me if I could possibly arrange to be in San Francisco when the office opened the next morning. I said I could, and would, but could she give me some idea of what the urgency was. This brought on more distress and an apparent inability to clarify the situation over the telephone.

I therefore suggested that she try to compose herself, leave the matter to me, and that I would be there when the office opened in the morning.

"In all probability," I said to Roger, "the problem has to do with internal operations; therefore you had better come along with me." I then took off for the airport, he went home to pick up his overnight bag, and the next morning at 9:00 A.M. we entered our office at 605 Market Street. (Note that our offices in California opened at 9 A.M. That is because the New York office opened at that hour; most offices in California start the day at 8:00 A.M. and close at 5:00 P.M., but we closed at 4:30 P.M.—minor indications of how our New York office failed to understand the way business is done in California.)

As we entered it was obvious that during the night the girls had not regained their composure; instead, at our appearance the one who'd called the day before became hysterical while the others were only marginally less so. The additional reason for this nervousness I later learned was that the hysterical one, who had never seen Roger Norton before, feared he might be a plainclothes detective looking for her because, as she had realized, she was involved in the problem, although innocently, and could be subject to arrest.

I introduced Roger, relieved the tension, and asked for an explanation of the problem. The secretary did most of the talking, because she was in the middle of the muddle. With fear and trembling, she told us that some Asians (who either distrusted banks or were insufficiently sophisticated to have checking accounts, but who evidently trusted us) paid their monthly mortgage installments in cash. Instead of the manager's depositing the funds immediately, however, she said he would sometimes pocket them, go over to Golden Gate Fields Race Track, across the bay, and bet on the horses.

He felt that he had a good chance to pick the winners, because he would be able to leave the office at 1:00 P.M. since the New York office was now closing at 4:00 P.M., get to the track early, examine the entries, and make intelligent choices.

The only trouble, she said, was that too many of his "winners" turned out to be "also rans," and some of the poor Asians's accounts were now as much as ninety days in arrears (which meant that notices of intention to foreclose would have to be filed by the following Wednesday). Imagine the consternation that would overtake a conscientious, partially illiterate mortgagor when an interpreter told him that he was in immediate danger of losing his house because of nonpayment of the monthly mortgage installments!

The outlook was almost as traumatic for our manipulating manager as it was, potentially, for the homeowners. Consequently, the secretary told us that McDonald (I think that was his name), realizing that draconian measures would have to be taken immediately, had decided to abandon race horses and try Reno. He would spend most of Thursday night at the gaming tables and would call the office Friday morning to tell his secretary how he'd made out. If he found that the odds in Reno were no better than those at the racetrack, he would decide what to do next and tell her.

Shortly after nine o'clock, our trusted employee called. His secretary took the call and signaled to Roger and me; we picked up two phones and listened. He told her that, although he'd stayed up until daybreak and had used all the money he could spare, dame luck had deserted him. There was now only one thing left to do: he would make a mad dash to Long Island, New York, and importune his parents to pull him out of the hole. He would have to accomplish this in time to put the amount of the purloined proceeds into the mortgagors' accounts before next Wednesday (it was now Friday morning). Otherwise, notices of intention to foreclose would automatically be spat out by the computer, New York would become aware of them, and the correspondent bank, which owned the loans, would have to be notified. They, in turn would require an explanation of the circumstances surrounding the "default" and what we were doing to cure it.

It was now Friday afternoon in New York and a practical certainty that my partner Smith, along with one or more of the others in authority, were not only out to lunch but, were probably having what President Carter referred to as a two-hour, three-martini (and, I might add, tax-deductible) lunch. I therefore could not reach them immediately after the Reno call. But since I had decided that the matter made it necessary for me to go back to New York without delay (I had not at this time moved to California), I headed for the airport and called them from there.

After briefing them, I asked that Smith and our operations officer meet me the next morning (Saturday) at my apartment in New York; I also said I thought the boy's father should be notified that at that moment his son was probably breaking the speed limit in an effort to arrive at the earliest possible moment at his father's house—alive and in one piece, or otherwise.

A person more deft at defalcation would have found a way to make such a round trip to New York by air; but McDonald didn't have the money or a credit card but he did have one of the company cars and a credit card good at gasoline filling stations. So he had to take the chance of covering the distance, something like 2,500 miles, in about 72 hours of elapsed time. If he preferred not to sleep while driving he might have snatched a few hours at refueling stops; but he had to average better than thirty-five miles per hour, allowing for pit stops, tie-ups, and occasional city traffic; "snacking" could take the place of eating. It sounds incredible; it also suggests that he may have missed his calling as he was obviously more adept at auto racing than horse racing, for he did, indeed, arrive alive at his father's house some time Monday morning.

So also did a representative of the surety company that bonded all of our employees, who placed the young man under house arrest, forced him to sign a confession backed up by his finger prints, and demanded that the father provide the amount of cash necessary to cover the defalcation. This formality blacklisted the boy, so that no bond would ever again be given in his favor by that or any other surety company.

Although our company was made whole, our troubles were far from over: under all servicing contracts the servicer is required to make full disclosure of any irregularity, discrepancy, or malfeasance of this nature. And if the correspondent (investor) considered the circumstance serious enough, he could terminate their servicing agreement and withdraw the mortgages being serviced without paying a red cent—which is the equivalent, in a physiological sense of withdrawing red blood: withdraw some and you become anemic; enough, and you die.

We were especially vulnerable to criticism and a vote of no confidence, inasmuch as this episode occurred not too long after Connie's death. It might easily have been assumed, therefore, that the two successors, Smith and Bussing, didn't have the necessary experience, knowledge, or capability to run a mortgage banking business. We were in a delicate situation.

I managed to put the burden of disclosing the incident to our investors upon Smith, inasmuch as admitting this potential thief into our fiduciary organization had been his contribution to the company. Fortunately, none of our investors took advantage of their privilege. Good. Smitty must have written a good letter before one of his three-martini lunches.

But now we had a vacancy in the San Francisco office and we had better put the right person in charge, because a second boo-boo would be inexcusable. The trouble was that the two men in the New York office, who knew enough about internal operations to handle the detail, were reluctant to make the move for various reasons. We had capable women, but in 1955 they had not been sufficiently emancipated to be considered for a managerial job, one that only a man would be "qualified" to fill.

We had one young man who did not own a house, did not have children in school (inasmuch as six-month-old children usually aren't), and who did not think that, beyond Hoboken, there was little else other than wilderness and Indians; most of all, he had the viewpoint of entrepreneurial big shots—as distinct from the bookkeeping mentality of the other two boys in the New York office.

But he had two strikes against him: one, he was not a detail man (and if your mind is not interested in detail, you're not going to be happy in a servicing job); and two, he had been in the office less than a year after returning from military duty in Korea. Many people would say that is too short a period in which to learn the ins and outs of mortgage banking.

So we were faced with a dilemma: either take chances on an inside man who lacked experience or go outside, as we had with McDonald, and run risks of another kind. In the end we chose the former lieutenant from Korea, John Bussing.

He immediately ran into trouble for two reasons: first, he was interested in people, not papers yet mortgage servicing requires paperwork ad infinitum; and second, Bussing, like his father, was interested in the larger outlook for the company—making acquaintance with builders, mortgage officers of banks and loan associations, and mortgage brokers. This brought him into conflict with the New York members of our organization, who preferred to think small, take no business risks, sit at a desk and use the telephone, and go home at 4:00 P.M., only two or three hours after finishing their two-or-three-martini luncheon at the Commodore, across Forty-second Street.

Differences of opinion do not necessarily lead to serious consequences, so long as they do not radically affect the bottom line; but differences in dollars in a monthly report to an investor can be quite embarrassing, especially if the investor discovers it first. Something of this sort, like a defalcation, can undermine investor confidence in the qualifications of the servicer. For bear in mind that the investor has little people working for him, too, who are paid to pore over papers (servicing agents' monthly reports) and reconcile them (to the penny) with the investor's controls.

Son Jack didn't run into accounting problems, partly because Gladys (otherwise referred to by employees on her level as "Glad Ass") Morgan, who had been in our accounting department in New York for a few years, was transferred to the San Francisco office at this time. Incidentally, I might add as an aside that she and her retired husband decided to buy a new car and drive to San Francisco instead of flying. A few weeks after her arrival, she received a friendly "welcome" letter from the state of California informing her that she owed a sales tax on her new car. "How could that be?" she asked, as the car had been bought in New York.

She was told that since New York did not have a sales tax, she is assumed to have bought the car there instead of in California, thus avoiding the California tax. "Not true; never heard of such a thing," said she as she explained the circumstances to the state. Wanna know who won the battle, or do you know that the law is so rigid the car could have been impounded if the tax was not paid? This left a bad impression on Gladdy until she found how easy and enjoyable it is to drive up to Reno Friday evening and spend the weekend at the fabulous hotels and gambling casinos. She soon was willing to forget the whole thing (and take a deduction on her 1040?).

Getting back where we left off, son Jack, with the help of Gladys, didn't run into accounting problems; but he did have trouble with the management in New York, as might have been expected, primarily because his mind was more on external production than internal procedure, more on making new acquaintances than sitting at a desk and poring over pages of numbers.

But that is not what he was sent to California to do, and he soon found it out. The first disheartening disagreement occurred when he learned through circulating outside the office and making contacts, that a certain savings and loan was about to offer several million dollars of FHA loans for sale, servicing released. To a person in the mortgage banking business at that time such an event was the equivalent of what the pigeons at the church called manna from heaven.

Competition among buyers, therefore, was as keen as that among wholesale bread bakers in New York, referred to in an earlier chapter. Heaven only knows what kind of hanky-panky offers were being made under cover or behind closed doors by our competitors for all or a sizable slug of these most attractive, seasoned assets.

Moreover, our competitors generally were principals; they could write a check on the spot. Their word was their bond. They didn't have to call up a partner in New York, a bookkeeper mind, and ask for permission to talk to the seller for fear that to do so might be interpreted as a commitment or an obligation. In short, we were at a distinct disadvantage when it came to every aspect of the business except accounting; and when one of our employees could pocket trust funds and bet them on race horses or risk them in Reno, one might ask in all fairness whether we actually were as well-qualified even in the servicing and accounting end of the business as we liked to say we were.

In spite of these handicaps, however, this young fellow, who was supposed to keep his mind on the books and not on the balance sheet, actually managed to get a written offer from the S & L that was offering this large block of loans. How he did it, without being able to put up a deposit or having authority to sign a commitment I do not know. But we got a substantial volume of seasoned mortgages in this deal, for which we had a ready market. Thus a very profitable transaction was completed.

Unfortunately, it's difficult to supervise office detail and circulate among builders, brokers, and banks at the same time; consequently, while this deal was pending over a period of two weeks or so, there was an accounting slip-up in the office, not too serious, one of the nickel-and-dime variety but nevertheless the sort of thing that shouldn't happen. So what was the reaction? The New York office had a conniption fit over it. No compliments or commendation was ever offered for the achievement of garnering a big block of saleable seasoned assets but plenty of carping criticism of the clerical error.

This was the first of a series of disappointments that went on for seventeen years, during which time Jack acquired an ulcer while Roger, in the Beverly Hills office, was having nightmares for different but equally frustrating reasons.

Finally, saying that his tour of duty in Korea, harrowing as it was, was not much worse than trying to work with the clowns in the New York office, he said good-bye to all of us in June 1972, sold his sixty-foot yacht, as noted above, went to Florida, bought another sixty-footer, and set sail for the Caribbean. To make a long story short, the two big shots in New York died, which left Roger, Bill, his number-two man, and me. I soon began to taper off, and that left Roger and Bill in Los Angeles to carry the burden of running the company. As a major stockholder I decided to sell my stock to the company, and the other stock-holders followed suit.

The critical question is, How are these two men making out now that they are free to run the business without interference? In one word, magnificently. Assets and earnings are higher than ever before. Men who at one time were competitors are now working with us, some of them for us, as a result of fundamental changes in the business that have taken place in recent years to which our two young men have been able to adjust.

Likewise, if you think that I degraded my associates in defense of my son, here, in brief, is the later story about him. He landed in Saint Thomas in the Caribbean after taking off from Lauderdale. (I think he had visions of continuing on to the Mediterranean, but the passage to Saint Thomas was so rough that he must have had second thoughts about that idea.)

What next? How it happened I am not clear; but the fact is that he suddenly became assistant manager and mortgage officer of the Bank of America in Saint Thomas. This was a 180-degree reversal; instead of trying to beg, borrow, or buy mortgages in California, where he was at a distinct disadvantage in an extremely competitive business—a David against Goliaths—he was now under no pressure. His price was fixed by the head office, the buyer would have to agree to it if he wanted to do business, and that was all there was to it. He was now Goliath, and this one could not be felled by a sling shot.

How he went from being a bank officer to financial vice president of one of the largest real estate development projects in the Caribbean on the island of Saint Thomas (which almost went belly-up when interest rates soared in the early 1980s) and how he next landed on his feet as president of a mortgage-banking company in Los Angeles, has been covered in an earlier chapter.

A couple of years after he made this connection, the company merged with an eastern building organization and he would have had to go east or opt out. He chose the latter, primarily, I think,

because his leukemia condition was worsening and also because
there was enough income in the family to keep the wolf from the
door.

So one might say that he had a less than agreeable experience
in his first job, a satisfying one with the B of A, a disappointment
with the real-estate venture in Saint Thomas, and a lack of interest
in continuing with the Los Angeles company after its merger.

A year or two after becoming a man of leisure he decided that
he and his wife should go to France, his favorite vacation spot. While
there he became inexplicably ill, the symptoms being loss of appetite,
fever, and weakness. Suspecting leukemia to be the cause, they
returned to San Francisco (not Palm Springs, because it was summer). The doctors here were baffled also but treated him as hematologists generally treat patients with a blood disorder. Practically
every diagnostic device in the hospital was used; nothing cured the
mysterious condition.

Finally, one of the hematologists decided to take a long shot—to
call in an MD, whose specialty was the digestive system. He didn't
spend much time reviewing all the procedures that had been tried
during the preceding three weeks but sat down beside the bed and
began asking questions. What had Jack been doing in Paris before
he began to feel debilitated and unable to partake of the gourmet
food for which the city is famous?

Among other things, Jack told him about a dinner they had had
on the left bank in which he'd had steak tartare (which, if your
memory fails you, is seasoned raw beef). When the doctor heard this,
he disappeared in a hurry and reappeared likewise. "You have
toxoplasmosis, my friend. The raw beef you ate was mildly contaminated. The microbes in the meat are multiplying in your body and
practically eating you alive."

The hematologists became as red in the face as the meat, but
they wouldn't admit their oversight. A simple medication was prescribed, so ordinary that it was available over the counter. A long but
successful period of rehabilitation followed.

Several months later Jack was attending a get-together of Connecticut Wesleyan University alumni, when a man came up to him
and said he was glad to see him on his feet rather than in a hospital
bed. Jack responded, with his usual sense of humor that, while many

people had visited him, he'd been so sedated that he didn't always recognize them and, if he did, he soon forgot them—and thanked the gentleman.

"Oh, mine was not a call of kindness," the man said. "I am the one who told you that you were being eaten alive by some French microbes."

Jack was overwhelmed with a mixture of gratitude, embarrassment, and humility. After reviewing in laymens' language the etiology and prognosis of the case, the two reminisced about their respective lives at Wesleyan, from which the doctor had graduated four years after his patient.

While on the subject of my son, I might as well finish it. One of the effects of leukemia is an enlargement of the spleen, a somewhat mysterious organ in the human body, which presumably becomes larger in leukemia patients because it has more work to do. Some doctors advocate removing it in extreme cases and providing medication as a substitute. Jack was considering having his spleen removed but was putting it off, preferring to delay another hospital visit as long as possible, if not altogether.

On May 11, 1991, he was carrying a box of something or other from his car to a trash bin when he missed his step at a sidewalk curb and fell, presumably on the box. An ambulance was called and, although the cause of his discomfort and other symptoms was not immediately determined, he gradually lost consciousness on the way to the hospital. An autopsy disclosed that the enlarged spleen had burst and he had bled to death internally, at age sixty-two.

Chapter 36
Commotion in the Cathedral

If you have read some of the earlier chapters you don't have to be told that in my married life, if I went to church it was to fulfill an obligation to my wife, rather than for other reasons.

On one such occasion recently it was not the statues of emaciated saints (who probably got that way from fasting as penance for their sins) that attracted my attention, but the two rows of pews closest to the sanctuary that were occupied by a group of well-dressed adults and two infants in the arms of two women.

Rather stupid, I thought to myself, for people to take infants to church; the brats won't understand what's going on (any better than some adults will); and to prove it they'll probably start kicking and yelling, especially when the congregation is supposed to get a message from the officiants. On the other hand, that might not make any difference, because it will probably be a repetition of what the faithful have heard many times before; but that, apparently, is not the way the faithful see it: they don't object to going over the same ground Sunday after Sunday.

Sure enough, no sooner had the ritual begun than the little darlings began to compete with it. One of them could have been fathered by Pavarotti, at least as far as his volume was concerned. But suddenly, fortissimo faded into pianissimo and then into fine; this occurred when a male member of the group, presumably the father, handed the little one to its mother for the purpose of fulfilling a need for which the father (either due to a flaw in male physiology or as a form of sex discrimination) was ill-equipped.

Thus, the mother was able to capitalize on the fact that the child's noise-making organ is also used in feeding himself and can't be used for both purposes at the same time. Smart woman (or stupid creator). The fact that breakfast, lunch, and dinner all taste the same from her delectable pacifier seems to be quite acceptable to her offspring.

The mother of the other child evidently had some sort of problem with her fast-food facility, because I noted that she tried to stick one of those nonparental pacifiers into the kid's mouth. But the latter by his gestures said, in effect, "To hell with that tasteless, synthetic substitute for something edible. Either give me a decent snack, like the one that other kid is getting, or take me out of here."

At this point a clandestine conference took place in which the less productive mother apparently persuaded the child's (presumptively) legitimate father to take the child out. (Which did not impose a hardship on him, I learned later, because he was a lukewarm believer and a reluctant member of the party, preferring golf to the gospel any day of the week.) However, he brought the kid back a few minutes later, having been as successful in quieting this little involuntary convert as the mother of the other one had been with her luscious physiological-anatomical feature. How the father managed it I did not find out.

At this point in the service the preacher felt called upon to compete with the two little ones. As the scene shifted from the altar to the pulpit, the kid who'd managed to squeeze a second breakfast out of its mother had decided to take a siesta; while the other one, who had had nothing but an empty synthetic substitute for a more succulent snack still had adequate energy to meet the preacher at least half way, drowning him out and deprecating the doctrine at the top of his two-month-old voice. The preacher, however, was not perturbed: he said he would rather deal with a doubter than with a dozer, of whom there were a number in the congregation (who probably were in their second childhood, so to speak). They were among the doubters, also, but probably too valuable as contributors to be ushered out.

As a matter of fact, the preacher showed that he really was a Christian: in spite of the irreverent interruptions, he said that he welcomed the cheerless little cherubs and would admit them to the family of Christians through the sacrament of *baptism*, here, this very morning. So I relaxed and decided once more to listen to the propaganda from the pulpit. If the preacher could carry on his dialectical dialogue in spite of the disturbance, I ought to be able at least to decipher enough of the dogma to know what I was missing—or rejecting.

Indeed, I think I understood most of the ideology that was being offered. The biblical reference that was intended to blend with baptism was taken from Matthew, the parable about the mustard seed—which, according to biblical botany, is one of the smallest seeds, despite which it grows to become one of the greatest trees. My mind may have been on golf rather than gospel, or profit rather than parable, however, for I failed to grasp the connection between big trees and little babies.

I can't say how other members of the congregation (those who were awake) reacted to the underlying subject of multiplication, both human and horticultural, which was implicit in the sermon; but, to an economist first, a monetarist second, and a Malthusian third, it seemed to me that it would have been at least as prudent as anointing the heads of the two little involuntary candidates for membership in the community of Christians with (polluted) water, whether holy or mundane, to open savings accounts for them and let the multiplier effect turn $100 into $200 in twenty years at 4 percent compound interest. That probably would do more for them in this life than holy water on their heads would do for them in their afterlife; especially since the church no longer holds that compound interest is usurious.

This could also inure to the benefit of the religious establishment, i.e., if the little cherubs, later in life, could be persuaded to part with some of their compound interest in exchange for such spiritual support and supplication as this religious organization would allegedly provide for the benefit of its faithful and especially its contributing members.

The problem, however, was to get on with the business at hand. The infants, the priest admitted, were not there to hear the sermon or sing the hymns (although they did their damndest to chime in from time to time), but rather to benefit from the sacrament of baptism. Whereupon he descended from the pulpit and beckoned the mothers, the two (presumptive) fathers, the two stand-ins who had agreed to be Godparents (so called), and a few others, who apparently also had more than a casual interest, to gather around the baptismal font. The mothers, either for reasons of modesty or otherwise, did not make their physiological facilities available to the little ones, so they continued to squawk, squirm, and serenade as they approached the font, which was just inside the narthex.

This led me to think that something other than candles, clerics, and cassocks must be bothering the little sweethearts. Could they be suffering from some kind of hereditary mental mutation? Hardly, I thought to myself: far from being able to think in psychoanalytic terms, about all they'd been able to do in their lives so far was suck, sleep, and soil.

Soon I began to get the point. When the parson proceeded with the baptism, he said that these innocent little kids were suffering the contamination of *original sin*, and he was going to get it out of their systems. He then did so by pouring a little water on their heads. That caused them to hoot and holler louder; a member of the congregation standing beside me told me that this was an outburst of anger (not hunger) at the fact that they were guilty of sin even before they were old enough to commit one, much less enjoy it. They didn't know when, where, or how it had happened; whether to blame their father, their mother, or a disembodied spirit which might have gotten into their mother's body when their father did.

Not until they were old enough to read about the shacking up of Adam and Eve would they get an explanation—provided, in the meantime, that it had not been expurgated from later editions of the best-selling fiction ever written, or thrown out by an ecclesiastical court for lack of evidence. Snakes should never have been considered credible witnesses.

Then came the ceremonial centerpiece, the portentous punchline: as he was wetting the heads of the little ones while they wet other things, he explained that not only were they being cleansed of the sin they had not committed, but they were also being *born again*. When the little ones heard that, their personal pandemonium broke loose: their screeching became loud enough and the waves of sound strong enough to cause, what I, at least, thought were the bells in the belfry directly above us to toll, though ever so lightly as they tend to do when a moderate earthquake reminds us that nothing is sacred. Not until then did I know why so many of the leaded glass windows of the cathedral were cracked. In addition to the stress of earth tremors, they have been subject to periodic assaults of the kind we were experiencing this morning.

To the faithful, this behavior of the babes seemed ungrateful. Consequently, after the service (or disservice) I asked one of the mothers if she could explain why the brats had been so agitated when the parson was, in fact, doing them a favor. Her answer was that her child had been that way from the moment he was born; he had been just as bad after breast-feeding as he'd been after a bottle. As a consequence, she said she had considered consulting a psychiatrist. But her husband said that would probably be a waste of money, because psychiatrists deal with *subsequent sin*, not original sin. However, this not being the first time she did something behind his back, she'd gone to see Dr. Goldstein, a reputable psychiatrist.

Sure enough, he'd had the answer, although he couldn't throw any light on original sin, his specialty being the real thing—the kind of sin we all like to commit (partly because we are enjoined from doing so by the same parson who worked on the innocent-but-guilty infants in the service). "The reason babies raise such a fuss after birth," the doctor said, "is that they would rather be in the womb than in the world. They feel that somebody has played a dirty trick on them, since in the womb there was total equanimity—no noise, no pollution, no parson, no diapers, no formulas, no rules, no regulations, no inhibitions, nothing but peace, serenity, comfort and complacency."

"Being born once," he added, "was enough to arouse the child's ire and resentment; but when the child heard it was going to be born again, that was too much. That added insult to injury. *That's* why it hollered so loudly that the bell tolled—it tolled for him. To your child, the baptism wasn't a sacrament; it was a sacrifice, in which he was the paschal lamb."

I don't know how the mother felt, but to me this was the only explanation that held water (whether holy, purified, or polluted). After the service we all went our separate ways, some feeling they had done their duty, while others had lingering doubts as to whether the doctrinal diagnosis was right, and, if so, whether the treatment would be effective. For my part, I sidled up to the two mothers and voiced the opinion that the children would be free of sin for only about thirteen years. By that time they would probably be involved with their high school playmates in restoring modern versions of it, and they would not need the inducements of a snake, or of anyone or anything else. (I got no thanks for this fornicating forecast.)

Chapter 37
Hobbies, Health, and Happiness

Hobbies have considerable psychological value; and the farther they are from one's daily routine, the better.

My first traumatic experience was that of being placed in fourth and fifth grade classes in the public school when I was transferred from the parochial school: at my age I should have been in the sixth grade. All my playmates of my age were in the sixth grade or above; so why wasn't I?

I was stigmatized as either a retardate or rebel—except after school hours, when I was the master mechanic in the construction of our pushmobiles, and the steering mechanisms thereon, or in the building of a playhouse in our backyard with glass windows and a small cookstove. I made drawings of and helped the other boys make weather vanes. In a word, I was a leader, and this restored my confidence. Compared to schoolwork, these activities were hobbies and they had therapeutic value for me. Although I didn't think of it at that time in those terms, I do now.

Much later in life, when I found myself in the wrong place at the Corn Exchange Bank, it was my insatiable interest in history, psychiatry, and sociology that enabled me to endure the tedium of the job until I could respectfully break away from it and return to graduate school.

Working for a doctor's degree and conducting classes left little time for recreational hobbies, but I was able to get my mind off the academic routine with a daily game of handball in the university gymnasium.

My greatest trauma developed when Connie Lowell, my valuable business partner, died shortly after I joined him, leaving me with the associates he had planned to eliminate from our company because of their ineptitude. I was still living in New York when this tragedy occurred, but had sold our house because I was traveling so much of the time. (The buyer, incidentally, was the playwright who wrote "Death of a Salesman" and many others, Arthur Miller.) With the house went my "hobby shop" in the attic, which my family ungraciously referred to as my playpen. But I still had my wood-working tools.

In May 1948, my son said that he and one of his college friends were thinking of going to Mexico during the summer vacation. I made a counter-proposition. I had acquired ten acres of land in Coldenham, New York, about eighty miles from the city and seven miles west of Newburgh. I therefore said to son Jack, "Why don't you and your friend do something more productive than going to Mexico? Also, if you plan to come into my business after college, it won't hurt you to have some firsthand knowledge of construction. Since we deal mainly in FHA loans, why not get a copy of the FHA construction manual and build a weekend cottage?"

He and his classmate agreed; I then bought a quonset hut from an army-surplus outfit, had a well drilled, acquired a camper's cooking stove, hired an earth-moving company to dig a basement, and we were ready to go as soon as college closed for the summer.

You have, by now, concluded that I am accident prone; you know that if I have two options, one of which will be a mistake, I'll choose the latter. Accordingly you are probably asking, How is he going to screw up this undertaking? Okay, I'll tell you.

After the earth-movers dug the hole for the basement, the next step was to put in the footings for the foundation, which are the functional equivalent of the genes in your nervous system: your genes determine whether you are a genius, a moron, or something in between.

So it is with the footings for a house. And although you can't do anything about your genes, you can do everything that is necessary in connection with footings. All you need is enough God-given common sense.

My plan called for a building with four square corners—a rectangle—something simple so I wouldn't get into any trouble. I had a measuring tape, a try square, and presumably my quota of common sense. So I measured one side, and laid my try square at the end of it. That gave me the exact (?) direction of the next side, and so on back to the point of beginning. Forms were then nailed together and concrete poured into them. That comprised one weekend's work (play).

The following weekend we began laying concrete blocks on the footings, i.e., "laying up the walls," as the tradesmen say. We soon noticed, however, that one wall was higher than another; in fact, no two sides were the same height, even though the same number of blocks was laid on both. Obviously the footings had not been laid on level ground. Okay; we'll simply have to shim the floor joists to compensate for the irregularities—a tedious, time-consuming operation. When it came time to put on the roof we had to shim everything again.

The interior walls were to be covered with knotty pine; each and every board had to be cut and trimmed to fit because, by this time, we'd found that the corners were not right angles. Evidently my try square was not adequate for the job: we had a house that was a parallelogram, not a rectangle. Since all cutting tools make straight cuts at right angles, practically every piece of wood in the house had to be cut by hand and trimmed to fit. Doors were the biggest problem of all. To swing properly, a door has to be hinged to a perfectly perpendicular jamb; and to fit right, the other three sides have to be at right angles to each other. If they aren't—and they weren't—there will be cracks around the edges, which will admit cold air in the winter, flies in summer during the day, and mosquitos at night. (I should know, thanks to Margaret Casey).This problem can be overcome, to a limited degree, by tacking strips of plastic on the edges of the door—as is sometimes done on dog houses and chicken coops!

The biggest problem was the four-by-six-foot plate-glass window. It, of course, was square; the opening was not. Fitting a rectangular window into an opening in the shape of a parallelogram is a challenge even Archimedes would have found exasperating. We managed more or less to cover up the mistake with draperies.

Notwithstanding the tedium and tinkering necessary to compensate for the fact that we did not have a surveyor starting us off properly with a true and level foundation, we wound up with a cozy, weather tight, architecturally tolerable little weekend-and-vacation cottage. It was even snug enough for us to spend time there in the dead of winter, and my son and his bride spent their honeymoon there.

Although we had a well-equipped kitchen, there was a first-class dining club only a few yards up the road, which was run by a White Russian immigrant, a Mrs. Mekishen. We usually had dinner there. On weekends her house was filled with White Russians from New York, all of whom were from the upper stratum of Russian society before the revolution.

We were all seated at one large dining table, where we would hear loud protests against Stalin. Ivan Ivanavich Aplaxin, who spoke English fluently, would translate for us. It's too bad none of them lived long enough to know that now Stalin is hated as much by the Russians in Russia as he was by them back in the 1940s and '50s. Aplaxin, incidentally, was a "stress engineer," who worked for General Motors during the war.

It was during this time that my wife was promoting dry skim milk for Borden's, a time when we felt the more knowledge she had about cooking the better she could do her job. As a result, she observed Mrs. Mekishen's cooking, which was superb. Borscht became a staple of our diet; if you ever come to our house for dinner we shall be glad to offer you some, made with a chicken or other meat broth (after the fat has been skimmed off), beets, cabbage, potato, sugar and vinegar to taste, and any kind of meat we may have available in small pieces. It's almost a meal by itself.

All of the people at the table had escaped Russia through one hair-raising method or another: some had swum across rivers in winter; others, like my employee, had gotten through Siberia, to Japan, to California, to New York. (Incidentally, he subsequently managed to own a small apartment house at 113th near Broadway, only to die young of cancer.) One of the group had been an officer in the czar's army but couldn't hack it in America; instead of joining the congenial crowd at the dining table, he drowned his depression with the contents of a bottle.

Mrs. Mekishen's husband had been a sculptor under the czar. They'd been intercepted when they'd reached the border but, if I remember correctly, she said she'd given her jewelry to the border guard to let her escape. (At last I've heard of a good reason for owning jewelry.)

When we moved to San Francisco in 1957, we had to abandon the imperfect little gem in the country. It was bought shortly thereafter for the amount of money I had invested in materials, which was $4,700. Instead of playing golf on weekends, we made something useful and enjoyed doing it. Of all my hobbies this one was probably the most interesting, in spite of the mistakes and frustration. Two years ago I drove up to the place from New York City. Much to my amazement, I found the present owner had added several rooms, and had beautified the surroundings; it is an extremely attractive suburban house.

Here in San Francisco when I was having so much difficulty with my New York partners, it became more important than ever to relax, which I was able to do, in my workshop in the basement of our house. My first project was a grandfather's clock. I bought a kit, put it together, installed the movement, made the necessary adjustments, and placed it in the entrance hall; that was twenty-nine years ago. It keeps time perfectly and chimes every quarter hour, and plays the Westminster melody on the hour.

Shortly after that there was a revival of interest in the Bay area in the precursor of the piano, the harpsichord, due very largely, I think, to the influence of Loretta Goldberg, who is a devotee both of Bach and of the keyboard instrument of his time. Although technically a musical illiterate, I am so fond of classical and operatic music that I whistle to the best of my ability melodies and arias, day and night. My brother-in-law says I would never be a successful burglar, because I would whistle while I worked. About the only time I don't whistle is while I'm asleep. My wife's nurse says I am the only person she has ever seen or heard of who would come home from a dental appointment whistling. The neighbors call me "the whistler" (without my mother, I'm sorry to say), but she bought a player piano when I was a kid—one of those things you pumped with your feet. We had a cabinet full of classical music, which I learned to appreciate.

Building the harpsichord was the most difficult hobby-category project I have ever undertaken. I visited the Zuckerman "factory," in Greenwich Village, New York City, just as Pinchas Zuckerman was going out of business. I think I bought the last kit he had for sale. It was a single-string model. Later I bought a three-string, five-octave concert grand—a much more complicated model, the instructions for which came in seventy-six single-spaced pages. After about a thousand hours of leisure-time labor, I was close to having a playable keyboard instrument and Lorette arranged for an ensemble—consisting of the harpsichord, a wind instrument, and a violin—to dedicate it. The only trouble was that my tuning left something to be desired.

The hour had come. The guests had arrived; the performers were tuned and ready; but the harpsichord was not: it was not completely in tune. (Chipping up to pitch—on 183 strings, the first musicological operation on a new instrument is, I discovered, exceedingly difficult, especially for one who lacks the sense of perfect pitch.) But one of the guests, a famous builder of harpsichords, John Phillips, got the thing in tune and the concert took place in our living room.

My wife read notes and was able to perform; I could not. So I signed up with Lorette. Up to the time I started this memoir I had not mastered the art; but when I finish this lousy thing I intend to go back to the keyboard, tune it, and try again to make music—the difficulty of which will be compounded by the fact that Dupuytren's Syndrome has shortened the tendons of three of my fingers, one of the concomitants of old age. (Me, old?)

If the harpsichord was my most challenging and difficult hobby project, winemaking was my most famous. Our basement is large (ninety by twenty-five feet); more than half of it is screened off from the furnaces, where the temperature does not vary appreciably from sixty-five degrees Fahrenheit the year round. Napa Valley, where some of the finest vineyards in the world are located, is less than one-hundred miles away. So why not make wine? Indeed, why not?

Well, one good reason would be that to buy a ton of grapes in Napa, haul them home, and then up the twenty-two steps to our basement is more manual labor than I prefer to indulge in, no matter how fascinating the hobby. But I had young friends and neighbors who were ready, willing, and able; all they needed was a room with a cool and uniform temperature, a concrete floor, hot and cold running water, and an adequate drainage system. I had all of these. The only thing we lacked was the equipment and the knowledge to convert the grapes to wine. We had all heard of the master who, some two-thousand years ago, turned water into wine, but as none of us thought it would be worthwhile to try that we resolved to go about it in the conventional way, using Wagner's book on winemaking as our guide and hauling tons of grapes from Napa.

To make a long story short, during a period of some ten years we made about ten varieties of white and red wine, and had nary a failure. I became so well known as an amateur vintner that when people met me the first question usually was not, "How are you?" but rather, "Are you still making wine?"

For a number of reasons my partners became unable to carry on, and we had to let the project die several years ago. I have less than a case of white wine left at this point and it will have to be consumed soon, because white wine doesn't improve after it reaches a certain age. On the other hand, I also have four bottles of Cabernet that are twenty years old, and they are supreme. We open one of these on a special occasion, and everybody has to be satisfied with a sip.

Bread. Do you buy that stuff they call bread? If so, I'd like to suggest that you try one of my other hobbies and start baking your own. But remember, yeast, like people, will multiply if left to its own devices and will overpopulate the bowl just as people do the earth. But not being inhibited in this case by religious prejudice, you can step in and prevent reproduction from getting out of hand by adding flour, whole wheat exclusively, vegetable oil, a bit of salt, and whatever other ingredients you wish to give it a distinct flavor. I add raw sunflower seeds, poppy seeds, rolled oats, chopped nuts, and heaven knows what else that may come to mind.

I have boiled chopped onions, used the onion water in the first step, and then added the onions along with the other ingredients. I sometimes add cottage, parmesan, cheddar, goat, and roquefort cheese. Then I add more flour and stir until the dough no longer sticks to the mixing bowl.

Now it is time to knead. The more you knead it the better; kneading develops the gluten in the flour and gives cohesiveness to the loaf. After, say twenty minutes of kneading, I may put the dough back into the bowl and let it rest (in a warm, draught-free place) for an hour or two, during which time the size of the batch will continue to grow because the yeasts are incorrigible. Then I knead it again and shape it into loaves.

If you want to save time and work, you do not need to use a bread pan; pans have to be greased, and later washed. I have been using a cookie sheet: sprinkle a little cornmeal on the sheet, then lay the loaves on it; let them rest for an hour or less then bake.

If you have homemade whole wheat bread, some equally good cheese—brie, gruyere, or cheddar—a bottle of wine (even if you didn't make it), and a green salad, then I say you have the makings of a gourmet lunch, provided that the salad has been made correctly.

I am as much of a crank about salad dressing as I am about bread and wine. A good salad dressing should be made with wine vinegar, olive oil, garlic, rosemary, blue cheese, mustard, salt, pepper, and a spot of sugar; mix that into some fresh lettuce, chopped celery, diced jikama, shredded carrot, toasted sunflower seeds, and a sprinkle of parmesan. That's my salad hobby.

Soups are as important as bread and salads. I start with broth. Since we eat meat sparingly, I either buy or make broth; the kind I make is as superior to the canned variety as homemade bread is to store bread. I buy five pounds of chicken backs and bones and boil them in about two quarts of water; discard the bones, let the liquid cool, refrigerate it overnight, and remove the fat the next morning. Beans, or lentils, that have been soaked overnight, and barley, chopped celery, onions, carrots, beet tops, bay leaf, rosemary, thyme, garlic, and pot liquors of all kinds added to the mixture make a delectable dish.

People who have hobbies are better adjusted to life and living than those who don't. I know how to spell boredom, but I have never experienced it.

Chapter 38
Two in a (Single) Bed

Back in chapter 24 mention was made of southern hospitality; this chapter has to do with a bit of Bussing hospitality.

After the two babies had, without their consent, been initiated in the cathedral services (chapter 36), my wife and I invited two members of the congregation from out of town to lunch at our house.

After lunch we learned that they had not made a hotel reservation, to which I responded that we had a perfectly good guest room they were welcome to use. My wife, although quite agreeable, reminded me that the accommodation had only a single bed. "Oh, so it does," I said, "but I think we can take care of that," whereupon I proceeded to expound upon my way of adjusting to nocturnal nuisances in general, and to the limited dimensions of a single bed in particular.

"There are several ways," I told them. "The first thing to do is give up the idea that there are two sides to every bed: in a single bed there's no such thing as *your side* and *my side*; the one who gets there first has squatter's rights and the other one takes what's left, which will be only a few inches. Then it's a question of whether the first-come-first-served occupant can be persuaded preferably by peaceful means, to move over sufficiently so as to consolidate the few inches on each edge, thereby doubling the number of inches on one edge."

"In the 'olden' days," I went on, "courtliness determined that one's female bed partner got in first and the gentleman took what was left—that is, until gravity took the place of gallantry and he landed on the floor. But now that gallantry is gone and women have equal rights (at least in the Western world), each partner may claim squatter's rights. However," I added, "in practice this usually inures, at least temporarily, to the advantage of the male, because he does not go through the bedtime ritual of applying oleaginous substances (worth fifteen cents a pound in the raw and fifteen dollars an ounce at the beauty counter) to the face, and removing eyelashes, eye shadow, and other embellishments. This enables the male, who seldom tries in some such similar way to improve the face and features God has given him, to fall asleep in the preferred position in or on the bed."

I also included in my anatomical addendum, a speculation as to how two people can accommodate their double width to a single space by juxtaposing their respective surfaces front to front, back to front, front to back, or back to back.

In any case, our guests concluded that the invitation was sincere and our accommodations acceptable; whereupon we took them on a tour of (everybody's favorite) city, including Golden Gate Park, Twin Peaks, Coit Tower, and other points of interest. After returning home and a brief rest, we took a cable car to Fisherman's Wharf and had a dinner of Dungenes crab. (Time was when we would start a seafood dinner with bay shrimp; but these rare and dainty delicacies have now been polluted to perdition. Crabs also began leaving the watery environs of your favorite city when, with our gracious hospitality, we began offering them sewage flavored with sea water, or vice versa. In the opinion of shrimp and crabs, we are the dumbest, most careless creatures on earth.)

After dinner, back to the cable car; a short hop in a taxi, and we were home. In those same "old days," the cable car ran on our street, Pacific Avenue; but while we were fouling the habitats of fish, shrimp, crab, and other delicacies of the delta we were also pouring asphalt over our cable-car tracks, so as to make the streets more "user friendly" to motorists, and the air even more polluted than the bay. (If we will only be patient we shall soon have managed to pollute everything that is pollutable.)

After a full and rather eventful day all four of us were inclined to intone the words of the late Samuel Pepys (1633–1703), who ended each day's entry in his diary with, "And so to bed."

Normally, Paul (the male in this case) would fall asleep while the nocturnal necromancy (mentioned above) of the wife, girlfriend, or partner for the evening was going on; except that in this instance he did not fall asleep, apparently because his conscience was bothering him: he couldn't forget the stock transaction he'd undertaken a few days before, in which he'd used inside information to his advantage at the expense of the persons on the other side of the trade; following which, adding insult to injury, he'd passed the information on to a few friends in exchange for a share of *their* ill-gotten gains. Thus, what was left of old-fashioned romanticism in his makeup caused him, in his wakeful state, to offer his preferred position to his partner when she had finished erasing or removing parts of her facade. He resigned himself to making out, to the best of his ability, with what little space was left.

If you were ever in this sort of situation you probably came to the conclusion, sooner or later, that there ought to be (and probably are) better ways for two people, when necessary, to share a width that was intended for only one; but how?

This was taking place, be it remembered, the night following the morning baptismal service at the cathedral, at which the reverend pastor read a biblical anecdote about another chap named Paul, who was riding a horse in what is called a holy land a couple of thousand years ago. He said he was headed for Damascus and the Garden of Eden to get some fruit and vegetables. These were preferable to Judean produce, because they were thought to be grown organically—free from pesticides, since all bugs and pests, like Adam and Eve, were told never again to commit the original sin. So as soon as that generation of pests died there were no more.

Some of his friends laughed at this "organic" explanation; they said he had a girlfriend in Damascus, that they ate forbidden fruit regularly, and that at this particular time her parents undoubtedly were out of town.

Whatever his reasons, the story read by the parson from the Book of Truth that morning related how Paul, in some mysterious way, was knocked off his Arabian horse as he trudged along the dusty road and was told by a voice from heaven to forsake Judaism and embrace Christianity. (Some of his Jewish friends and relatives called the episode not a conversion, but a conviction for riding an Arabian nag; weren't Hebrew horses good enough? "Too bad he didn't break a few bones," some said.) Whatever it was that knocked him off, it did indeed result in his chucking Judaism in favor of Christianity. What that had to do with us in church that morning I never did find out, unless it was supposed to prove that God is on our side—that God is a Christian. Or else that if you're not a Christian, don't ride a horse.

Meanwhile our overnight guest, who, like Paul of Tarsus, had been deposed, not from a horse but from a bed, now lay prostrate on the bedroom floor—wondering, like the other Paul, what in heaven's name had gotten him into his predicament—until he, too, got a flash of insight, so to speak. That is, he reasoned, "If Paul the horseman was able to remount and go triumphantly on his way, maybe *I* should try one of those mounting positions our host was talking about, instead of trying to squeeze side by side."

At this juncture, as if by mental telepathy, his bed partner awoke. "What goes on?" said she, as she beheld him on the floor.

"I'm not sure," he said, "but I must have had a dream about the church service we attended this morning. I didn't pay much attention to it at the time, because I didn't see any relevance to my life in it; but a few minutes ago when I came to, here on the floor, it occurred to me that the horseman and I had both had the same experience; but instead of lying there in the middle of the road, he got up, got on, tapped the nag in the ribs and continued on the road to Damascus."

"I think I see what's coming," she said. "You think we should try getting on top of one another in this damned bed in one of the ways suggested by our host."

"It's a solution worth trying," he said. "It couldn't be worse than what we've tried so far."

"I'm not so sure," said she. The underdog in the middle of the bed, she reasoned, would be in danger of suffocation (or if you will pardon the expression, *ass*phyxiation) and the top dog, in a back-to-back deal, although inoperative biologically, could suffer injury (unless he happened to be a big shot like Paul of Tarsus and got miraculous first-aid from heaven). Inasmuch as she was a 36-30-48 and he no better at 33-38-40, if he was on top, back-to-back his distance from the floor would be the sum of her width (not less than fifteen inches if our geometry is right), plus the thickness of the mattress and box spring, and the length of the bed's legs, a total of about thirty-six inches. Even if there was a pad under the carpet, no one would consider the risk of falling three feet off an otherwise cozy cushion of human flesh a satisfactory tradeoff for the cost of a hotel room. So they hesitated.

In their preoccupation with positions they evidently forgot that blankets for single beds are never wide enough to cover two people and be tucked under the mattress at the same time, and consequently, tend to fall off, which led to a different sort of "solution." That is, since all efforts to accommodate their sleeping arrangement to the limitations of a bed built for one had come to naught, they finally decided to divide the covers and roll up in them individually, in sleeping-bag fashion, he on the floor and she on the bed.

So far so good; both actually fell asleep. But soon she was awakened by what sounded like a confused monologue in which he seemed to be perplexed by some sort of anthropological nightmarish mixup. As nearly as she could understand his mumblings, he apparently was troubled by one of the suggestions of their host earlier in the day regarding the various postures two people may assume in a single bed when their primary purpose is to sleep. Evidently his subconscious was trying to reconcile a postural question he never had thought of before, namely that our biological ancestors, the anthropoid apes, co-habitate front to back (the front of the male facing the back of the female). If we are their descendants, how come we mate, whenever we get a chance, in the front-to-front position— face to face as it were? When, where, and how in the anthropo-evolutionary development of man did this revolutionary anatomical modification take place? Or did it? Is man's face-to-face position evidence of divine creation as the biblical literalists would have us believe? Or is it the result of evolution?

When daylight came his partner told him how his nocturnal necromancy not only kept her awake for another part of the night, but was now arousing as much curiosity in her as it was in him.

But they had to put this evolutionary enigma on the back burner for the present as it was now time to get on with the problem of making a living so that, among other things, if opportunities presented themselves in the future to spend a night together they would have enough wherewithal to pay for a room in a hotel, where presumably they would have the luxurious option of *two* single beds if they preferred a monotonous, though 100 percent restful night or a double, queen, or king size in which they could vary the agenda without risk—or at least the risk of falling.

P.S. This author is as confused about the mating question as Paul was. I do not recall (in the limited amount of reading I have done in anthropology) any explanation as to how it came about that man "makes love" face to face, and our presumed anthropological ancestors don't. I don't know if anyone other than the publisher's proofreader will take the time to read the stuff I am writing; but if by chance someone with a knowledge of anthropology happens to do so and can throw some light on how, when, and where the change from front-to-back among the apes gave way to face-to-face among us occurred, it would be gratefully received. There are many religious fundamentalists and biblical literalists in our midst who agree with the late Clarence Darrow who, seventy-odd years ago in the Stokes trial in Kentucky, pleaded with tears in his eyes that the biblical version of the origin of man be taught in schools of the state with at least the same respect or reverence we have for evolution, although you can be sure he made no reference (God forbid) to the difference between the way we manage to (over)populate the world and the way monkeys do. But if he did give it any logical libidinous thought, he could have cited it as "proof" of divine creation rather than continuous evolution.

In rejecting "creationism," how do we explain the shift from the front-to-back posture of our friends and relatives, the primates, to our face-to-face posture? Was it a mutation or a gradual, evolutionary development? If evolutionary, what kind of intermediate positions occurred in the distant past? And what reason is there for thinking the process has stopped? Is it not conceivable (and I use the word advisedly) that future Mesdames Bobbit may find the butcher's knife a less useful weapon because our sexual apparatus will have evolved to such an extent it no longer resembles that of monkeys. ("There he goes again" I hear you saying. "He can't discuss anything without making fun of it.")

Chapter 39
A Few Outlandish (?) Observations

I was born too soon. Several days ago a forty-year-old divorcee of my acquaintance said to me, "I'm glad I'm not dating anymore; the risk of AIDS is too great."

To a more or less hidebound nonagenarian this sounded like a non-sequitur; my recollection of a date was an occasion when a male and a female of about the same age took a walk in the park, had dinner together, or sat on the front porch while the parents went to bed (with a clear conscience).

On the other hand, this middle-aged gal's lifestyle may not be new or novel; if you were old enough in 1922 to read the *New York Times*, you will recall the vociferous altercation between Bishop Manning, of the Cathedral of Saint John the Divine, and a New York City jurist, Judge Lindsey, who openly and avidly advocated what he called "companionate marriage," which was somewhat akin to the kind preferred by then-Mayor Jimmy Walker and his live-in girlfriend. (The judge had probably reached his conclusion as a result of presiding over numerous marital squabbles. Undoubtedly these came to his court because of the difficulty some couples had in adhering to the Bishop Manning type of contract, which was indissoluble "until death.")

The bishop couldn't base his objection on one of the ten commandments, because the only one that deals with sex proscribes adultery; and since neither Jimmy nor his girlfriend was married, there was no adultery. In fact, said some nonchurchgoing observers, only people with "dirty" minds would assume that because they were living together they were sinning together.

The bishop was in enough hot (holy) water with his defense of the traditional marriage system; but he was about to get into more of it (along with his regular occupation of helping people get passports to the everlasting trouble- and tax-free, felicific life after death). This additional problem involved raising money to finish the over-size cathedral. The latest gimmick was to call it "the Church of *All* People," hoping thereby to get contributions from nonmembers, disbelievers—even companionate couples.

I don't know how much money came rolling in but, judging by the amount of uncut stone and marble that remained on the grounds of the cathedral, my guess is not much. Soon the whole PR fundraising campaign came to a screeching halt when a couple who were not Episcopalians but who apparently preferred the bish's kind of marriage to Judge Lindsey's, asked to have their marriage solemnized in "The Church of All People."

"No can do," said the bish. "You have not been confirmed; you are not Episcopalians." That made headline news throughout the United States. It even pushed the Waldorf Astoria's diplomatic dilemma off the first page. That occurred when Queen Marie of Rumania ordered broccoli for dinner. Not only didn't the Maitre d' have any—he didn't even know what it was. The botany department of Columbia university had to tell him it was not a wine but a "wegetable," that he wouldn't find any in the produce market, and that the poor Queen and King Ferdinand would probably have to do without it until they returned to Bucharest. Even when they returned to Rumania and were able to get it regularly, however, broccoli proved not to be a cure-all, for Ferdie died a short time later.

Inheritance

In my anecdotage I have gotten off the track. What I started to say was we might as well face the fact that monogamy is primarily an economic mandate which, to please its affluent members (and contributors), the church wove into the fabric of the faith, in order better to facilitate its enforcement so that the financially able members would be under less pressure to pick up the tab for little bastards. The church and its affluent members ultimately lost the battle, however, when the welfare state began taking care of everybody, including the unfortunate little so-and-so's who seem to have no fathers—not, I should point out, because their mothers have learned the technique of immaculate conception, but, rather because their fathers have learned the art of deception.

Not having a responsible father is only one of the handicaps these newcomers will have to deal with. When they become old enough, say, to be supplied with schoolbooks and condoms, their teachers will probably tell them that they have inherited an enormous debt that was caused by, and is increasing at least in part as a result of, the irresponsible behavior of certain missing male members of society.

If a teacher has not, up to this point, been shot to death by one of the pupils, he may try to give them some idea as to how big the debt they have inherited actually is with this blackboard illustration:

One thousand, $1,000
One hundred thousand, $100,000
One million, $1,000,000
One billion, $1,000,000,000
One trillion, $1,000,000,000,000

The debt that all Americans are responsible for is nearly four times the last amount, and it is growing at the rate of about a billion dollars a day. "In the last thirty minutes," the teacher will say, "the government has spent about $21 million more than it collected through taxation, which means that the debt you and other citizens are responsible for is increasing at the rate of about $300 billion a year."

"What'll happen if we say 'Nuts' to the whole thing and tell 'em what they can do with their debt?" asks one of the boys.

"That has happened in other countries; and when it does, bondholders tell the government that they want cash when their bonds mature," said the teacher. "And the government gives it to them."

But little Willie Wiseaker, one of the smart kids in the class, pipes up, "If they can produce money that way, why didn't they do so originally, instead of getting it by selling bonds?"

"Good question," says the teacher, stalling time because he isn't sure he has the answer; but in fact he does when he says, "The round-about process of selling bonds, instead of printing money, is based on the hope that money obtained through taxation will be available to pay off the bonds when they come due. If it isn't, then there is nothing to do but print more of the stuff."

"I don't get it," says one of the girls in the front row. "Sounds screwy to me. Yesterday you told us that, if more peanuts are produced than the market usually absorbs, the price declines. So if the government printed money instead of selling bonds, or if it sold bonds and printed the money later, it all comes to the same thing: there has been an increase in the amount of money and its value should go down, like in peanuts."

"Then what happens?" asks otherwise dull David.

"It's obvious," shouts Willy. "Inflation."

The bell in the hall rings; the period is over.

Some of the youngsters go to the manual-training class, some to a history class, and others to the class in social studies, where, after learning some of the consequences of increasing the quantity of money, they will now hear some of the consequences of increasing the volume of humanity.

Population

The first bit of information they hear is that it took *four million years* to produce the first *four billion people*, or a net increase, on average, of 1,000 people per year; we now produce that many in less than six minutes. By this time tomorrow there will be about 260,000 more people on earth.

"Are the mothers of all these children able to feed, clothe, and educate them?" the teacher asks.

"I saw a picture on the TV yesterday of thousands of starving people," said one of the girls. "Most, if not all, of them were half-dead babies less than a year or two old. The mothers evidently go on having babies, whether they can keep them alive or not."

"I saw that picture, too," says another girl, "and I couldn't figure out why the women don't make their boyfriends put condoms on, like we do."

"Yeah," pipes in little Betty Buxom. "I always tell my boyfriends that they have to use those things, whether they want to or not; and if they don't cooperate, they don't copulate—not with me."

"Me too," says Susie. "If my boyfriend tries to get out of putting one on, I grab him and force it on. If I tear it, which sometimes happens, I always have some in my purse as Miss Amoral, the English teacher, says we should."

"Right on," adds Penelope (whom the boys nicknamed "Pussy" for short), "and if you want my advice you will take your pill, too, regularly, as prescribed. Don't neglect it. You know you are going to play with one of the boys as soon as you can find a place, and pills plus condoms make it more fun, because you don't have to worry."

"But," says the teacher, "what happens if you don't play it safe or something goes wrong?"

"Everybody has a little bad luck once in a while," says little Peter Paterno. "If a gal gets knocked up, she either has an abortion or she has a kid without a father."

"Why not make the boy who got her that way responsible?" asks the teacher.

"How can she know who was responsible?" says Penelope. "She might have had three, four, or even more guys that month."

"It's not important," says Pete. "The government will take care of the kid."

"Is that one of the functions of the welfare state?" asks the teacher.

"Sure!" the class practically sings in unison.

"Then is that one of the reasons why we have the big national debt you learned about in the civics class? How about that?" the teacher asks Henry (whom the kids called Hank, or Hanky Pank, because of his after-school habits).

"I guess it is," says Henry.

"Then why did so many of you say it's a dirty trick for the public debt to be passed on to you all?"

Silence. No one has an answer until Alice Avery (whom the boys called AA, for "always available") says defensively, "What's a government for, if not to take care of its citizens?"

Ding-a-ling. There went the bell in the hall again, as this class, too, ends without solving any problems.

Although girls in schools can avoid pregnancy if they use the equipment provided at the public expense, teachers have to provide their own protection against the hazards of their occupation;

male teachers, for example, can wear bulletproof vests. Although women teachers have not been rubbed out by pistol packing pupils as male teachers have, they are considering wearing the vests for dual protection, both from firearms and from the harassing arms and hands of their male colleagues.

TV

One of the differences between TV and TB is that the latter is curable. TV can be entertaining and educational; it is also seductive and addictive. The educational possibilities are enormous and mostly neglected. The American public school system is frightfully expensive and woefully ineffective, one of the main reasons being that attendance is required, instead of being offered as a privilege.

I suggest that we expand TV for home study and arrange properly supervised examinations, give credit, and award diplomas. I would start with college work. Ultimately it is possible that the cost of education could be greatly reduced; the time required to earn a certificate or diploma, likewise; and, where necessary or desirable, the student may have a part-time job at the same time (provided some stupid legislative body doesn't prevent it by way of a minimum-wage law).

I would emphasize basic subjects for home study; to learn a vocation, employers are the best teachers. They have to train workers in most cases today anyway, even though the applicant may have had scholastic preparation; so the present educational program could be short-circuited as a time- and money-saving policy. An apprentice may or may not be paid, depending on his qualifications. Leaving basics in the public education system and practical education in the domain of employers would prepare young people for the responsibilities of learning and living much better than our present system.

Drugs

If our educational system costs more than it is worth, our handling of the drug problem can't be far behind. We continue to think we are our brother's keeper. Many years ago, a group of moralists decided that nobody should have an alcoholic drink because some drinkers are gluttons. What we got was bootleggers, bedlam, and baneful booze. Eventually the Volstead Act was repealed, only to resurface again in the legislation outlawing narcotics. This has turned out to be even a greater failure than Prohibition.

What is the solution? There is no simple answer; but we have found that we can't eliminate it by law. Drug addiction is an illness in an epidemic; it is not a crime, and the addict is not a criminal. To an addict, a drug is mandatory medication, not an illegal substance, and it should be made available in the open market, preferably in pharmacies ("drugstores," as they are called improperly). The addict should not be permitted to buy the junk, however, unless he can show that he is enrolled in an approved clinic. If this doesn't rationalize the problem, the patient may have to be considered a lost cause. Sterilize him first; then treat him as a medical case. The rest of us may then be less afraid to go out at night, because these people will not have to resort to violence to obtain what, to them, is a life-sustaining substance.

Sterilization

If you don't mind stirring up a hornet's nest (or a love nest), recommend that sterilization be *de rigueur* for at least two classes of people: those retarded mentally, and those on welfare who have two children (to limit to that extent the burden of public welfare). The most compelling reason for the marriage system, presumably, lies in the fact that parenthood and parental responsibility go together. If they in practice don't, society has the right to protect itself and children from the consequences.

The Insurance Business

This is not an appropriate function of the government. If you disagree, please explain how the Savings and Loan industry managed to leave us taxpayers with a liability of something like $200 billion (nobody knows the actual amount because the liquidation process has not been completed). Whoever heard of an insurance company that rated all risks equally and charged premiums accordingly? FSLIC did; it may still, for all I know.

Governments are generally unqualified to operate any kind of business enterprise, including the insurance business, where the risk of loss is unusually high. Through FEMA our government has gotten into the casualty field: we have assumed liability for loss due to flood, hurricane, earthquake, wildfire, and, as we go to press, prospectively some of the cost of universal health insurance. Although the cost of the proposed health insurance plan is supposed to be paid for in part by adding it to the cost of production (and thus to the cost of living and the difficulty of meeting foreign competition), the remaining portion, to be borne by the government, will facilitate and expedite the expansion of our national debt beyond the back-breaking level where it is today.

Social Security

Social Security is another insurance program that is likely to run into major difficulties at some time in the future, one of the reasons being that the reserve for future obligations is turned over to the U.S. Treasury in exchange for government bonds. The reserves are then used for whatever purposes Congress chooses, all of which will be non-self-liquidating. Therefore, when it becomes necessary for Social Security to draw on its "reserve," it will receive paper money fresh off the printing press, or bank credit in the federal reserve system, which comes to the same thing. The purchasing power of the funds is likely to have fallen in the meantime, because of the deleterious consequences of deficit financing, but will be "offset" by means of a cost-of-living adjustment, which will further augment the money supply and elevate the price level additionally.

"Okay, Gramps," says one of my critical granddaughters, "I have to take your word for it, but why don't you suggest solutions for some of these problems, starting in this case with insurance?"

"Smarter people than I have tried that," I say. "But you remind me of a 'solution' one of my distant relatives had, many years ago, for one kind of insurance that didn't cost anything and that was not screwed up by government interference. Maybe it could be applied to some insurable risks."

"For example—" she says.

"Well, it's quite simple, really," I say in reply, and tell her the following tale:

"When I was a little boy we had some distant relatives, the Biltmans, who owned a farm in Vanderburg county. Occasionally my little sister and I were guests of Aunt Mayme and Uncle John during a few weeks in summer.

"One night a thunder storm erupted, and my sleep was interrupted. Between flashes of lightning I saw Aunt Mayme walking about with a kerosene lamp in her hand. I couldn't figure out what she might have been looking for. Do mice come indoors when it rains, I wondered; if so, wouldn't the cats make it unnecessary for her to try to catch them?

"Then she walked over to the bed where Uncle John was sleeping; he must have had such a clear conscience that he was able to sleep through it all. She seemed to be waving something over him; so in the morning I asked her why was she trying to wake him up. Did she want him to see the lightning?

"'No,' she said, 'I wasn't trying to wake him up, honey; I was using the blessed fronds from Palm Sunday to protect him from the lightning. I passed the fronds over you, Lucille, and me, to insure our safety, too.'

"'Does that protect the house, too?' I asked.

"'Yes,' she said. 'It's better than insurance: it protects; insurance only compensates.'

"'Does it protect the barn, the cows, and the horses?'

"At this point Uncle John came in with a bucket of milk, which showed that the palm leaves had indeed kept him alive. And something must have kept the cows alive, too—at least I had never heard of getting milk out of a dead cow; buttermilk, maybe, but not sweet milk. Also, when I woke up I had heard a rooster crowing to wake up his girlfriends, which meant that they were okay too. He always woke them up, I decided, so they would get busy scratching up a good breakfast, especially after a rainstorm, when there were worms risking their lives to enjoy crawling about in the mud. Worms helped the hens produce good eggs, and good eggs made healthy chicks—if the hen sat on them long enough. Intelligent roosters, Aunt Mayme told me, made the hens do this, because roosters think like popes: the more of them the better.

"So I concluded that Aunt Mayme or Uncle John must have put some of those dead palm leaves in the barnyard, too. Good thing they didn't have goats, because goats would have eaten the blessed fronds, which I don't think protect lives and property when they're in an animal's stomach or a pile of fertilizer. I always wondered why my mother kept those dead palm tree leaves so long. Now I knew."

"More nonsense," said the granddaughter. "I like your sarcasm better than your solutions."

Euthanasia

Since I have shocked you at least once with what many would call my extremist ideas, I might as well go whole hog and suggest that when a person is in an incurable, painful condition, with tubes sticking into and out of him, brain dead, and kept half alive by artificial means, some arrangement should be available to end the suffering. More and more people are making living wills, empowering members of the family to authorize medical authorities to terminate such a tragedy; but, where there is no such authorization, a consensus of medical authorities should be permitted, with the consent of relatives, to end it. With the growing proportion of extremely old people like me in the population, hospitals are becoming overburdened with patients who are there only to die; whether death takes place now or a few weeks or months later is of little or no consequence to the half conscious, unconscious, or suffering patient; but it is of extreme importance to society, which is facing increasing difficulty in providing adequate medical care to people who are curable.

Abortion

It's a messy business, but you and I have no right to interfere with a woman who chooses it. I can understand how those opposed feel justified in demanding that their tax dollars should not be available to organizations offering abortion services; they do not, however, have the right to interfere with agencies that do so without government funds. Meddling in such matters is more of the same busybody behavior that tried to legislate abstinence from beer and now treats drug addiction as a moral, rather than a medical problem.

Immigration

Our generous welfare system is a magnet that draws citizens from other countries. Employers and consumers tend to be more kindly disposed toward them, because they are usually willing to work for less, while native workers deplore them for the same reason. As time goes on, however, our attitude is likely to change, due to demographic factors that lie ahead in the United States.

For example, as noted above, and because of its significance may be mentioned again, in 1945 there were forty-two working Americans for every retiree; in 1980, there were 8; today, there are 3. In about six years, there will be only two Americans working for every one retired, unless the proportion of younger people increases—as could be the case if more immigrants were admitted, since they tend to be younger people. On the other hand, when the new arrivals discover that, like the rest of us, they, too, have to pay, one way or another, for the goodies that are being given out in our "modernized" slipshod welfare society, they may conclude that life here is no longer a bed of roses, perhaps not much better than the life they had at home—the home to which they might return, then, without so much as a nudge from the INS.

Chapter 40
Odds and Ends

Christmas was only ten days away; and being neither an oniomaniac nor yet an irreconcilable member of the "bah humbug" club, I found myself in the usual situation—without gifts for a few friends.

The dilemma could be minimized, I decided, if I could find some things in the house I didn't want, and that others could use, in which case we could get some gift-wrap and ribbon, tie the stuff up, and pass it around. It was the word *tie* popping into my head that gave me an idea that took care of the problem for the 1992 season.

Here's how it went: I would write a letter or note and attach it to a small, gift-wrapped package. The note would say, "If this is the season of sharing or giving, the purpose of this note is to tell you what *you* may give *me*." (Then, before proceeding with the message, I would say that the attached package was not exactly what it seemed—although it contained nothing lethal, could be kept in the house, and could be opened, when the time comes, without the services of a bomb squad.)

Confusion would be further compounded when it was found that the "greeting" (the attached note) seemed to wander off on a totally irrelevant subject as follows: "Centuries ago, a necktie was a *bib*, whose purpose was to protect one's shirt—it being easier to launder a rag than a shirt. Then some smartalec, probably a haberdasher like Harry Truman, visualized the profit possibilities of adding bright colors to the drab linen or woolen cloth then in use and hiring an advertising agency to tell men that, if they want to be 'stylish,' they must don the latest improvement in menswear, the new brightly colored bib. That, it was hoped, would cause them to discard their old ones and buy the new (at a 'slight' markup in price). The fact is, they did; and in that respect they acted like women, in the sense that both have inferiority complexes—as evidenced by the fact that they don't feel comfortable unless they follow the crowd and wear what's 'in style.'

"Having succeeded in this endeavor, these self-appointed arbiters of fashion, these merchandising manipulators of the human mind decided that their next promotional ploy should be to propagate the idea that linen, wool, and cotton are plebeian materials, and that, if he wished to be accepted socially, the only tie fabric that a man could wear was *silk*.

"Therefore, the elite and many others who had aspirations in that regard—all of whom lacked sufficient self-confidence to defy the dictum of these dictators of decorum—fell in line to buy, and henceforth wear, bibs made of *silk*.

"In all probability (it might be noted in passing), the Associated Dry Cleaners International contributed to the budget of the Haberdasher's Guild and the Silk Merchandisers Association to help cover the cost of this advertising and promotional campaign, because dry cleaners knew (what I didn't) that silk should be dry-cleaned, not washed."

Then the note would have to jump from the Middle Ages to the Yuletide of 1992, if it was to deliver any kind of seasonally appropriate greeting; so it would continue, "Years ago, when I worked for a living, I didn't pay much attention to household expenses; but today, when the Open Market Committee of the Federal Reserve delights in forcing interest rates down, parasites like me, who depend on interest income, have to budget more carefully and watch expenses more closely. So when I asked my housekeeper one day why our dry-cleaning bill was so high, she replied reluctantly, 'Well, you know . . . ' and then hesitated, as if trying to avoid answering the question. After a few moments of toying with her apron and looking at the floor, she finally came out with it, 'It's the ties.'

"She didn't have to elaborate, because we had both noticed that, all too often, after a meal there are signs of soup, sauces, or salad dressing on my (bib) silk tie. However, the ties in my wardrobe are always spotless when I come to put one on, regardless of how I might have mistreated it the last time I wore it. If I gave any thought to it at all, it was probably that she'd washed and ironed the tie as she does practically everything else in the house. Which left me still in doubt about our dry-cleaning bill.

"So I made further inquiry and finally found out (what every-body else seems to know) that you don't wash silk ties: that's the best way to ruin them. That's why my intelligent servant takes them to the dry cleaner. (I, myself, have been 'taken to the cleaners' more than once in my lifetime, but that's a horse [not a tie] of another color.)

"The next thing I learned was that it costs as much to relieve a silk tie of spots as it does to buy a washable tie; so at that point I said, 'To hell with silk ties,' and decided to give them to my less cost-conscious friends, of whom you unfortunately are one, thus relieving me of this drain on my declining resources. That is *your* gift to *me*, which I referred to at the beginning of this message.

"Merry Christmas,

"Irvin.

"P.S. If you don't like the color or design of the tie I am giving you, I shall be glad to exchange it, provided there are no signs of soup, sauces, or salad dressing on it."

Nothing Endures

What has happened to IBM is similar to what is happening in the United States today.

During the period of the 1950s to the mid-1980s, IBM was preeminent in its field—so much so that management, and a large segment of the investing public, considered the company virtually invincible; which, in turn, enabled the management (or so I thought) to rest on its laurels, almost to the point of becoming cataleptically complacent, otherwise known as going to sleep.

But while they were somnambulant, a few bright youngsters here and there were tinkering with circuits, chips, and calculators in their garages and hobby shops, and by the mid-eighties were able to turn out amazingly sophisticated devices that were competitive with IBM, and at lower prices. Competition turned into catastrophe: IBM stock fell from 175, in 1987, to 49 in 1992; thousands of employees were retired or discharged; plants, closed or abandoned; and dividends to stockholders were reduced substantially—as was the credit rating of the company. No such corporate financial collapse, on so large a scale, had ever happened before in this country—possibly in the world.

The same kind of complacency may underlie the American economy today, as a consequence of the cataclysmic events of the last three quarters of the twentieth century. That is, although we were slow in entering the First World War, our ability to convert quickly and efficiently from peacetime to wartime production amazed everyone; after the war ended, these facilities were just as quickly reconverted to peacetime production, again to the astonishment of the rest of the world, while Europe had an uphill struggle to recover. We thus were, or appeared to be, preeminent in the industrial world—until depression took the wind out of our sails in the 1930s. Depressed conditions persisted—in spite (or because) of efforts by the Roosevelt administration to "program" and "manage" the economy—until the Second World War broke out in 1938. That pulled us out of the Depression; then Pearl Harbor drew us directly into the conflict and we again, as in 1917, startled the world more than ever with our capacity to produce, produce, and continue producing ships, tanks, armor, and airplanes—in unbelievable quantities, incredibly fast. We had become, indisputably, the world's greatest industrial power.

But nothing endures. No sooner had this war ended (in 1945) and we had begun to relax, than the Cold War developed; this time *we* would be the primary target. As a result we began another massive military build-up, which dwarfed in magnitude anything that had ever been undertaken anywhere heretofore. If anyone, up to this time, still doubted our industrial prowess, he now was forced to concede that no other country could match our performance, duplicate our achievement, or compete with our competence: and, most remarkable of all, we did it without lowering our standard of living, without reducing the supply of consumer goods, and without serious inflation.

As a result, we also became overconfident and self-satisfied (as IBM had been before the mid-1980s). What we overlooked was that, while we had been producing weapons for a market where cost was of secondary importance, producers in other countries were developing their capacity to turn out consumer goods at costs that *were* competitive in free markets.

Thus, when the Cold War ended in the late 1980s, we were left with prodigious facilities that were capable of producing the wrong things for the wrong reasons, and with a labor force whose wage scales and fringe benefits were not adjusted to the competitive market for consumer goods. We even had labor contracts that obligated an employer to pay wages to workers laid off due to lack of demand. Many foreign producers were thus able to underprice us even while using old, labor-intensive methods. As a result American producers began moving their sophisticated machines abroad and teaching low-paid foreigners how to use them, thus reducing demand for our workers here at home. This process has now reached the point in the United States where the number of people employed in federal, state, and local government exceeds the number of workers in manufacturing. All of this has been going on while we have been patting ourselves on the back for being the greatest industrial nation in the world.

At last we are discovering that it is difficult to pat ourselves on the back and produce at the same time. Indeed, we are beginning to see, but are reluctant to admit, that a socioeconomic leveling process is taking place throughout the world as a result of the current industrial-communication revolution. Wide discrepancies between the so-called "rich" nations, like the United States, and the many "poor" nations—in terms of their living conditions, production methods, education, health, and welfare—are diminishing; productivity in poorer countries is rising, but their costs, proportionately, are not, partly because high birthrates keep labor cheap, and partly because welfare and work are looked upon as separate concepts. Consequently, our competitive advantage is shrinking and our standard of living is falling. The communication revolution is as potent an economic force today as the industrial revolution was a century and a half ago.

Our efforts to adapt to this new world order are and will continue to be handicapped by the necessity of using funds to pay interest on and reduce our overwhelming national debt; and at the same time maintain our elaborate welfare and entitlement programs.

Reduction of the national debt deserves a high priority, not only because of the interest charge (one of the largest items in the budget), but also because we have to depend to a degree on foreign investors to buy our bonds. They, however, will not continue to buy them if we do not break the habit of "paying off" maturing obligations with new (refunding) issues, which continue to decline in value as the dollar does. If foreign investors, for one reason or another, become less interested in our government securities (as lenders have done with reference to IBM), they might well demand cash at maturity of their treasury obligations—which monetizes the national debt to that extent, thus increasing the volume of currency in circulation without reference to economic activity; and that lays the foundation for inflation.

The only way a government can pay or reduce its debt is through taxation, either direct or indirect, the latter being inflation. Since deliberate inflation is unconscionable—a means of confiscation of property without due process—direct taxation at rates sufficiently high to pay current expenses of the government and reduce the debt besides tends to become as confiscatory *with* due process as inflation is without due process. If the tax bite reaches the point where the return on private investment is insufficient to cover the basic costs of doing business, entrepreneurs, venture capitalists, corporations, and others who produce goods and employ workers tend to transfer their operations to countries where fewer taxes and other burdens are imposed by government on the productive process. In other words, a country that is deeply in debt is, practically speaking, in a no-win situation. There are good reasons for thinking that we may be approaching a no-win situation today. If so, the long run outlook is less than encouraging.

When a young friend who was more interested in entertainment than economics and finance read this she asked, "What can an economic illiterate like me do to counteract the effects of higher taxes or inflation or both on me and my standard of living?"

"Not much" I had to tell her, especially because of her lack of knowledge of tax-avoidance devices and tax shelters.

"Tax shelters?" she said. "What are those?"

That gave me an idea. Christmas was only a few weeks away and I had not bought, designed, or composed a greeting card. Could I combine tinsel and taxes this year as I did with Santa and silk ties once before? That would not be easy, said I to myself because Santa giveth, but taxes taketh away. They are incompatible opposites, aren't they? Yes, but I'll give it a try. Here is what came out:

"Since it has long been customary to call a Chicago ball club White Sox (instead of White Socks), why couldn't a shelter for tacks be a tax shelter? All you need to know is how to construct the shelter (See sketch.) So here are the directions: (1) cut the solid lines; (2) fold the dotted lines; (3) place two carpet tacks in the structure (but leave the facade open to enable you to see if any insider trading is going on). This little gift should cheer you, not only during this yuletide, but also on or before April 15 every year.

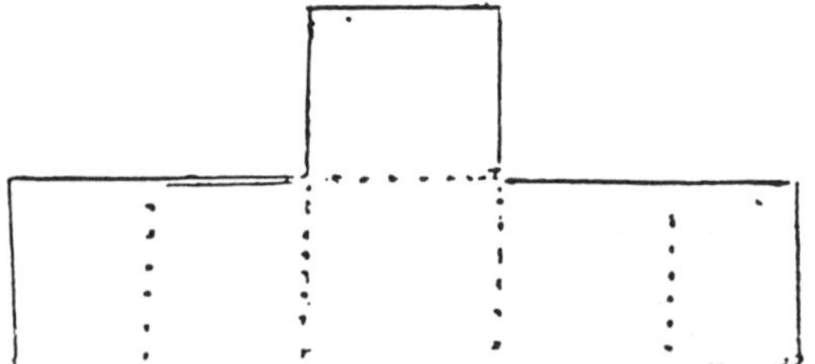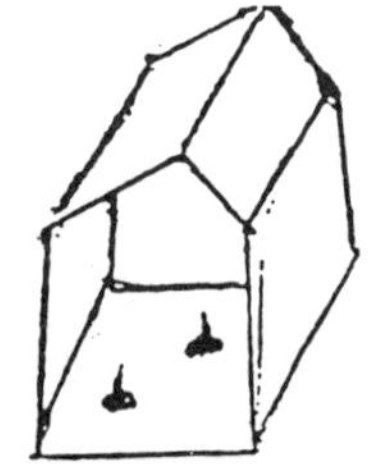

"Counsel has advised that I add an exculpatory clause, to the effect that my recommendation has not been approved or disapproved by the IRS; that there are no warranties, either express or implied, and that I am not the SOB you see in the upper-lefthand corner: that's the star of Bethlehem.

"Irvin"

Preferring to be more facetious than factual whenever possible, I decided to do another home-made greeting card in December 1993 with the following message:

"We are still running a hospice of sorts for my dear wife of 92, which has raised the question in my mind as to how soon Santa will become a victim of her kind of disability (Alzheimer's), the first symptoms of which will be that he will leave a doll for David and nothing for Nataly. His ultimate demise will probably occur, I imagine, at about the time when so many people in the United States will have come from cultures where there never was such a character that he will not be missed—except by department stores.

"That led me to realize that in a few years I'll not be missed either, although I shall leave about a three hundred-page calling card which I started writing on my ninety-second birthday and finished a few months ago on my ninety-fifth. So although I'll not be missed, I may be remembered as the jackass who thought or hoped that people would read an autobiography of a nobody.

"Also, before I forget, I hope you will have a happy new year too; but we are both likely to be disappointed in this respect if we read newspapers, listen to the radio, or look at TV.

"In spite of which, best wishes,

"Irvin"

When the story of the twentieth century is written, preferably by historians, not humorists, they are likely to say it was a period of revolutions—a continuation of the industrial revolution of the nineteenth century and the information and sexual revolutions that are occurring in our midst today.

For example, if you had said seventy-five years ago that co-education should include co-habitation you would have been considered amoral, immoral, or subversive. And if you went to the extreme of licentiousness and recommended that children in high school be taught (if they didn't know) the difference between "safe" sex and "other" sex, and that sexual materials should be issued to them as a part of their education as books are, you would have been called a lunatic libertine and removed to a public institution for crazy people.

But now that we raise no objections to an active sex life of adolescents and, in fact, provide them with certain materials that do not necessarily facilitate fornication but do tend to decrease the risk of infection and pregnancy, and no one has been sent to jail or to an asylum for the insane for doing so, has not the time come for progressively minded members of society to advocate that we provide libidinous laboratories in school buildings where youngsters could try out the recommended practices and procedures during study periods or after school hours? After all, you wouldn't have a ball team without a playing field or a swimming team without a pool, would you? Providing equipment without a place where it can be used or tried out is negligence, is it not?

Then, as part of the expanded educational program, if a pupil finds or thinks he has found either a valid criticism or has a constructive suggestion concerning a recommended procedure or prophylactic, shouldn't he be encouraged to discuss it with his faculty advisor? And in that case shouldn't the teacher have the right, if not the obligation, to test the pupil's opinion, with the cooperation, including copulation if necessary, of another member of the teaching staff (preferably but not necessarily one of the opposite sex) in another lascivious laboratory reserved for the faculty?

Revolutions, however, usually spawn counterrevolutions, and the sexual revolution is no exception. Just when we thought we had finally thrown off the yoke of virginity, a plague arises that threatens to foreclose our newly found freedom (which those who believe in divine intervention tell us is punishment for our sinful relaxation of sexual restraints).

But there are many disbelievers. A little more than seventy years ago, for example, when I was an undergraduate at Columbia University, Hartley Hall, a dormitory for men on the extreme end of the block between Amsterdam and Broadway between 115th and 116th Streets was as far away from Furnald Hall, a dormitory for women, as it was possible to build them and still have them on campus. If a Hartley student happened to be curious as to whether the layout of the floors above the lobby was the same in Furnald as in Hartley, the only way he could find out would be by looking at the architect's drawings because the housemother (usually a middle-aged matron who, like the dean of women for the university as a whole, probably had never been married or anything) stood guard over the residents in three shifts, day and night, to make certain that the virtue of the girls would not be imperiled.

The closest I ever got to one of these co-eds was when one of the theaters in Times Square "papered the house," i.e., delivered a bundle of orchestra seat tickets to the university book store for sale at fifty cents apiece, apparently because the public was not buying them at five dollars apiece.

When one of the Furnald girls appeared at the university cafeteria for lunch one day and I was working at the salad counter, I impulsively asked her if she would like to go to the theater that night. Yes, she would.

Getting her out of the dorm that evening required, first, that the housemother see and size me up. I don't think I was fingerprinted and we didn't have social security numbers in those days, but when she was assured that I lived across South Field in Hartley and that I probably could be apprehended and appropriately penalized if the theater turned out to be a ruse for a deleterious purpose, she was willing to entrust the girl to me and had her sign out and indicate her expected time of return.

For two nickels we were whisked to Times Square via the subway; after the performance, back to 116th Street by the same method, and direct to Furnald, where the night matron on duty unlocked the door. I was permitted to say good-bye by shaking the girl's hand. After signing in, she was subject to the additional surveillance of the twelve o'clock bedcheck. (What responsibilities a housemother had in days long gone!)

Turn now to the year 1990, some sixty-eight years later, when I revisited Hartley. I found women in the lobby—not particularly unusual, since the undergraduate school also was co-ed—but what seemed more unlikely was that the fair sex were also in the elevators, which took them inevitably to the inner sanctum of the upper floors, which in my day were never even seen, must less occupied, by anyone but males.

This called for further reconnoitering. Thus, when I stepped out of the elevator on the tenth floor where my room was in 1922, the first person I saw was a girl (young enough to be my great-grand-child) who had a bag of books over her shoulder and obviously was not a chambermaid; so said I to myself, *I guess this is the girls' floor; I'd better get out.* So I walked down to the ninth floor, but girls were down there, too. So I said to one of them, "Is this a girls' dorm now?"

"No, sir," said she. (Yes, she really did say "sir," which pleased as much as it surprised me; she evidently was from a family old-fashioned enough to think that the young should speak respectfully to older people, whether agreeing with them in general or not.)

But her response left me confused. Since I had now found women on two floors, I said, "How come they don't call this a women's dorm?"

"Because men live here, too."

"On what floors?"

"Any floor, all floors."

"You mean men and women live on the same floor?"

"Yes, sir. But in separate rooms."

"Do they have separate bathrooms, I hope?"

"Yes, sir."

"Thank you," I said. "You have been very kind in answering what must have sounded like foolish questions," which caused her to chuckle a bit as she rushed to the elevator.

But I had now to go nostalgically to my old room, stand outside, and do a silent meditation. In my day the boy in the next room had a baby grand piano on which he played Chopin's nocturnes and Mozart's *Eine Kleine Nachtmusik*. Now the baby grand was gone, but a babe had taken its place. In the long run, I wondered to myself, which was better? Sixty-eight years before, I was a victim of the "cold shower" solution of the president of Indiana University and the self-flagellating fortitude of the Reverend H. R. Mott of the YMCA.

What a change! Has there ever been a cultural revolution as profound and pervasive in so short a time as our attitude toward sex in the latter part of the twentieth century? Even the parents of the young lady who answered my questions, who must have believed in old-fashioned virtues, judging from their daughter's courteous demeanor, apparently were sufficiently flexible in the sociosexual sense to allow her to attend one of the many universities where students of both sexes occupy the same residence halls.

And what has happened to the holy house mothers and deans of women? Have they managed to survive by changing their character? Have they been able to shed their inhibitions as tadpoles shed their tails, becoming ambivalent ideationally as the tailless tadpoles become amphibian? If not, are they now employed in housing the homeless?

In a broad sense, what we are talking about here are changes in lifestyles as a result of the weakening of two pillars of society that in the past influenced social behavior to a considerable degree, namely, religion and the family. Religions are accepting sexual freedom mainly because they no longer have sufficient influence to suppress it, and increasingly the family is sexual freedom in fact. More and more children think there is nothing unusual, if they think about it at all, in one-parent families or two-parent families in which the parents are not married. Young couples living together refer to each other as "girlfriend" or "boyfriend" and no stigma attaches to it. In time the marriage system as we know it will be vestigial.

This should come as no surprise. The original reason for marriage was economic since only one person was a wage earner; now that both parents are likely to be wage earners, it is unnecessary to bind them together.

Chapter 41
Of Mastodons, Monkeys, and Man

This may be almost the end of the tale, but not quite the end of the teller; I've got to hold out for at least six more years to validate the title of the book. Otherwise, I may be cited for mislabeling. I wonder if, when the end does come, it will be absolute—without continuation in any form or place—or whether life here will be a prelude to something better or worse later on. And, in either case, will "they" "up there" then tell us, more convincingly than "they" do "down here," what the purpose of the whole business is?

The "revelation," which the mysterious overlord of the universe is alleged to have put out for the benefit of "the one-book" man (beware of him), is far from convincing to many of us, although it is amazing how many believers there are and how they are growing both in number and fanaticism in a few places in this world. Some of the followers of the "prophet" Muhammad, for example, evidently believe that they will receive a one-way prepaid ticket to an everlasting life of bliss in heaven if only they "liquidate," "rub out," or just plain kill someone who differs from them whom they label "infidel." And, not to be outdone, an Orthodox Jew will tell you that Jehovah gave the Israelites a quitclaim or grant deed to a parcel of real estate here on earth long before Muhammad ever was heard of. Nobody else has a right to occupy it without first receiving the express consent of these earthly, heavenly endowed landlords.

Just who and what are we, anyhow? The so-called scriptural "revelations" may be folklore at best, and wishful thinking at worst. May we, in fact, be little more than potential piles of compost? Or, alternatively, are we spare parts in a worldly warehouse, waiting for our turn to be spot welded or bolted into the latest version of a supernova and shot off at other planets for the purpose of extinguishing life, such as a dinosaur population, or, just for the hell of it, to knock a planet off its axis? On the other hand, is there a competing, more benevolent overlord who sometimes uses his power and influence to create rather than destroy planets? In that case, if I happen to be hanging around when he (she) is planning the next job, I'll suggest that whatever comes up from earth will better serve the purpose of destruction than creation, because we have had more practice in, and are more adept at, the former.

Is that because, to us, this world seems more like a doctor's waiting room, with dim lights, shabby chairs, and last month's magazines, where we wait until our name is called? And is this what causes many of us to become restless and inclined to plunder, pollute, fight, fornicate, and overpopulate?

The question is further complicated by the fact that the former tenants of this earthly domicile, the dinosaurs, kept it in good condition and developed a self-sustaining ecosystem that after millions of years was at least as wholesome as it had been when they'd inherited it from the fishes (following their decision to return to the more congenial environment of the sea after giving up the experiment of living on land). True, the carnivores among them ate the more docile herbivores; but never were there any world wars.

By comparison we are such shortsighted simpletons, careless housekeepers, and demographic dumbbells that, during the few minutes of cosmic time we have been here, have managed to uproot rain forests and clear-cut the rest, lose or contaminate much of our topsoil, and dump refuse into lakes, streams, and bays because the money for sewage treatment and fertilizer plants goes for sports arenas and parking lots instead.

If there is such a thing as the Heavenly Holding Company, Inc., a lot of heads must have rolled when it was discovered that good dinosaur tenants had been killed off and their domicile turned over to monkeys who, everybody should have known, would not only neglect the place, but overpopulate and ultimately destroy it.

In view of the easily accessible Library of the Lord and the complete Encyclopedia of Omniscience, there was no excuse for this biological blunder of turning the whole planetary kit and kaboodle over to us by way of our inexperienced, tree-dwelling ancestors.

In the annals of the angels, this dinosaur-monkey debacle ranked as one of the greatest blunders of all time, and seems unlikely ever to be exceeded, and indeed wasn't, until a few months ago, when IBM managed to pull off a bigger one.

The reminders of the end of one species and the succession of another may not throw much light on the probable end of us, the end of the book, or the end of me. So having reached, in a manner of speaking, a "dead" end, I relax, turn on my CD, and listen to the incomparable performance by Van Cliburn of twenty-six compositions of piano music. What impresses me is not only Cliburn's genius, but also how few masterful composers there have been since the time of the dinosaurs—not more than fifty or sixty out of the billions of us who have come and gone. The fact that an auditory disturbance called "rock" passes for music and is overwhelmingly popular, while a comparatively small auditorium is usually large enough to accommodate those who know the difference between racket (rock) and music, is simply one more reason for thinking that the intelligence quotient of the race, although it may have improved somewhat in the last four million years, is now declining on the average to the level of our simian relatives before they came down from the trees.

Including mine—inasmuch as I haven't been able to think of a suitable valedictory or word of appreciation for your forbearance in wading through so many pages of this text; at which juncture Cindy, my middle-aged granddaughter, came to my room.

"After glancing through parts of the MS," she said, "I think, Gramps, your ideas on inflation might justify your critics in saying that your mental capacity really isn't a heck of a lot better than that of your four-legged relatives."

"Why do you think my idea is more simian than sensible?"

"Well, in the first place, I remember the story you once told me about the proud father who watched a victorious regiment march up Broadway in a ticker-tape parade some years ago; and how he told everybody his son was one of the soldiers in the parade, and the only one in step."

"So, what's the connection?" said I.

"I don't read the financial news much," she replied, "but lately, even first-page news headlines have quoted authorities from the chairman of the Federal Reserve system, former and current members of the Council of Economic Advisers, economists who have been awarded the Nobel prize—in fact, practically everybody but you says we don't have to worry about inflation; it's under control. So it looks like everybody is out of step but you."

"I see what you mean. However, the difference between what these respectable people are saying, and what I have said, is in the time factor: they are talking short term; my outlook is long term. The political crowd, particularly, tend to think in cycles of four years or less: the president starts running for reelection the day he is sworn in for the first term. Investors, securities dealers, and brokers hope to show a profit in a few weeks or months; many people, when they buy a stock or bond, start checking quotations the next day or week.

"Our government has carried on fallacious fiscal policies for sixty years; the fact that no disastrous consequences have occurred thus far is no guarantee that they will never happen. Historically, upheavals have always followed unsound fiscal policies. Can it be that our government is the only one in step?"

"Okay, Grandpappy," said she, "but, in general, how short is short run and how long is long run?"

"If you will tell me the difference between individual psychology, rational psychology, and mass or mob psychology, I might be able to give you a reasonable answer. No one can predict mass behavior, when faith will give way to fear, confidence to confusion, or optimism to pessimism. When an event or series of events starts a reaction up or down, it tends to spread throughout the public consciousness, slowly at first and later like wildfire; optimism gathers momentum more slowly than pessimism, because, in economic matters, it requires money to take advantage of 'opportunities for profit'; but when pessimism gets into the public psyche everyone tries to get out 'before it's too late,' which often means it's already too late. It may take years to develop a 'bull market,' but only a few months or less to 'correct' it—'correction' being a Wall Street euphemism for misdirected mob psychology."

"So you're going to stick to your guns—your portentous prediction, in Chapter 29, that we are sitting on what we in the old days would have called a powder keg and what today is better described as an atomic stockpile?"

"No, not an instantaneous occurrence; rather a gradual process that gathers momentum and accelerates until it reaches a climax."

"What can we do to slow down or reverse the trend?"

"Damned little. Since we get into trouble by borrowing heavily and spending more, the only antidote is to pay the debts, and save more. But that brings about 'depression' and unemployment; there is no quick fix. Does that make me a pessimist or a realist?"

In came now my second granddaughter, Bethy. She, too, said she has read my tale of woe, but she would like to know if I could list the salient points so that he who runs may read. "If people have to correct their mistakes," she said, "they will not have time to read stuff like your book."

My answer was that, although abbreviation may be the soul of wit, it also tends to shortchange logic and reason and may not be convincing; but I'll try to hit some high spots in the next chapter.

Chapter 42
Looking Ahead

When this tale was started three years ago the intention was to see if a superannuate had enough of his marbles to write a lighthearted anecdotal account of his life in at least two centuries and, with a little luck and a bit more longevity, three centuries. At the moment it looks as if this objective might be realized.

As the story unfolded, however, it seemed desirable to include various social, political, and economic changes and developments during my ninety-five years in so far as they have affected you, me, and millions of others and which are likely to affect future generations even more.

As a result, some of the lightheartedness has been lessened by the inclusion of a few unfavorable forecasts, most of which our children and grandchildren will have to deal with unless certain social and economic measures currently unpopular and others practically inconceivable are accepted and activated. A few of these may be mentioned in abbreviated form to enable those who run to read:

Population

Man was asleep at the switch when he became responsible for controlling his numbers; he let the population spigot run on and on regardless of consequences. Although it took four million years to produce the first four billion people, we are able (with the help of the right-to-lifers, the pope, rabbis, ayatollahs, mullahs, Mormons, the religious right, and little schoolgirls) to produce again that many worldwide in less than thirty-eight years, which amounts to about 260,000 more by this time tomorrow and 1.8 million a week from now. Our priorities are so disorganized that we produce people before we arrange to have food and shelter for them.

It seems never to have occurred to us that if the population were stabilized at an optimum level it would not be necessary to provide more of everything year after year but rather only enough to replace what wears out or what we destroy while fighting each other (for the preservation of peace). What we saved thereby could be made available for new or improved goods and services to enhance our standard of living.

The optimal level of the world's population might be roughly calculated by determining the number of acres of land required to produce food (a balanced diet) and the basic amount of clothing and shelter for one person and relating that figure to the amount of arable land in the world. Such calculations have been made, and they show that we have exceeded our productive capacity for even a minimum standard of living and that starvation awaits a continuously increasing population worldwide. More so than ever before, the right-to-life in many parts of the world will be a right-to-die of disease and starvation after birth. We could have halted this holocaust in the early part of the twentieth century when the world's population may have approximated more nearly an optimum level.

One of the most unfortunate side effects of the population explosion is the differential rate of increase among races. If one racial group, for example, increases numerically in a community while another group does not, the latter begins to feel less secure and conflict between the two tends to develop. Strategists in race relations have even been known to recommend that members of their race have more children to increase their numerical strength. If such a practice leads to more dependency on welfare, a few members of the racial minority tend to take matters into their own hands—which unfortunately does not always avoid bloodshed. (P.S. If I can think of anything in favor of increasing population, I promise to include it in the next edition.)

Big Government

That government is best that governs least. If there is a more heretical slogan in modern society, or indeed has ever been, I'd like to know what it is. Governments everywhere either take more power by force or are given more power by the governed as they rely on government to do more and more for them that they should be endeavoring to do for themselves. The original and primary function of government is to preserve law, order, and justice.

Even in this country where we have faith in the productivity of private initiative, we have departed so far and so completely from this concept beginning with the New Deal that we are unable to undertake even minor ventures without first hiring lawyers and accountants, consulting bureaucrats and government agencies, and digesting reams of instructions put out by the government printing office (when it is not turning out more paper money).

The tentacles of government grew in size and sensitivity during the New Deal as a consequence of the belief that the private sector was unable to manage the economy and that the government could do so if it assumed the responsibility, as Russia had.

This train of thought was in the air when the Second World War broke out and when in time we were caught up in a life and death struggle in which the economy became subservient to the military and completely subject to government domination. The ideal of the New Deal was realized.

The Cold War made a continuation of many government controls expedient as we became chief policeman of the world to put down local squabbles and political uprisings, many of which were presumably inspired or implanted by Russia to harass us.

The psychological impact on American citizens of this expansion of activities and seemingly altruistic foreign policy was that if we can spend billions to fight big and little wars in other parts of the world and give away millions more to repair the damage, we should be able to provide more, bigger, and better welfare programs for our people at home. Since, however, our government didn't have enough hard money without raising taxes to do both, it did so with borrowed funds, thus boosting the national debt from less than a trillion dollars in 1982 to more than four trillion in 1993. At the present rate of burning the nation's candle at both ends, our public debt will come close to six trillion dollars in a few years—unless we, to paraphrase the late Hon. William Jennings Bryan, refuse to be "crucified on the cross" of perennial deficits and a rising national debt. The only trouble is that there's no way to stop deficits except by spending less and taxing more, neither of which a legislator is likely to vote for unless he plans to retire from political life when his term expires. Likewise, there's no way to reduce the public debt except by taxing more directly and (more insidiously) by indirect taxation, i.e., inflation.

Inflation

Inflate a basketball beyond its normal capacity and there'll be no bounce, no game. Increase currency independently of production, and the price level in the long run will tend to rise sufficiently to equate the two; and the (economic) game will go on. Some will call it "prosperity."

The ethical standards of our government do not permit it to create money except for purposes such as offsetting budgetary deficits incurred in carrying out mandates of Congress. If and when, under these circumstances, the volume of currency approaches the critical mass, chapter 29 suggests the scenario that tends to unfold at this juncture. Those who foresee the consequences buy gold, productive mines, oil wells, land, and other productive real estate, assets that in general increase in price as currency decreases in purchasing power.

"But," said one of my friends, "if we've been running deficits ever since Roosevelt and Keynes got their heads together, why haven't we had more than the 3 or 4 percent annual inflation rate, which is bad enough, but not cataclysmic as it should have been according to your theory?"

"Good question; hard answer," I said. "The probable explanation is at least twofold. First, that our productive capacity is so great that we have been able to combine welfare and warfare without creating shortages of consumer goods. But items that can not be increased as rapidly as the volume of currency have risen substantially. The price of gold in current dollars, for example, is fourteen times greater than it was prior to the New Deal. The reproduction cost of the house I am sitting in is twelve times what it was in 1960, and close to 150 times what it was when the New Deal (or rather the New Deficits) began. Likewise, the financial markets; would stocks and bonds have risen as much if the volume of currency (measured in part by the size of our national debt) had not risen as much as it has?

"Precisely when the critical mass of currency, or loss of confidence in the dollar, is in danger of occurring is unpredictable because it is a manifestation of massive psychological behavior or mob psychology, a mental attitude that spreads like wildfire when triggered by an unsettling occurrence of one kind or another, real or fancied."

Taxation

Congressmen do have consciences; and when they see handwriting on the wall, even though some of them don't seem to be able to read it, as a body they conclude that steps should be taken (after the next election) to at least balance the budget. (Overbalancing it to provide a surplus for reducing the public debt is probably too much to expect.)

But my granddaughter at this point suggested that criticizing Congress was like a pot calling the kettle black. "You made a big mistake many years ago," she said, "when you took that bookkeeping job at the Corn Exchange Bank and later another boner when you accepted an uncongenial assignment at Met. Life—both instances of either bad judgment or stupidity (as you call some of my decisions). So how can we be sure that your ideas about deficits, debt, and democracy aren't equally flawed?"

(One of the results of criticisms of this kind is that they are a sign of intelligence; and if they come from one's blood relative, at least some of that intelligence must have come from you and that restores some of one's self-confidence.)

I had also to admit she had a good point. Only time will tell. The fact that so few economists seem to take as dismal a view of the future as I do may only add credence to the opinion that the economic system is so complex none of us is able to comprehend the interrelationship of all markets, and forecast completely and accurately the consequences of a business venture or a broad policy of government. That is the risk factor. That may be why business enterprises generally confine their operations to single markets and why conglomerates frequently run into trouble, "downsize," and sell off operations not closely related to their core business.

But if "something should be done" (but not until after the next election!) to balance the budget and reduce the deficit how shall we pluck the goose to cause the least squawking? "We refuse to curtail welfare," legislators will say for publication; and privately, not for publication, "because that will cost us votes. Why not tax corporations? They don't vote, and they've got lots of money. And the rich too. We'll probably lose their vote anyway, but there are many more poor folk who will vote for us than rich who will vote against us."

This narrows the alternatives down, as usual, to the corporate and personal income tax, the government's major source of revenue. The result is that we have developed in the last sixty or seventy years an internal revenue code of about 2,000 pages, close to 10,000 pages of regulations, and 200,000 pages of judicial rulings, comprising one of the most confounding, confusing, frustrating, administratively expensive, and economically destructive bodies of law conceived by man since the days of Hammurabi or even Moses. It is practically incomprehensible even to tax attorneys and accountants, including agents and employees of the IRS. Submit a tax problem to the latter and you are likely to get as many different answers as respondences.

In addition to which, as individuals we spend billions of hours every year keeping tax records and either filling out tax forms ourselves or turning the data over to our accountants for completion of the complicated form 1040; multiply our time by its value per hour and you come up with an incredibly large cost before you write a single check payable to the IRS.

The present body of laws, regulations, and court decisions not only make compliance costly and nerve-wracking, they make it necessary to research and consider the tax consequences of every investment or business undertaking, as well as its economic soundness. Many otherwise desirable business ventures are abandoned after the tax consequences are factored in or else the undertaking is transferred to another country (evidence of which is our unfavorable balance of trade).

A national sales tax, properly drawn so as to eliminate its regressive feature, would raise more revenue, eliminate most of the unproductive costs of compliance with the present law, minimize the warping of business undertakings, reduce if not eliminate a huge underground tax-dodging network, and generally improve taxpayer morale. The only losers would be tax attorneys and accountants, but the stimulus to the economy that would come if a sound and equitable tax system were in use would go a long way toward filling the gap in their operations. In any case, the income tax must go.

Welfare

In the twentieth century schizophrenia became a geopolitical disease as many nations developed dual or split purposes, that is, a foreign policy designed to wipe a neighbor or competitor off the face of the earth and a domestic policy designed to improve the welfare of its citizens, even if there was not enough tax income to pay for both. Foreign policy involves death and destruction; domestic policy, the opposite. Both are extremely costly. We have adopted, in a broad sense, a three-way method of footing the bill in which the government, the beneficiary, and an employer (if any) jointly cover the cost. The part paid by the government is one of the large items responsible for the budget deficit, about which enough has been said. What are the implications as far as American business is concerned?

Companies that operate solely in the domestic market have to compete only with producers subject to the same expenses, and to a greater or less degree they can shift the burden to consumers; but if they are in competition with foreign producers here and in the international market, they are at a competitive disadvantage if foreign producers are not required by their governments to share similar costs. Under these circumstances American producers try to avoid at least the taxes levied to cover welfare either by hiring "temporary" workers or by producing some components abroad, by "farming out" jobs to home workers or, as a last resort, by moving the entire business to foreign soil.

Our Standard of Living

Our government has become a sty and the U.S. Treasury, the trough. As a welfare state it does many things for its citizens that they used to do for themselves, and we have come to think of this as normal. Although there may be no legal requirement or logical reason for governments to provide old-age insurance, health care, and various other benefits, justification for doing so, if any is needed, is that it redresses to a degree the disparity in well-being between those who have more and those who have fewer necessities of life, the only question being, where to draw the line. This is further complicated by the fact that beneficiaries, who greatly outnumber benefactors, hold the purse strings of government in a democracy.

If any additional complications are needed they include the fact that with the development of our monetary or exchange economy, we as individuals produce practically nothing we consume and are therefore totally dependent on an income of cash. The subsistence homestead, an economic anchor to windward, once a source of satisfaction and family security, is a long-forgotten, impractical way of life in our industrial, exchange society—to our disadvantage, one might say.

The nearest substitute to the degree of security of a subsistence homestead is cash in a savings account, a concept too often replaced by a debit balance in a credit card account (that being a part of the monetary-exchange economy many consumers have learned so well).

Although the standard of living in a country depends on many factors, the question in the United States today is how our standard is or may be affected by budget deficits and an unusually large public debt.

If direct taxation of consumers and corporations is one of the fiscal methods employed to reduce deficits and the national debt, the standard of living of individuals will be adversely affected because (1) the consumer will have less to spend by the amount of the tax, and (2) if corporations are required to pay more taxes, this may necessitate increasing the price of finished products. Since foreign producers may not be subject to the same kind of expense, they may be able to undersell us. We may find ways to reduce costs, including wages, but if that proves to be insufficient the temptation will be to move the business operation to the competitive country. If you don't lick 'em, join 'em. In either case, our standard of living suffers.

But from the long-term point of view, a counterbalancing worldwide adjustment may be taking place. That is, as the economies of Third World countries begin to improve—in part due to the migration of industry from countries like the United States—wages rise, savings begin to accumulate, the necessity of a large family to provide old-age security for parents subsides, population grows at a reduced rate, the bargaining power of labor improves—in brief, their standard of living tends to rise with industrialization, while ours tends to decline under the stress of global change and competition. The ultimate, long-term result will be an approximate leveling of standards worldwide as a result of international trade and communication.

Future generations in this country will feel the impact of these developments more and more due to the increasing proportion of old people and the declining proportion of wage earners to support them. The standard of living of both groups will be under this additional pressure arising from the demographic dilemma we face.

Drugs

Some people never learn. Maybe the eugenists are right when they say the intelligence of the human race is declining because the growth of population is occurring among those with the lowest IQ. How else explain that in trying to solve the drug problem we are using the same methods that failed to eliminate the liquor problem? For the benefit of those who can't read and others who can't remember, prohibition fostered an underground economy; made gangsters rich (being tax dodgers); increased the production, sale, and use of firearms, which were necessary to rub out competitors; and introduced an aperitif more commonly known as bathtub gin and other libations not greatly different from rubbing alcohol. Importing the real thing from Canada and Europe expanded international trade but did not affect the balance of payments because the "ports" of entry were muddy beaches shrouded in darkness; smugglers are smarter than senators. After about a dozen years of deception and duplicity, the Roosevelt administration killed the Volstead Act. They failed, however, to emphasize the futility of fighting personal and private behavior by law.

Consequently, when drug trafficking and use became widespread, and since legal bodies have only one remedy for everything, it was decided to eliminate drugs by enacting yet another law. As a result, what we now have is an army of "enforcement" agents and formidable interdiction facilities costing billions of dollars, the effect of which is to encourage murders, robberies, muggings, gangsterism, an underground economy, counterfeiting, and tax dodging—which does little to solve the drug problem. If anything, this cumbersome bureaucracy worsens the problem by making the junk scarcer, addiction more expensive, robbery more "necessary," killing more common, and arrests routine. Jails and prisons are now so overcrowded that the criminals of last week are turned back to the streets to make room for those brought in this week. Mental patients and misfits are likewise turned loose to become homeless. The situation will be "taken care of," however, if we okay the several-million-dollar bond measure at the next election so we can build more and bigger jails and houses of detention. The trouble is that it takes years to build new jails, the completion of which is held up because the cost of construction is always greater than was estimated and a supplementary bond issue must be voted. Meanwhile, the streets and our homes become more dangerous; only new windows, practically unopenable from the outside, prevented an uninvited guest from paying a nocturnal visit to our bedroom a few months ago.

In this connection, I have to tell a relevant tale about my experience with the drug problem, not however as a user. One Monday morning my maid told me that her daughter had been mugged the previous Saturday night, her jaw badly broken, and that her mouth was wired shut after emergency treatment at a hospital (at our expense). The mugger's motive, the daughter said, was snatching her purse. (I wondered why a mugger would break a person's jaw if the motive was money, but I let it go at that.)

A week later on Sunday afternoon, a person I had never seen before rang my doorbell. Unsuspectingly I opened the door and there was a young woman whose mouth was wired shut; she handed me a note, which read substantially as follows; "The car Mother bought some time ago has been impounded by the police because there are $200 worth of unpaid parking tickets against it; she is being held by the police in the city jail until she pays up. I have $100; Mother would be grateful if you would advance me another $100 so we can get her out of jail and regain possession of the car."

Although I did not know her, I had also studied the law of probability in a math class in college seventy-five years ago, and I remembered enough of it to believe that people with broken jaws and mouths wired shut do not occur at random and that this, therefore, must be Mattie's daughter.

She arrived at my house in a taxi, so I said, "Hold the cab and let's go over to the bank and I'll draw out $100." Then I gave her $10 to cover the taxi fare, went back home, and continued reading about crime in the Sunday newspaper.

Monday morning Mattie arrived as usual. "Glad to see you're no worse for wear," I said.

"Nothing worse than my arthuritis [sic]," she said.

"How did they treat you?" I asked.

"Oh, everybody treats me okay; like you."

"I mean the police," I said. "Didn't they threaten to keep you there until you paid the $200?"

"Dr. Bussin', I don't know what you-all's talkin' about."

"Well, didn't they take your car away because of the unpaid traffic tickets you didn't know about when you bought the car?"

"I got no idea what you talkin' about. My car was right in front of my house all weekend, and I was home, too, 'cept Sunday mornin' when I went to church."

I then told her what had happened. She was extremely apologetic, but apparently less than surprised. She immediately tried to reach a parole officer in the Police Department, to report that her daughter evidently was either violating parole or being used by an addicted boyfriend. Just how the broken jaw fit into the scenario I do not know, but there must be some connection.

I concluded that the author of this scheme could make more money writing plots than panhandling.

Drug addiction should be treated as a condition, not a crime;

and with commiseration, not contempt. Narcotics should be available at market prices in pharmacies (mislabeled drugstores) to habitual users, who would have to show that they are undergoing treatment; or better still, at clinics under the health-care system. Clinics could be provided at a fraction of the billions we now spend on interdiction, which only makes the stuff less readily available and higher in price, thus making pushing more profitable and crime more common.

Some of the billions we would save, for example, could be used to provide "bed and breakfast" accommodations for the addicts and others who no longer would have to spend their nights robbing, assaulting, mugging, and murdering; we could even include croissants for breakfast, in place of that lousy puffed-up store bread.

Privatization

All efforts to reduce the spreading tentacles of big government have failed. Every administration tries to out-do its predecessor with a new and broader version of some sort of Great Society program. It began with the New Deal, which tried one alphabetical "reform" after another, all of which only hampered the economy until Adolf Schickelgruber Hitler came along. Some abuses in the financial markets were corrected; but bureaus and agencies that have long outlived their usefulness are still in existence, such as the Farm Bureau, which has over 100,000 employees, a budget of $61 million, and spends more than a dollar in overhead for every dollar it delivers in government payments to farmers. (As we go to press there are signs that Congress is going to correct this.)

We haven't begun to explore the possibilities of turning over more of the services now performed by government to companies with the lowest bids. Private enterprise with the profit motive can perform practically any function at lower cost than a government department. Margaret Thatcher proved that in Britain.

Minimum Wage Law

A well-intentioned humanitarian effort to compensate for the unequal bargaining power of two contracting parties. The result is to perpetuate a class of unemployed individuals. In desperation, many of them become disillusioned with society and, as a last resort, turn to robbery, holdups, drug trafficking, and burglary, or become welfare cases. Most of them are capable of doing something and, in our own self-interest and theirs, more effort should be devoted to placing them in jobs and paying them according to their productivity. In the process they might even learn to be more productive.

"Litigitis"

In the latter half of this century another epidemic has developed in this country for which we have no "vaccine," although Great Britain does. In the United States today, practically everybody is suing everybody else. One of the reasons your medical doctor charges so much, for example, is because he has to buy expensive liability insurance policies to protect himself from "malpractice" lawsuits.

The British "vaccine" that put an end to this menace requires the plaintiff to pay the legal expenses of a defendant if the plaintiff loses the case. Why can't we do likewise?

Term of Office

Until such time as we have reduced the national debt to a level at which we can pay maturing obligations and current interest out of income, the party in power is going to be under pressure to collect unusually large amounts of revenue and reduce expenses and outlays at the same time.

Under present conditions, however, elected officials are reluctant to do either for fear of defeat at the next election. Consequently they tend, while in office, to do what will appeal to the largest number of voters, and thus they avoid upsetting them by imposing the taxes and reducing the services that would balance a budget and restore fiscal integrity.

One way to remedy this stalemate would be to limit officeholders to one term and hope they will act, while in office, in accordance with the best interest of the country in the long run, i.e., by reducing expenses and increasing taxes. In attempting to justify such painful new policies, it would be necessary to admit that they had gotten us into the predicament of actually having to go into more debt every year just to pay interest on our existing debt, a situation a citizen would be in if he or she had to borrow money every month to pay the monthly mortgage installment. If that continued one's credit rating would decline, further borrowing would ultimately be denied, and foreclosure would follow. (Whether, when, or to what extent our government may be exposed to the same eventuality is the trillion-dollar question. Chapter 29 suggests a conceivable scenario, one we hope never develops.)

Hate and Holiness

Looking ahead to the twenty-first century, religious "fundamentalism" is likely to take the place of nationalism as a cause of conflict. Muslims will feel a sense of obligation to dispose of non-Muslims (infidels), which they may do, not with Big Berthas, submarines, aircraft carriers, and other monstrous forms of matériel, but with the help of fanatically devout members of the faith who, as their last earthly act of devotion, will become human bombs, in return for which they expect to be welcomed in heaven with open arms. Hindus, Buddhists, Sikhs, Orthodox Jews, and Orthodox Catholics all have their God-given revelations and their willingness to fight to protect them, although they are less militant. All of them, however, are growing in numbers faster than Christians in this century; and unless education overtakes superstition, voodooism could become the dominant form of worship in the next century.

Chapter 43
Political Platform, 1996

This will be the last presidential campaign of the twentieth century. The party in power will tell us how well off we are, how good they have been to us, and how it will be to our advantage to continue their leadership. The other party will find fault with most of the policies of the previous four years, but neither will "tell it like it is" in the true sense of the word, will speak in generalities, and will offer "bigger and better" public assistance programs. No mention will be made of what you can do for your government by either party; instead they will vie with each other in making generous promises (without reference to the "technical" question as to who is going to pay for them).

A third party, small in number, weak in influence, and hoarse from hawking, but sound, sincere, sensible, and far-seeing will probably rise to the occasion in a patriotic effort to fill the intellectual vacuum left by the two major parties (somewhat reminiscent of the valiant effort of the late Teddy Roosevelt and the Bull Moose party in the early years of this century).

It will probably prove to be a disappointment to these crusaders, however, because they will call a spade a spade and tell the people where we are, how we got there, and what the consequences are likely to be unless they stop reading the lips of self-promoting candidates and demand more logic in and less unfunded largess from the government. That kind of talk, will bring about their defeat because the truth is not what the public wants to hear.

Since the objective of the third party will be to point the way to the long-term well-being of our country by avoiding if possible some of the pitfalls that lie ahead, here are some of the planks this party is likely to use in building its platform for the all-important turning-point election of 1996:

1. NO SECOND TERM. The new party will recommend that henceforth, no elected official shall be permitted to succeed himself, the reason being that office holders tend to vote for proposals that will help them get reelected regardless of the longer-term consequences for the country as a whole. A legislator who voted for a pay-as-you-go program, for example, would face defeat in a campaign for reelection, while his opponent would give the impression that he could pull a rabbit out of the government's fiscal hat, thus removing the burden from voters without mentioning that the hat already has a $4 trillion hole in it through which the rabbit either has escaped or will do so soon.

2. DRUGS: LEGALIZE THEM. The new party will declare that our attempt to control the production, importation, and consumption of drugs is a leading cause of the growth of violent crimes. An addict will rob, steal, break in, assault, and murder to obtain money for the only substance that can quiet his craving. Since our purpose is to make the stuff scarce, we also make it more costly, crime more frequent, and "pushing" more profitable. Addiction is a disease, but we treat it as a crime. There is not enough jail and prison space for dangerous criminals and drug offenders, however, with the result that all too often prisoners who are a threat to all of us are paroled to make room for individuals who are guilty of little more than the disease of addiction. On top of which we try to solve the problem by building more prisons. Isn't it time we came to our senses?

Common sense tells us that drugs should be legalized and made available to addicts at pharmacies at fair market prices, provided the individual is undergoing rehabilitation at a certified clinic. Only a fraction of the billions we now waste in futile efforts at enforcement of the drug law would be required for a constructive, curative program.

3. KILL THE INCOME TAX, AND ADOPT A NATIONAL SALES TAX with appropriate and equitable provisions to offset the otherwise regressive features of the latter. The income tax and our drug policy are the most unsatisfactory, unsettling, unproductive, uneconomic encroachments in the United States today upon our right to life, liberty, and the pursuit of happiness.

4. ESTABLISH A "POPULATION" POLICY. Nothing is

gained and much is lost as a continuously growing population overloads public services, housing, schools, health facilities—practically everything, including pollution. Indeed, an expanding population is a kind of pollution. Penalties of one kind or another should be imposed on families that have more than two children, and bonuses or other inducements should be offered to families or individuals who agree to some form of sterilization. It would be desirable from the demographic point of view to provide no additional welfare payments to a parent or couple who have more than two children, the only objection being that it would impose a hardship on innocent offspring rather than irresponsible parents.

5. ABORTION is a personal matter, and government has no right to interfere with an individual's decision.

6. EUTHANASIA. An individual with an incurable disease who is kept alive with expensive artificial life-support systems or who is brain dead draws upon and greatly decreases the limited resources, financial and professional, of the health care system that would or should be available to patients who are curable. In view of the enormously increasing proportion of old people, the time has come to require all citizens in one way or another to make Living Wills authorizing euthanasia under appropriate circumstances.

7. WELFARE. The Realistic party platform will "tell it like it is" when it comes to welfare also. It will say that printing money and doling it out to rich and poor alike, as we have been doing ever since Mr. Roosevelt started it in 1933, will have to stop. If we don't stop, we shall soon have to TAX MORE.

But to support our enormous WELFARE and ENTITLEMENT programs with tax dollars would so brutalize our economy that industry would call it "cruel and unusual CAPITAL punishment" and by degrees move its resources, robots, and research to countries where the government does what governments are supposed to do—maintain law and order; where citizens provide much of their welfare, and business enterprises do what they are supposed to do—produce what the community wants as efficiently as possible and not be financial cogs in a system of public welfare. (We have wandered so far from the natural functions of government, industry, and individuals that it will take a hundred Realistic political campaigns to get us back on track.)

8. REPEAL MINIMUM WAGE LAWS. The mere suggestion that a minimum-wage law is not in the best interest of those it is designed to help is another reason why one who would make such an outlandish comment had better give serious consideration to the purchase of a metal chest protector. The fact is, however, that minimum-wage laws probably do more harm than good to the people they are supposed to protect. A worker should not be denied employment simply because he is unable to produce, say, $4.75 worth of value in an hour. What if he is able to produce $3 worth? Should he be employed at his rate? Common sense says Yes; common law says No.

Is it reasonable to think that if employed at $3 he might learn sufficiently in time to produce $4.75 worth? If given such an opportunity, will his opinion of himself improve? Will he be a more satisfactory member of society doing a $3 an hour job than as a drifting, unemployable panhandler? Is he in danger in such a situation of being drawn into the drug trade? Common sense says Yes to these questions; the law says No.

Minimum-wage laws grew out of conditions in which the demand for workers declined due to mechanization, while the supply increased due to persistent growth of population. This imbalance continues but is more pronounced in so-called Third World countries. A partial, long-run solution in a country such as the United States is two-fold: first, limit the supply of labor by limiting immigration and achieving zero population growth (ZPG); and second, eliminate or alter the income tax to remove the penalties imposed on saving and the capital gains tax to make capital more liquid, thus providing more funds for expansion and more jobs for workers.

9. PRIVATIZATION. Big government attempts to manage the economy for the "protection" of consumers from the "rapacity" of big business but is incapable of providing full and continuous employment. Big business endeavors to ward off what it calls "unnecessarily restrictive" or "confiscatory" regulations by influencing public opinion and the opinions of elected representatives with the help of congressional lobbyists.

Democracy and big government have won the contest: big government has become bigger and government controls more numerous during the latter part of this century, primarily because there is general disbelief in the potency of competition as an equitable regulator of the economy, despite the fact that it is the only method that is in harmony with the instinct of self-preservation and the acquisitive nature of man.

That form of government is best that confines itself to the preservation of law and order; the corollary to which is that many activities undertaken in recent years by big government could be done more efficiently and less expensively by private operators stimulated by the profit motive under competitive conditions.

The Realistic party, therefore, advocates turning many operations now performed by government over to private enterprise, for which there is no substitute.

10. PROSTITUTION. Legalize it, not because we favor it but because (a) it takes up too much of the time of police and courts; (b) nothing is accomplished in the process; (c) practitioners could be required to pay license fees, thus converting an expense to an income; and (d) the spread of disease could be curtailed by requiring medical examinations as part of the licensing requirement.

11. RATIONALIZE THE LEGAL SYSTEM. It is easy to sue, costly to settle, and nerve wracking to defend. Everybody is suing everybody else; many lawsuits are frivolous, but no cure for the epidemic has been found. Or maybe the Realistic party has: it will propose a federal law (thus adding one more to the intolerable number on the books) that will require the PLAINTIFF to pay all legal expenses incurred by the defendant if the plaintiff loses the suit.

Epilogue

It is with some satisfaction and a bit more trepidation that I wind up this valedictory—gratified for having completed what I started three years ago but somewhat disquieted by the fact that my outlook for the twenty-first century not only differs from that of practically all contemporary economists (and political leaders) but may also be called subversive or "un-American" (whatever that means) by others because of its generally unfavorable view of the future for our beloved land.

I tried to soften the blow and mollify the "message," but nothing would be gained by refusing to look facts in the face (as I see them), the only question being whether many of the "facts" are in reality unwarranted assumptions; that is where the dialogue, not to say the dog fight, will develop. I assure you, it would have been more pleasing to me if logic had led me to a more optimistic outlook for our economy.

The missing link in the forecasts, however, is timing. Although I have had the audacity to suggest that in the next century there are likely to be more problems than solutions, I haven't enough confidence to say *when* this or that development is likely to begin because mass behavior or mob psychology is unpredictable. Who foresaw, for example, the sexual revolution that has changed life, living patterns, and social mores in this country so suddenly? Not long ago sex and sin were (and you should pardon the expression) synonymous. No longer. Even hide-bound, church-going matrons, who have never been married or anything, don't seem to be shocked when virtuous young ladies become live-in partners with men; sexual activity for reasons other than procreation are permissible. (But if the old man is right, what present generations have gained in sexual liberation will be offset by the obligations they will inherit due to the prodigality of us, their forebears. Rearing offspring and caring for an increasing proportion of us old fogies at the same time by these on-coming generations is going to require the wisdom of a Solomon, plus perhaps the platform of a prudent political party.)

Another major social change that we did not forecast is the greatly improved economic, professional, and independent status of women in this country since the end of World War II.

Also, how in only a few weeks in the autumn of 1929 there was a complete turn-around in the mental attitude and mass behavior of the American people. Our expanded and improved communication network creates awareness, spreads an idea nationwide, and influences and unifies the public psyche as never before. Ability to read is not necessary, only the ability to hear the ubiquitous electronic transmission of the spoken word.

The consequences even of a minor change in a major policy tend to be small in the beginning, but influential in the long run; and it is the long run with which I have tempered my opinions and forecasts because at the time of writing investors still "love" our government bonds, inflation is not following deficit financing, American industry still seems able to cope with competition from lower-cost producers elsewhere, and the recession is gradually receding. So why worry?

Why indeed do I worry? Because in my opinion we have sown the wind (of unsound economic policies) and shall reap the whirlwind unless we take time by the forelock and make a herculean effort to balance the books.

As usual, I have gotten off the track. What I intended to say in this farewell is how grateful I am for your taking the time to read this bit of reminiscence and reflection. My publisher looked askance at the project at the outset, saying in effect that nobody would read an autobiography of a nobody. But you have generously done so.

If you drop me a line (a postcard will do) to 2469 Pacific Avenue, San Francisco, CA 94115, regardless of the amount and intensity of your criticism, it would be appreciated.